SAGE was founded in 1965 by Sara Miller McCune to support the dissemination of usable knowledge by publishing innovative and high-quality research and teaching content. Today, we publish over 900 journals, including those of more than 400 learned societies, more than 800 new books per year, and a growing range of library products including archives, data, case studies, reports, and video. SAGE remains majority-owned by our founder, and after Sara's lifetime will become owned by a charitable trust that secures our continued independence.

Los Angeles | London | New Delhi | Singapore | Washington DC | Melbourne

LEFT FRONT AND AFTER

LEFT FRONT AND AFTER

UNDERSTANDING THE DYNAMICS OF *PORIBORTON* IN WEST BENGAL

JYOTIPRASAD CHATTERJEE
SUPRIO BASU

SAGE SERIES ON POLITICS IN INDIAN STATES–III

SERIES EDITORS
SUHAS PALSHIKAR
RAJESHWARI DESHPANDE

Los Angeles | London | New Delhi
Singapore | Washington DC | Melbourne

First published in 2020 by

SAGE Publications India Pvt Ltd
B1/I-1 Mohan Cooperative Industrial Area
Mathura Road, New Delhi 110 044, India
www.sagepub.in

SAGE Publications Inc
2455 Teller Road
Thousand Oaks, California 91320, USA

SAGE Publications Ltd
1 Oliver's Yard, 55 City Road
London EC1Y 1SP, United Kingdom

SAGE Publications Asia-Pacific Pte Ltd
18 Cross Street #10-10/11/12
China Square Central
Singapore 048423

Published by Vivek Mehra for SAGE Publications India Pvt Ltd. Typeset in 10.5/13 pt Berkeley by Zaza Eunice, Hosur, Tamil Nadu, India.

Library of Congress Control Number: 2019951240

ISBN: 978-93-532-8723-8 (HB)

SAGE Team: Abhijit Baroi, Syed Husain Naqvi, Mahira Chadha and Kanika Mathur

CONTENTS

LIST OF FIGURES

LIST OF TABLES

LIST OF ABBREVIATIONS

AIFB	All India Forward Bloc
AITC	All India Trinamool Congress
BAC	Bangla Congress
BJD	Biju Janata Dal
BJP	Bharatiya Janata Party
BSP	Bahujan Samaj Party
BUPC	Bhumi Uchhed Pratirodh Committee
CD	Community development
CPI	Communist Party of India
CPI (M)	Communist Party of India (Marxist)
CSDS	Centre for the Study of Developing Societies
DGHC	Darjeeling Gorkha Hill Council
GCPA	Greater Cooch Behar People's Association
GJMM	Gorkha Janmukti Morcha
GNLF	Gorkha National Liberation Front
GTA	Gorkhaland Territorial Administration
HDA	Haldia Development Authority
HYV	High yielding varieties
IMF	International Monetary Fund
INC	Indian National Congress
KLO	Kamtapur Liberation Organization
KPP	Kamtapur People's Party
LF	Left Front
MGNREGA	Mahatma Gandhi National Rural Employment Guarantee Act

MLA	Member of Legislative Assembly
MP	Member of Parliament
NES	National Election Study
NFSA	National Food Security Act
NSM	New social movement
PCAPA	People's Committee Against Police Atrocities
PDF	Progressive Democratic Front
RKSY	Rajya Khadya Suraksha Yojana
RSP	Revolutionary Socialist Party
SAP	PULF:
SBBS	Sara Bangla Bastuhara Samiti
SC	Scheduled caste
SKJRC	Singur Krishi Jomi Raksha Committee
ST	Scheduled Tribe
SAP	Structural Adjustment Programme
UCRC	United Central Refugee Council
UF	United Front
ULF	United Left Front

SERIES NOTE

The *SAGE Series* on *Politics in Indian States* aims at developing comprehensive, contemporary political histories of Indian states looking at the past two and a half decades. The series will consist of volumes covering important trends in the politics of major states of India. Each volume, devoted to one particular state, would situate the politics of that state in the larger socio-historical context and present a detailed analysis of the significant patterns of competitive politics in the state with a focus on framework of party competition, rise of new social forces, role of leadership and the context of regional political economy. Going beyond state-specificity, each volume would also attempt to situate the politics of the state in the larger all-India context.

Besides analysing the state-specific trends in party politics that have led to the rise of many state parties, these volumes would also carefully look at the social bases of parties and their electoral fortunes in the backdrop of fluctuations in voter choices during elections of the past quarter of a century, making use of the rich data archives of Lokniti.

The unfolding dynamics of politics since the 1990s, which manifested at the state level at slightly different moments and sometimes even preceded the 1990s, have forcefully brought back the states in the consciousness of students of Indian politics. It has also led to a renewed interest among sociologists and economists about the political processes at state level and their interconnections with socio-economic developments in India. At the same time, there is a glaring absence of detailed documentations of the state-specific political processes during the past two decades. The series will address this gap in the literature on Indian politics. The series will also propel more informed cross-state comparisons as a starting point to truly grasp 'all-India' politics.

INTRODUCTION

In a sharp contrast to the political trajectories of most of the states in post-Independent India, West Bengal has exhibited an altogether different contour of politics marked by the unprecedented continuity of the Left regime for no less than 34 years. Under the leadership of the Communist Party of India (Marxist), hereafter CPI (M), the Left Front (LF)—also comprising the Communist Party of India (CPI), Revolutionary Socialist Party (RSP) and the All India Forward Bloc (AIFB) along with some other minor allies—came to rule West Bengal in 1977 and remained in power till they were defeated by the All India Trinamool Congress (AITC; also called Trinamool Congress [TMC]), a breakaway faction of the Indian National Congress (INC), in 2011. This is undoubtedly an exceptional trend as far as state politics in India is concerned. In the history of state politics in postcolonial India no political party or alliance has had such a long and uninterrupted stint at power. It is true that the INC in pre-1990 Maharashtra had experienced a relatively long stint at power in the state. Mention can also be made about the Bharatiya Janata Party (BJP) in Gujarat and the Biju Janata Dal (BJD) in Odisha who have been ruling these states since 1995 and 2000 respectively. But in all these states the ruling parties or coalition either did not or are yet to rule the states for more than three decades continuously like the Left coalition in West Bengal. Moreover, the speciality of West Bengal lies in the fact that here a communist coalition had ruled the state for such a long time, negotiating successfully with the overall bourgeoisie democratic political framework of India. The story of the CPI (M) in West Bengal is also distinct from the ruling parties of these three states, since the former always restricted itself from joining the central government, while the latter or some of their allies at times have formed the central government. It is a fact that the party ruling the central government often has a comparative advantage in the context of state politics in India. Amidst all the talks about regionalization of Indian politics, what is often witnessed is the tendency of the regional or state parties to ally with the national parties to bolster their electoral fortunes in the states concerned. A reverse trend can also be noticed where the national parties, in order to extend their influence in the states, seek to join hands with the state parties. The idiosyncrasy of the CPI (M) rule in West Bengal should be traced in its refraining from these electoral calculations of alliance formation with the parties in command of the national government. However, as a social scientist having interest in the political processes unfolding at the social level, one needs to look deeper into the nature of this exceptionality of West Bengal. This will involve an examination of the contradictions and dynamics prevailing at the socio-political rubric of the state which might have some distinct bearing in shaping up the political processes here. Such a scrutiny would necessarily touch upon the emerging social forces and their decisive role in shaping up the political institutions and associations, thereby creating a political culture congenial enough for a communist government to remain in power for more than three decades.

The long durability of the LF rule in West Bengal has been approached and analysed from a number of standpoints. Some scholars have attributed it to the solid organizational grip of the LF especially over the rural electorates and to the successful implementation of the land reform programmes along with substantive extension of democracy to the grassroots via panchayats (Bhattacharyya 2004, 2010; Chattopadhyay 2005–2006; Kohli 1987). Others have talked about the effective delivery of the livelihood demands of the political society (Chatterjee 2004), LF leadership's successful drawing upon the cultural elements of power (Ruud 2003) and development of an environment of clientelism (Bardhan et al. 2009; Sarkar 2006) as the primary factors for its long stint at power in West Bengal. A brief focus on these will help us to understand and analyse the social and political processes associated with the exemplary rule of a Left coalition.

Kohli (1987, 1997) has dealt at length with the socio-political factors responsible for the LF's, primarily its spearhead the CPI (M)'s, success as a ruling coalition/party in West Bengal. Although his analysis is restricted to the CPI (M)'s first two decades of rule in this state, but that by no account is an insignificant time span for any party to rule a state in the Indian context. It is a fact that the CPI (M)-led coalition continued to rule the state for almost one and a half decade thereafter, but Kohli's analysis of the factors based on the first two decades of its rule holds for that period too. In his view, a well-organized and disciplined party composed of the middle and lower socio-economic strata is the key for the success of the CPI (M). The exemplary achievements of the two flagship programmes of the successive LF governments in West Bengal namely the land reform and revamping of the panchayats through their politicization, also owe much to the well-knit party organization of the CPI (M). The two major components of land reform programme have been tenancy reform through the implementation of Operation Barga and redistribution of land. Operation Barga has resulted in the granting of tenurial security to a substantial number of sharecroppers, thus widening the scope for improved incomes (Kohli 1997; Lieten 1992; Ramachandran 2001). The extent of land redistribution has also been encouraging as, 'one-fifth of all ceiling-surplus land distributed in India was distributed in West Bengal' (Rawal and Swaminathan 1998, 2598). Besides the land reform programme, the politicized panchayats have paved the entry of the lower and lower middle classes into the arena of institutional politics by transferring substantial power and resources to them to decide about the trajectories and shapes of local development. This is indeed a radical shift from the past when organs of local governments were primarily under the control of the propertied elites and elements of the bureaucracy. By instilling confidence among the rural lower stratum, the CPI (M) in this fashion has limited the scope of unorganized and deinstitutionalized rural populism, which has resulted in considerable consolidation of its rural support base. Coupled with better wages and moderate improvement in quality of lives under the new LF government, a shift in the rural power structure, which replaced the power of the landlord families by the institutional power of the village panchayats, has been witnessed. By paving the way for, 'institutional politics with a broader social base' (Majumdar 2009, 89), the new regime has also dealt a significant blow to the feudal power base of the then West Bengal polity. In both these programmes, namely the land reform and decentralization of power, the organized and disciplined party cadres have played the roles of facilitators as well as supervisors. (Bhattacharyya 2004, 2010; Kohli 1987).

Along with the effective intervention by the LF in transforming the rural power structure in West Bengal, its long sustenance at power is also a function of its efficient managerial skill to provide welfare and solutions to various livelihood issues and problems of the population of the political society (Chatterjee 2004). Drawing on the Foucauldian notion of governmentality that refers to the transition, '...from a regime dominated by structures of sovereignty to one ruled by techniques of government...' (Foucault 1991, 101), Chatterjee (2004) conceptualizes political society in contrast to that of the civil society. While the civil society is connected to the nation-state on the basis of, 'popular sovereignty and granting equal rights to citizens' (ibid., 37), the political society is founded on the interlinkages between the population and the 'governmental agencies pursuing multiple policies of security and welfare' (ibid.). Civil society, in this sense, is composed of the citizens of a sovereign state, who are law abiding and have inalienable rights. The elites of any society as law abiding and rights-conscious citizens, hence, essentially figure in the domain of a civil society.

The transition from sovereignty to governmentality also marks a simultaneous shift in the aim of politics: from ruling the citizens of a sovereign state to governing the population by a government. While law is the 'intrinsic instrument' of the former, 'a range of multiform tactics' or procedures to govern the population is the instrument of the latter (Foucault 1991, 95). Thus, far from imposing law on men, governmentality is constituted on the rationality of disposing things in ways which can produce the desired ends. From this art of government, which rather than assigning importance to laws puts emphasis on managing and controlling the population, Chatterjee derives his notion of political society in the context of democratic politics in India.

In India, the expansion of civil society or the 'bourgeois society' (Chatterjee 2004, 38) and its institutions, practices and characteristics are limited to a small section of people. Although the Constitution and the associated laws treat every Indian as a citizen with equal rights and, hence, a member of the civil society, to Chatterjee (ibid.) they are mostly the rights-bearing citizens as imagined by the Constitution. Hence, they are not proper members of the civil society, but that does not anyway imply that they are outside the reach of the state or the politics concerning it. Being a part of the population inhabiting its territory, the state and different governmental agencies have to control and look after the well-being of these population groups. As targets of governmentality, these population segments are governed by the state. Thus, the interaction of the population with the governmental state turns out to be political although its substance might differ from the one which is expected in liberal political discourse to exist between the citizens or the members of civil society and the sovereign state. The members of these population groups, in their striving to live and earn a livelihood often cross the limits of legality or legal conceptions of citizens, compose the political society.

The emergence of political society in India can be traced during the 1980s. It is the period when the discourses and practices of development produced the 'Third World'. In radical opposition to the dreams of the advocates of development regarding material prosperity and economic progress of two thirds of the world, we have witnessed underdevelopment, impoverishment, exploitation and oppression to rise at a massive scale during this period. Hence, the field or targets of governmentality have been prepared by the practices of development itself, which, '...proceeded by creating "abnormalities" (such as the "illiterate," the "underdeveloped," the "malnourished," "small farmers," or "landless peasants"), which it would later treat and reform' (Escobar 1995, 41). Obviously, these categories of population compose the 'governable subjects' (ibid., 147) of an overall regime of governmentality which allows them a political space, which Chatterjee calls 'political society'. Thus, political society or the domain of the politics of the governed is informed by the emergence of the governmental state which happens to be a political reality constructed by the development discourse of the post-World War II era.

Following the logic of governmentality, it can be said that political society is developed out of a mutual perception of both the state and different population groups that the government is morally, and to some extent politically, obliged to deliver certain services and benefits even to those who do not properly fit in the republican model of citizenship. This is backed or reinforced by the contemporary expansion of democracy to the grassroots which has brought in these so called 'marginal' categories of population under the ambit of electoral politics. In the expansion of the field of political mobilization or widening the scope of popular politics, various agencies—governmental or non-governmental—assume active role. Among these, the agencies of the political parties are very crucial since party competition in a democracy is all about garnering the electoral support of the electorates. Hence, different political parties, active to gain the support of the electorates, mediate between the government and the categories of population to assure the delivery of benefits and privileges to the latter for furthering their electoral ends. In West Bengal context the CPI (M), with its well-disciplined organization, performed this role of mediation better than all other parties involved in the competitive democratic political sphere. This could be a plausible explanation of the long stint at power of the LF in West Bengal.

Apart from its well-disciplined organizational network, the CPI (M) could do this because of its professed ideology also. As a party committed to emancipate the lives and living conditions of the working class, it was rather easy for the party to expand the scope of such ideology to cover the different cross-sections of the marginalized and excluded population. As a programmatic party constantly engaged in 'ideology work' (Kitschelt and Wilkinson 2007, 9), the CPI (M), since its ascendance to the power in West Bengal, has tried to establish political linkage with these cross-sections of the population through its policies and programmes. Being a leftist party relying on programmatic appeals to win the confidence of the electorates, however, does not prevent it to be labelled as clientelist by a section of the scholars and researchers.

While discussing the LF government's land redistribution programme, Basu (2001) has found the existence of a patron–client relationship to exist between the CPI (M) and the section of the peasants close to it. He points to the illegal possession of undistributed vested land by the Krishak Sabha (the peasant union of the CPI [M]), the access of cultivation to which was restricted to, 'only those who find favour with the party bosses...of course with the condition that a part of the profits from cultivation will be surrendered to the local Krishak Sabha unit!' (ibid., 1337). Sarkar (2006, 346) talks about the 'increasing informalisation of the economy and the breakdown of the formal legal system' under the LF regime in West Bengal as the potential factors responsible for the growing vulnerabilities of the relatively disadvantaged and marginal sections of the population. These in turn led them to depend on the parties for patronage. The CPI (M) with its unmatchable organization proved to be the most efficient among all other parties to protect the vulnerable. Hence, he attributes the cause of the exceptional continuity of LF rule under the CPI (M) in West Bengal to the trade-off between growing insecurities of the electorates and their electoral support to the ruling CPI (M). Bardhan et al. (2009) also trace elements of clientelism in the relationship of the Left parties, particularly the CPI (M) with the electorates in the rural area. Analysing the data obtained from a survey of 85 villages in West Bengal, they find that the receipt of various governmental welfare benefits was positively correlated with voting for the Left. The hint of patron–client linkages, as the study reveals is also evident from the fact that those who attended the meetings of the CPI (M) regularly got more benefits than who did not. In a similar vein, Chakrabarty (2014) notes that as far as the distribution of the benefits of the governmental schemes for the rural population is concerned, the panchayats, under the LF rule, consistently discriminate against those who are opposed to the ruling party namely the CPI (M).

Such allegations have been plenty in the everyday life experiences of the common people in West Bengal, especially during the last one and half decade of the LF rule. In many instances of government appointments, more prominently in those of the schools, colleges and state universities, *party dhara* (arranging or fixing with the ruling party: the CPI [M]), more than the requisite qualifications, had allegedly become the means to get selected. One of the present authors has the experience of visiting a village in Paschim Medinipur district of West Bengal which remained unelectrified even after almost two decades of LF rule. This was unusual since most of the neighbouring villages were electrified. During the course of informal interaction, the villagers reported that the chief cause of it was the village being a traditional stronghold of the INC. Chakrabarty (2014) also holds responsible the patron–client relationship for the much publicized starvation death of five *adivasis* at Amlasol. Amlasol is a village in Belpahari Gram Panchayat of Binpur–II block of Paschim Medinipur district. The villagers of Amlasol elected a CPI (M) candidate from the village while the Jharkhand Party had the majority in the Belpahari Gram Panchayat. In the upper two tiers, namely the panchayat samiti (at the block level) and the zila parishad (at the district level), CPI (M) had the majority. The clientelist network was evident since the CPI (M) which controlled upper two layers of administration did not provide the necessary back up to the village panchayat as it was under the control of the opposition Jharkhand Party. Hence, clientelism stood in the way of implementing good governance through decentralization of political power to the grassroots.

The factuality of these accounts notwithstanding, points may be raised about their instrumental and ontological consideration of the practice and the notion of clientelism. To begin with, one may examine the potential reasons for any political party to adopt the course of clientelistic linkage with the electorates. Quite obviously, in a multiparty democracy all these boil down to garner electoral mileage to a greater extent or to achieve the crucial edge in the party competition. Thus, a party will cultivate the patron–client relationship not merely to consolidate its constituency but to inflate it further. Clientelism in the shape of extending benefits to those segments of the electorates who are in favour of a particular party, therefore, is intended to shrink the support base or vote bank of the opposition parties. During the long LF rule in West Bengal this, however, did not happen. Barring the Assembly Election of 1977, that brought the LF in power of West Bengal, in all the subsequent state assembly elections up to 2011, the main opposition parties or coalitions (primarily the INC and the AITC since 1998), constantly managed to get the support of about 35 to 40 per cent of the electorates, as reveals Figure I.1.

Hence, the apparent failure of the CPI (M) and other LF partners in extending their electoral support base further by instituting crack in the opposition constituency may be a pointer to the polarization existing at the level of the electorates. In such a situation where the political preferences are largely independent of electoral promises and performances of the respective parties, the incidents of partial treatment as mentioned above might be the outcome of the corrupt practices of faction leaders of the ruling CPI (M) and other LF parties (Chatterjee 1997). More than the alleged charge of clientelism, these may be the results of faction leaders' thirst to share the spoils of power and to develop their support clusters among the electorates to prove their worth before the party leadership. Patron–client linkage, perhaps, is more fruitful in an indefinite and uncertain electoral atmosphere, where the party preferences are rather open to the calculations of benefits given or assured by the contending parties than in

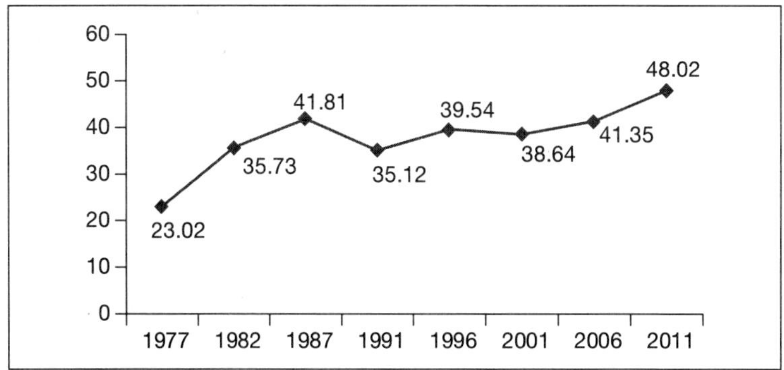

Figure I.1 *Non-Left Vote Share Since 1977 to 2011 in Different Assembly Elections in West Bengal*

Source: Election Commission of India.

a tight-knit polarized situation as encountered in the instance of the LF rule in West Bengal.

Considered ontologically, the ideological orientation of programmatic political parties acts heavily against clientelist proclivities being impinged into its policies (Kitschelt and Wilkinson 2007). The CPI (M) as a political party ideologically committed to work for the upliftment of the non-elite segment of the population, hence, could hardly afford to be clientelist. Rather than clienetelism, these relationships of the CPI (M) with the electorates, might be something not more than, 'a mutual arrangement of convenience' (Chatterjee 2004, 55).

Thus, clientelism cannot be a defining feature of a political party which follows the dictates of an ideology. Its policies, programmes and schemes, or put simply, its logic of functioning reflects the urgency on its part to achieve the general objectives set forth by the ideology. As a communist party, the CPI (M), perhaps, is also no exception to this. Corbridge et al. (2005), in their study on West Bengal, have noted an urgency among the CPI (M) leaders to make a public display of a progressive state government, committed to the cause of good governance through greater and meaningful participation of the common people. For its commitment to good governance, the CPI (M) cannot simply afford to be clientelist politically.

Often the low-level village-based leaders belonging to the Left parties, primarily the CPI (M), have been instrumental in bringing the developmental state to the common people. In West Bengal's rural social scene, mostly the school teachers, inspired by the communist ideology, have performed this role. They have been the key to develop what Bhattacharyya (2009, 2010, 2016) calls the 'party-society', or the chief mediators between the population governed and those who govern (Chatterjee 2004). In the rural areas they can be clearly identified by the term *mastermashai* or by the suffix 'master' attached to their names. In almost all the villages of West Bengal, at least during the LF period, these school teachers have enjoyed enormous respect from the people. More than their education, knowledge and wisdom, this is due to the belief of the rural folk in their ability to arrive at suitable solutions to various local disputes which are acceptable to all. As mediators between the government officials, the party and the villagers they perform an important role. By virtue of leading their daily lives in and among the villagers they develop an everyday understanding of the problems facing the villagers, which they can bring into the notice of the government officials and administrators in the appropriate language and manner. In the same token, being well-versed with the culture, lifeworld and method of cognition of the rural people they can also inform and make the villagers aware about the different government schemes meant for their development. Hence, these local leaders facilitate the process through which the villages become visible to the government and the government also enters the domain of public discourses of the rural society.

The school teachers as local leaders of the CPI (M) are also relied upon for their selfless character. This is primarily due to the fact that being salaried, these teachers have no genuine vested interest in land. Being organically linked to the village community and yet living largely independent of agricultural income, their informed opinion regarding any type of land dispute, thus, tends to be regarded as impartial and acceptable to all. Their educational attainment, simple lifestyles and free mixing with the villagers, inspire an awe that allows them the necessary space to build up the consensus in the rural society of West Bengal. Undeniably, such consensus has been instrumental for the CPI (M) to build up its successful hegemony strong enough to rule West Bengal for more than three decades.

The selflessness, modesty and politeness of the school teachers and some other local leaders of the CPI (M) are the assets which enabled the CPI (M) to build a strong support base among the rural folk in West Bengal. Their pattern of everyday lives and their relationship with the villagers endowed with such cultural markups develop a sense of confidence among the villagers. Ruud (2003) refers to this as 'symbolic capital' a notion developed by Bourdieu (1977), which is instrumental in legitimizing the position of village leaders. Symbolic capital signifies the image that people have of a leader, her/his reputation as an honest, learned, knowledgeable, polite and wise man built up and reproduced continuously within the ambience of social interaction with the villagers on a day-to-day basis. Beginning with the days of the peasant movements of the 1960s and continuing at least up to the first two decades of the LF rule in West Bengal, the village leaders particularly those of the CPI (M), had been successful in creating such an image of them in the popular imagination of the rural populace. It became commonplace to equate a communist leader as a knowledgeble person with full of simplicity, honesty, unselfishness and ever sacrificial nature. Such prestige and renown attached to a person, more than any material endowment such as money and other forms of wealth, turns out to be the basis of her/his legitimacy.

In the context of the village leaders in West Bengal, Ruud (2003) mentions about the practice of *len-den*, signifying 'taking and giving', that bears a close resemblance to Bourdieu's notion of symbolic capital. But there are shades of differences as well. The relationship of the village leaders with the villagers involving the practice of len-den, as argues Ruud (ibid., 177), creates 'trust, confidence and mutuality', which transcends the limits of gift-giving or the credit-debt expression of symbolic capital. This is not to say that len-den is not based on the principle of reciprocity but such reciprocation is expressed through the villagers' acceptance of their relationship with the leaders and commitment to maintain, strengthen and extend it. More than gift exchange, it assumes the shape of sharing with a generous expectation of assistance from the village leaders to stand by the villagers whenever they are in trouble, which is to be reciprocated through their political support to the leaders as and when the need is there.

At this juncture it is important to throw some light on the concept of 'party-society', developed by Bhattacharyya (2009, 2010, 2016). In his attempt to analyse the CPI (M)'s success in maintaining a solid support base among the rural electorates of West Bengal, he talks about the development of party-society: 'A specific kind of sociability' (Bhattacharyya 2016, 116) marked by the thorough prominence of the political parties in every aspect of social life of the rural people. Party-society emerges when the 'social' comes to be encompassed by the 'political'. In this sense, Bhattacharya (2009) claims party-society to be the specific form of political society in the rural areas of West Bengal.

The genesis of party-society can be traced by the fact of complete domination of the political parties over the rural social space so much so that no other viable channels of public transaction exist independently of the parties' intervention and control. In such a situation the villagers have no other option but to depend on the parties for any sort of assistance. The rural social institutions such as the family, education, religion and market turn out to be the sites for partisan contestations for exercising control by the rival political parties. It signals a complete overshadowing of the liminality existing between the private and the public sphere by the political parties to the extent that any matter of private dispute assumes a partisan shape. Even the quite intimate personal affairs become issues to be controlled and managed by the political parties. It is needless to mention that such a form of sociability depends to a large extent on the command over institutional sources of power by the different political parties. In the rural societies of West Bengal during the LF rule, the CPI (M), being a major partner of the ruling coalition and also being a well-organized and disciplined party, has proved to be quite efficient in managing and controlling the party-society. Through the successful devolution of institutional power to the grassroots in the form of panchayats, the CPI (M) has included the hitherto excluded population, mostly the poor agricultural population, into the orbit of power relations. It has been a story of decentring the power centre where power, unlike the earlier regimes, moved away from the rural elites and upper classes to the lower classes. Party-society in this fashion has largely contributed in democratizing the rural political sphere.

The panchayats, therefore, have been the principal tools of instituting the party-society. The CPI (M) as well as its peasant wing the Krishak Sabha, due to their predominance in a large number of panchayats, have been the primary agents to establish such a new pattern of political transaction. The new political climate set in motion certain new norms and language of politics to which every party, the ruling or the opposition, had to acclimatize. Party-society thrives on the notion of everyday politics where political parties are expected to create and nurture their support base or electoral constituencies on a daily basis.

Evidently, for its organizational cohesion and ideological inclination to the lower social strata, the CPI (M) has turned out to be the major beneficiary of this new politico-social formation. But to consolidate their constituencies, other political outfits also have become busy in carving out their niche by effecting certain changes in their ideologies and strategies, however, minimum or superficial it might be.

It is true that political society and party-society both facilitate the process through which the marginalized population enters into a political dialogue with the state, but there are differences between them as well. Apart from their respective areas of operation, that is, the urban for the political society and the countryside for the party-society, these distinctions pertain to their functionalities, objectives and modes of operation. First, while political society tries to inject a sense of shared interest in the shape of a community among the different population groups, the party-society makes inroad in the settled communities by splitting them into different political groups. Hence, partisan division of communities becomes more prominent than the existing social stratification along caste, religion or ethnicity. These traditional forms of social hierarchies, which had been the bases of patron–client relationship, simply failed to come into terms with the conceptual as well as functional representation of the party-society (Bhattacharyya 2009). Second, since in the political society political parties have to compete with other civil society and state agencies to deliver the services to the population segments, they cannot make electoral calculations their sole aims of operation, whereas parties in the context of party-society exclusively aim at maintaining, consolidating and enhancing their electoral support bases. Finally, the modes through which the political society operates are contingent and more flexible than that of the party-society since the former has larger and different institutional options to offer than the latter whose scope is limited to the institutional domain of the panchayat only. Although the local clubs, schools, cooperatives appear to be the important sites of operation of the party-society but its source of institutional power exclusively lies with the panchayat.

Through the party-society thesis, Bhattacharyya seems to contradict the opinion of Bardhan et al. (2009) and others who attribute the LF's success in maintaining a concrete rural support base for more than three decades to the logic of clientelism. Naturally, he also does not consider that the debacle of the LF is due to the erosion of the patron–client linkage claimed to be existing between the LF and the electorates at large, especially of the rural areas. Citing the findings of a survey conducted after the defeat of the LF in 2011, he argues that far from the attrition of clientelism, the defeat had been caused by the simmering discontent of the electorates with the local leaders particularly for, 'the latter's excessive interference in public matters and indulgence in corruption' (Bhattacharyya 2016, 26). The panchayats, which had opened up 'a field of political transaction' (Chatterjee 1997, 160) by ensuring wholehearted participation of most of the villagers, have become non-participatory due to the excessive control of the ruling coalition, particularly the CPI (M) (Bhattacharyya 2010). Moving away from its earlier path of democratizing the rural political space, the long stint at power generated within the party a sense of invincibility, strong enough to be less respectful to dissent and difference (Mukherji 2009, 14). Hence, failure in sustaining the extension of democracy to the grassroots, once achieved by the LF during the first decade of its rule, has detached the party-society from its very foundation, the consequent degeneration of which, in Bhattacharyya's opinion, might have some bearing on the downfall of the long-standing LF rule.

From the foregoing analysis it becomes apparent that the LF in West Bengal set in motion a new social and political process potential enough to sustain its rule for almost three and half decades. The cornerstone of this new politics lies in the attempt to democratize the sphere of institutional politics to include the people at the margins within the structure of formal politics. Another dimension of this had been the effort to introduce institutional reforms in agriculture aimed at transforming the property relations in the rural areas. These initiatives of the LF have been a classic expression of the intricate relationship between democracy and development. The analysts ranging from Kohli to Bhattacharyya, in one way or the other, have talked about this relationship and put the onus on the CPI (M)'s ideological stance and its solid, disciplined and coherent organization for its effective implementation. It is true that the ideology professed by the CPI (M) along with its partners in the LF have introduced a new language of politics which has paved the entry of the non-elites or the subaltern into the arena of power relations. At the same time, crediting the ideology exclusively for this without considering the social conditions prevailing at the period that prepared the congenial breeding ground of such an ideological orientation, also amounts to eulogy. Since every form of knowledge is rooted in the social texture (Manheim 1979), so analysis of a system of thought, or for that matter ideology, by detaching it from the overall social and political environment suffers from analytical and methodological weaknesses. In our case, if we accept the pro-poor ideological orientation of the CPI (M) as the important cause for the long sustenance of its rule in West Bengal, then the question that immediately springs up to the informed mind is, why it has failed to replicate it in other states where the poor and the marginalized people exist in no less significant numbers than West Bengal? On the face of this what seems to be more important, perhaps, is to focus on the idiosyncrasies of the socio-political history of West Bengal since the colonial rule extending up to the postcolonial period, which has infused greater salience to Left ideology and politics. Possibly, such an exercise can unpack the exceptionality of West Bengal compared to other Indian states which might have serious bearing on the long sustenance of Left rule here.

THE EXCEPTIONALITY OF WEST BENGAL REVISITED

Analysis of the political dynamics in West Bengal that has allowed such unprecedented regime continuity under the aegis of a Left coalition hence warrants a focus on the unique character of social polity of the state. The exceptionality of West Bengal in contrast to other Indian states definitely lies in its distinct political culture which has developed or matured during the long course of people's negotiation with the colonial rule. The intelligentsia, the social reformers, the peasantry and the anti-colonial forces of different natures and shades have been the chief architects of such a distinct tradition. A sociological and social historical analysis of Bengali culture and tradition hence is necessary to unveil the nature of exceptional political trends witnessed in West Bengal in the last three or four decades. This would bring into light two important factors which have been instrumental in marking off the society and politics of West Bengal from most other Indian states. First, unlike many other Indian states, West Bengal politics seems to have been minimally influenced by the caste vector. This is not to say that caste as a form of social hierarchy has little or no presence in West Bengal society, but to many critics the political processes have remained largely untouched by it. An attempt to analyse the possible reasons for the relative insulation of the political processes from the social forces represented by caste, religion, ethnicity and so on would bring into light the second one, namely the revolutionary proclivity of West Bengal politics. The traditions of 19th century social reform movements and peasant movements bear testimony to these. How far the second dimension is a necessary condition for the first also needs further investigation.

Formal Politics without Caste

There is no denying the fact that the social reality of West Bengal bears considerable imprint of caste-based stratification. Ghosh (2001) has portrayed quite vividly the nature and extent of caste discrimination which the members of the lower castes have to withstand in their everyday lives. Citing some glaring examples of caste discrimination suffered by the Doms and the Hanris (two scheduled castes in West Bengal) in their civic and religious lives, he has brought to light the quantum of social distance existing between the upper and the lower castes. Even after seven decades of independence with nearly three and half decades under LF rule, discrimination along caste line has not disappeared in West Bengal. In spite of this, caste fails to make its presence felt in public life here. Pointing to the unobtrusive persistence of caste in the customary practices of the civic communities, he comments that it 'is not the principal conduit of political power and contestation in the state' (ibid., 2).

The presence of caste in social life and its conspicuous absence in political life of West Bengal has been reported by a number of scholars (Chatterjee 2012, 2016; Guha 2016; Kohli 1987; Kumar and Guha 2014; Samaddar 2013; Sinharay 2014). They all get stuck by the double bind of the Bengali culture which allows caste discrimination to persist, however unobtrusively, in the everyday lives within the context of communities, while simultaneously restricting its entry in the political arena. They seem to be puzzled by the fact of the near complete insulation of the political ethos from the issues of caste. The sociologists find it quite paradoxical to explain the inabilities of the social arrangement of caste in informing the political matrix. Contravening the fundamental premise of sociology of knowledge that speaks about the social determination of every form of knowledge, thought and ideology, West Bengal presents a scenario where ideology, both Right- or Left-wing, remains unaffected by caste-related interest. The root cause of exceptionality of West Bengal politics, in contrast to most other Indian states, possibly, lies in this cultural double bind.

Sociologists, political scientists and political anthropologists have attempted to analyse the exceptionality of West Bengal political scene from different standpoints. Broadly, these can be clubbed into two streams of thought, namely the colonial modernization and the context-specific historicity thesis. The first, pioneered by N. K. Bose (1958), tries to see the diminishing influence of caste as an offshoot of the modernization process ushered in by the British rule in India, particularly in West Bengal—where it had a special interest. The second approach considers some of the historically specific social and political aspects of the society in Bengal that have prevented the spilling over of caste sentiment in the domain of formal politics. In this context, Chatterjee (2012, 2016) talks about the partition of Bengal and its influence in realigning the interests of various castes in the political mosaic. This has resulted in the 'mysterious' disappearance of caste in Bengal (Chatterjee 2016). Although the analytical strategies of the two orientations differ, but one can also notice the similarities since the context-specific historicity of West Bengal can hardly afford to do away with the unfolding of colonial rule here, which had an immense effect in altering the social rubric of Bengali society significantly.

Bose (1958) argues that the colonialists unleashed the process of modernization in Indian society primarily through an alternative system of production. As an impact of this, '...the chief basis of loyalty to the caste system was demolished very nearly to completeness' (ibid.,

410). Citing a local social worker's survey in a village in Birbhum district of West Bengal conducted in the year 1947, he has pointed out the noticeable shift in professing the hereditary and traditional occupation by the members of different castes. Another study, he reports, conducted by a student of the Geography Department of the University of Calcutta in 1956–1957 in Santipur town of Nadia District of West Bengal confirmed the same trend. The shift has been more prominent in case of the upper castes such as the Brahmins and Vaidyas towards higher professions such as medicine, law, office work, or landowning or land management. The almost complete reorganization of the economic life, an offshoot of western specifically English education, initiated by the British rule in Bengal, thus, have weakened the solid grip of caste in Bengal. Although, such a modernizing influence of British rule of late became a pan-Indian affair, but there is no denying the fact that it started its journey from Bengal and it is here that British commerce found a favourable roosting place in the late 17th century. The changes in the traditional economic activities of caste ultimately effected changes in the cultural realm to weaken its hold upon the mind of the urbanized, politically conscious people. Perhaps, this has led Bose (ibid., 409) to conclude that:

> In West Bengal, at least, caste has played a more negligible role than in the neighboring state of Bihar. One has to remember that, in Bengal as well as in Bihar, political parties bearing an all-India character, like the Congress, the Socialist and the Communist parties, or the Jan Sangh and the Hindu Mahasabha have been guided by considerations other than caste in the choice of the majority of their representatives.

As far as the context-specific historicity of Bengal is concerned, Chatterjee (2012) talks about the near total domination and control of the public political life by the upper caste Hindu elites of Bengal as a reason for the unique absence of caste in Bengali politics. To understand this he turns attention to another unique experience that the society in Bengal has underwent, namely the partition of Bengal in 1947 and its socio-political ramifications. The upper caste dominance of the Bengali society has its roots in the colonial land settlements. Due to the Permanent Settlement Regulations Act (1793), the upper castes, primarily the Brahmins, Kayasthas and Baidyas became owners of substantial amount of land which they controlled as absentee landlords. To them land was a productive asset that used to yield good amount of rent. Residing primarily in the urban centres in and around Calcutta they were totally ignorant about agriculture. Apart from collecting rent, an important source of their income, they did not have any definite interest in agriculture or agricultural productivity.

These upper castes had the opportunity to acquire English education, a direct offshoot of colonialism, in different educational institutions of the urban areas which gave them enough mileage in monopolizing the jobs and higher professions. The high positive correlation between literacy and engagement in higher professional jobs has been well documented by Bose (1958) and that for acquiring English education by the three upper castes by Chatterjee (2016). They were, in fact, the class formed by colonialism to act as the interpreters between the colonizers and the millions of people they governed in India, who were to be, as says Macaulay (1919, 116), '...a class of persons Indian in blood and colour, but English in tastes, in opinions, and in morals and in intellect.' Receiving the necessary backup of the colonial educational policy, the Hindu upper castes, the so called Bengali *Bhadraloks*, tightened their grip over the jobs and professions which had been instrumental in establishing their authority in the public domain. Far from caste, educational attainment especially English education became the crucial determinant of Bhadralok status, which '...became the ultimate stamp of respectability' (Chatterjee 1997, 70), of the upper castes in the new economic and political conditions of colonial Bengal. The shift in traditional occupation and the acquisition of high social status through English education thus turned out to be the foundations of the upper caste Bhadralok dominance. The British administrators also noted this, as they mentioned in the *Report of the Bengal District Administration Committee 1913–1914*, that in Bengal, '...the social order is a despotism of caste, tempered by matriculation' (Bengal Government 1914, 176). The authority of the upper castes or the Bhadraloks was so unquestionable that the members of the middle and lower castes used to consider their subordinated status as something natural.

In the 1930 and 1940s, however, the hegemony of the upper castes faced stiff challenge from the emerging groups of Muslim middle class comprised primarily of the substantial peasant proprietors. Although this section of the peasantry was socially quite similar to the dominant peasant middle caste in other parts of India, but their challenge to the Bhadraloks—comprising of the Hindu upper castes—rather than being caste oriented, acquired the communal shade. The situation was really threatening to the supremacy of the upper castes since everywhere, starting from the elected provincial government of Bengal in 1935 to the municipalities, universities and so on, this segment of the Muslim population posed serious challenge to the upper castes' political clout. Here in lies the significance of partition of 1947 that resulted in a massive migration of Hindu population from the then East Pakistan to West Bengal, particularly in the Kolkata suburbs and those of the Muslim middle class from West Bengal to East Pakistan. In this fashion the partition of Bengal came as a great relief to the upper castes since it guaranteed their continued dominance in West Bengal.

The partition of Bengal had extended the space of political dominance of the urban upper castes in West Bengal. With the migration of the Hindus from East Pakistan primarily into Kolkata and its suburbs, the urban population size increased considerably. This augmented the economic, social, cultural and political importance of Kolkata further. As most of the urbanites were from the upper castes, so, it also signalled a concurrent increase in their political significance. Since the upper caste Bhadraloks of Bengal historically had been detached from cultivation, they had no material interest in land as well. The same report of the Bengal Government (1914, 175) quite succinctly described the situation:

> The *bhadralok* castes have very little direct connection with agriculture. Our enquiries showed that in Eastern Bengal a *bhadralok* cultivating land with his own cattle and plough and with his own hired labourers, was indeed a rarity.... This dislike for cultivation on the part of the better castes is unequalled in any province in India.

This uniqueness of Bengal, as far as the aversion of the upper caste Bhadraloks to cultivation compared to other states in India was concerned, had its reflection in its political culture too. It entails that political disputes and conflicts centering on rights over land, cultivation and agricultural produce: the bones of contention of caste-based politics elsewhere, had never been directed against the upper castes (Chatterjee 1997). Hence, the historical specificity of West Bengal relating to the political supremacy of the upper caste Bhadraloks, earned through pursuits such as education, engagement in higher professions and the likes, other than the ones traditionally determined by caste has, perhaps, prevented the articulation of caste-based interests in the domain of formal institutional politics.

The ascendance of the upper castes in the political sphere can be gauged through their predominance and leading roles in every political party, the ruling as well as the opposition. This was true even for the Communist Party which had been very active in organizing and leading the refugee movement for protecting the rights of the East Bengal refugees in the 1950s and 1960s. The same pattern of the urban upper caste dominance has continued in the three decades of LF rule and thereafter in the present AITC regime. Tawa Lama-Rewal (2009) while analysing the profile of the West Bengal MLAs from available data finds out the upper castes' overall domination in the West Bengal Legislative Assembly since 1952. Echoing Kohli's (1990) opinion pertaining to the supremacy of the well-off upper castes educated minority in Bengali politics, she argues, '...no party in West Bengal has been able to challenge the upper caste domination of state politics' (p. 374). The trend, which she observes to be present since 1952 to little over three decades of LF rule, is also continuing in the present AITC regime in West Bengal (Chatterjee 2012, 2016). In a similar tune to Chatterjee (2012), she also asserts that there is no caste/community based vote banks in West Bengal since almost all the castes and communities find their places in most of the parties. Table I.1 which depicts the voting pattern of the upper castes and the Scheduled Caste (SC), in different elections (parliamentary and assembly) in West Bengal since 1999 also proves this.

The table clearly reveals that the upper caste vote share almost remained the same for both the LF and the AITC alliance since 1999. The scheduled caste vote share of the LF remained relatively high

Table I.1 *Voting Preferences of the Upper Caste and Scheduled Caste Electorates in the Assembly and Lok Sabha Elections since 1999*

	Left		AITC+	
	Upper Caste	SC	Upper Caste	SC
1999*	41	52	42	21
2001	41	52	48	30
2004*	46	57	38	30
2006	48	56	44	25
2009*	39	53	52	23
2011	38	43	50	37
2014*	27	25	44	42
2016	23	33	42	40

Source: CSDS Data Unit, National Election Studies (NES) and West Bengal Assembly Election Studies since 1999 to 2016.

Notes:

1. AITC + = AITC + BJP (1999, 2001, 2004) and AITC+INC (2006, 2009, 2011).
2. All figures are in per cent.
3. * Parliamentary election.

up to the Lok Sabha election of 2009. This may be due to the influence of the Left parties on the East Bengal refugees among which a sizeable section happens to be the SCs. Since 2011, perhaps due to the shift in the power locus in West Bengal, SCs have become more inclined towards the AITC alliance. This, perhaps, is a confirmation of the assertion that caste has very little role to play as a vehicle for the articulation of political interest in West Bengal.

The two explanations discussed above have significantly contributed to unmask the uniqueness of West Bengal politics reflected in its insulation from the interference of caste-based interests. While the modernizing view rests on the interaction of colonialism with the caste-based social structure of Bengal, the context-specific historicity approach takes the argument farther. Accepting the influence of colonialism in altering traditional caste pursuits, especially for the upper caste Bhadraloks, it also talks about the idiosyncratic experience of Bengal partition as a historical antecedent for rendering caste redundant in public political life of West Bengal.

The uniqueness of the caste-neutral political culture of West Bengal, as the two approaches suggest, however, needs to be revisited and revalidated in the context of contemporary West Bengal. Specifically after the 1990s the changes brought in the micro-level social network of the societies and communities by the macro policies of globalization and economic reforms have been dramatic. The policy of free market has not only reduced the functions and scope of the state but also effected significant changes at the institutional level of contemporary societies. The thrust of the reform strategy on liberty, individual freedom, autonomy and identity has been associated with a redesigning of the value structure of the societies, as well. How far these have reinvigorated the notion of identity of the people is a serious issue to be explored. In the specific context of West Bengal, the identity issues surrounding caste assumes significance in this context. It is true that caste had been absent in political discourse of West Bengal so far. But the renewed emphasis on identity brought in by the market economy and the emphasis of the economics and politics of neoliberalism on economic independence of the individuals might be a game changer. Moreover, the manner in which the long-standing communist government in West Bengal, with its avowed emphasis on class-based issues and priorities, interacted with such a new political, economic and cultural project should be an interesting subject of debate, discussion and analysis. In the overall context of dissolution of communism in the 1990s and simultaneous resurgence of identity-based politics throughout the globe, such an analysis has the potential to throw some new light on the sociology and politics of caste in West Bengal.

Left Politics

The Challenges

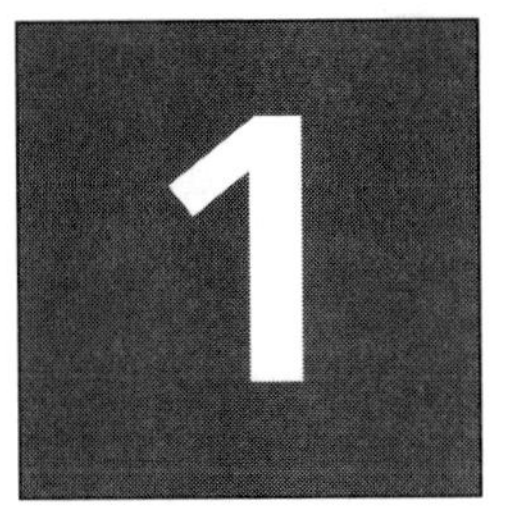

After a decade of political turmoil and violence the LF under the leadership of CPI (M) assumed state power of West Bengal in the year 1977. The period was also challenging since in the economic sphere West Bengal had been a poor performer among the major Indian states. Thus, establishing political stability and providing the necessary fillip to economic development of the state were the major concerns of the newly elected government.

The nature of the political turbulence of the time can be understood by the fact that during 1967 to 1977 West Bengal had witnessed change of chief ministers five times punctuated by imposition of the President's rule for four terms covering a total period of almost three years. The political turmoil of the period had its roots in the severe economic crisis affecting almost every cross-section of the West Bengal populace. Kohli has appropriately termed this decade a 'decade of chaos' (1997, 342). Repeated crop failures causing agricultural stagnation coupled with the poor health of the industrial sector turned West Bengal into a 'ship to mouth' economy. As a result popular discontent against the incumbent INC government was increasing very sharply so much so that the Congress Party in the state came to be divided in 1966. The breakaway faction, the Bangla Congress (BAC) contested the forthcoming state election in West Bengal in 1967 against its chief adversary, the INC. Like many other Indian states, the state election of 1967 saw the end of the Congress rule in West Bengal, which had been continuing here since the Independence of India. The defeat of the Congress could be attributed to the industrial depression and acute food shortage resulting from the poor performance of the Third Five Year Plan (1961–1966). The food shortage was severe enough to push the food movement, ongoing in different forms since 1959 under the influence of the CPI, to reach its zenith in 1966. In the meantime the CPI, the chief opposition of the INC in the state, also got divided to give birth to the CPI (M) in 1964. The split was the result of some ideological and tactical differences among the members of the CPI regarding (a) the party's stand vis-à-vis the Soviet proposal for peaceful transition to socialism (b) the differences of opinion within the party leadership about the side to be taken in the Sino-Soviet dispute about the nature and ideological scope of the 'national democratic state' thesis put forward by the Soviet leaders (c) the party's view and its stand in the Sino-India border conflict in 1962 and (d) the party's evaluation about the nature of Indian bourgeoisie and the Congress under Nehru's rule.

For the pro-Chinese wing of the CPI, among which the West Bengal lobby was quite prominent, the then Soviet-advocated strategy of peaceful and non-violent transition to socialism was nothing but revisionism since it directs the communists to leave the path of social revolution and to go for a coalition with the nationalist bourgeoisie. This resulted into the CPI getting fragmented into three camps: A conservative Right following the Soviet line and a radical Left professing the Chinese path of continuous revolution. The third group was composed of the centrist moderates who considered India at that period not as a national democracy but which eventually could become so. Unlike the rightist wing this group was critical about the reactionary policies of the Nehru government while at the same time moving away from the Left's all out opposition to the Nehruvian state. This faction was in every mood to support its progressive policies to establish the national democratic state. Finally in the seventh Congress of the CPI at Calcutta in October–November 1964, the CPI (M) comprising the Left segment of the CPI, was formed. The centrists got divided between the CPI and the CPI (M) while the bulk of its leadership joined the latter.

After formation, the CPI (M) became the major partner in the two successive United Front governments in 1967 and 1969. In the 1967 state election, the United Left Front (ULF) under the leadership of the CPI (M) won 74 seats out of a total 280 seats while the CPI and BAC-led People's United Left Front (PULF) got 77 seats and the INC got 127 seats. The post-poll alliance of the PULF and ULF saw the first non-congress United Front (UF) government in West Bengal in 1967 with Ajoy Mukherjee of the BAC as the chief minister and Jyoti Basu of the CPI (M) as the deputy chief minister. Initially the CPI (M), known for its radical political outlook, was hesitant to support the non-Left BAC—a party with a good representation of the landlords and the rich farmers. Keeping into consideration the precarious economic condition of the state arising out of the acute food shortage and the need to initiate class action from below to resist the landlords' and rich farmers' catalytic role in constituting a famine like situation in the state, it decided to join the government. Soon there was tension cropping up between the CPI (M) and other non-Left partners in the UF pertaining to the issue of procuring and selling of food grains at a controlled price from government-run shops. This resulted in the fall of the UF government on 2 November 1967. Subsequently, a new alliance namely the Progressive Democratic Front (PDF), supported by the INC, came to form the government. The weak PDF, however, could not carry with the government for long and after 3 months its collapse saw the imposition of the President's rule in West Bengal on 20 February 1968.

In the mid-term election of February 1969, the ULF comprising of all the Left parties formed a pre-poll alliance with the BAC to form the UF, which convincingly won the election defeating the INC. The CPI (M)'s seat share increased to 83 from 74 of the first UF, while the INC was reduced to 55 from the earlier 127. The CPI (M), although the largest party, left the chief ministerial position to Ajoy Mukherjee of the BAC and retained some important departments among which Home and General Administration, and Land and Land Revenue were crucial ones given the political dynamics of the period. In order to use the government as a means to further the interest of class struggle, the CPI (M) besides performing the legislative functions, also kept some space for extra-legal initiative by the party workers. Among these, recovering ceiling surplus land (as determined by the West Bengal Estate Acquisition Act of 1953), *benami* land (ceiling surplus land transferred to the names of the relatives of the landholders to avoid its legal confiscation), and to redistribute it among the landless peasants with the assistance of the rural mass organizations were important (Franda 1971). The police was also instructed to consult the officers of the Land Revenue Department before taking any action to suppress the legitimate democratic movements of the people. Such steps of the CPI (M) created considerable impasse to the smooth functioning of the UF government since the peasant units of all the major constituent parties of the UF engaged in mobilizing peasants to seize such lands from the *jotedars* (wealthy peasants) even if it required application of force at times. Under such a condition of near constitutional crisis the chief minister resigned and President's rule was imposed in April 1970.

Since its inception in 1964, the CPI (M) had been experiencing considerable strain arising out of the divergences in the opinions between the centrists and leftists regarding its ideological and practical approaches to politics. To begin with, it was about the decision of participating in electoral politics. While the centrists did not find anything wrong in it, to the leftists it was a deviation from the path of revolutionary politics. Then came the issue of entering the ministries and that too in collaboration with the landlord and rich peasants backed BAC. The centrists defended the position of joining the ministries as a tactical move to further the cause of revolutionary change. The leftists were rather apprehensive about it since joining the government could amount to being part of its protocol which often might clash with the organizational and ideological struggle of the exploited classes. In the context of recovery of benami land, Jyoti Basu, the deputy chief minister of the second UF government, argued that the UF government would support all forms of legitimate struggle of the people, but would not stand by their unlawful actions (Franda 1971). From his argument it was revealed that the leftists' apprehension was not ungrounded. This indeed was a justified statement from an efficient administrator, but seen from the angle of revolutionary struggle, such an assertion of a communist leader was bound to create enough confusion among the rank and files of a revolutionary communist party. Moreover to the leftists, alliance with BAC, which had been the representative of the rural upper classes, was a sign of class collaborationist approach. As members of a communist party committed to the cause of revolution, the leftists within the CPI (M) were doubtful about the fruitfulness of joining hands with the class enemies, however tactical it might be.

This pro-institution tendency of the CPI (M) appeared to them as the mark of neo-revisionism.

The dilemma within the CPI (M) came out into the open with the Naxalbari peasant uprising in March 1967 led by the CPI (M) affiliated Krishak Samiti. The movement originated in the three police station areas of the Siliguri Block of Darjeeling District of West Bengal, namely, Naxalbari, Phansidewa and Khoribari. Soon it spread to Srikakulam in Andhra Pradesh. Initially, the state CPI (M) agreed to provide support to the movement. During the preparatory phase of the agitation, when the CPI (M) was yet to join the first UF coalition government, the pro-Chinese leftist faction within the CPI (M) was quite optimistic about the revolutionary potential of the uprising, which the Communist Party of China (CPC) hailed as the 'spring thunder' over India. This optimism of the CPI (M) was there in the early days of the first UF government too as was evident from the statements of Harekrishna Konar, peasant leader of the CPI (M) and the Land and Land Revenue Minister of the first UF government, who favoured extraconstitutional means adopted by the peasant organizations to secure the benami land from the jotedars. The stand of the CPI (M), however, changed drastically with the Union Home Minister, Y. B. Chavan's ultimatum to the UF government on 13 June 1967 to put down the Naxalbari agitation, failing which the central government would be forced to intervene (Bhattacharyya 2016).

Subsequently, the CPI (M) showed its commitment to uphold the legitimacy of the UF government by embarking upon a massive police operation against the Naxalbari movement and its leadership. Consequently, the movement went underground and most of its leaders were arrested by the police within 4 months of the uprising. Such volte-face of the CPI (M) was perceived by the Naxalite leadership as an appropriation of the former by the reactionary Indian ruling class which resulted in the CPI (M)'s choosing the path of electoral democracy and getting deviated from the revolutionary politics of the exploited classes of Indian society. This was enough to initiate a process of rift within the CPI (M). Initially the Naxalbari leadership formed the All India Coordination Committee of the Communist

Revolutionaries (AICCCR) in November 1967—a national platform for all the radical communists. Ultimately on 22 April 1969, on the birth centenary of V. I. Lenin, the Communist Party of India (Marxist-Leninist) (CPI-ML) was formed, marking the second major split in the Communist movement in India.

In the sixth mid-term Assembly Election held in March 1971, the political instability continuing in West Bengal led the different contending political parties to redraw the maps of their alliance networks. The UF had split into the ULF under the leadership of the CPI (M), and the United Left Democratic Front (ULDF) primarily under the leadership of the CPI. This was a clear indication of the increasing distance between the CPI and the CPI (M). The prime reason, perhaps, was the growing affinity of the CPI with Mrs Indira Gandhi-led INC due to her 'pro-Left' populist policies backed by a nationalist wave and her successful army operation in liberating Bangladesh. As an outcome of the election, a democratic coalition government, formed primarily under the aegis of the INC and backed by the CPI, Forward Block and some other Left parties under the chief ministership of Ajoy Mukherjee of the BAC—which had won only five seats contesting in 131 seats (source: Election Commission of India)—came to rule West Bengal. The CPI (M), once again the single largest party (winning 113 seats contesting in 241 seats; source: Election Commission of India) with also the highest vote share (37.42%; source: Election Commission of India), came to compose the opposition along with some other Left parties allied to it. The government was indeed very short lived. It took office on 2 April 1971 to be dissolved only on 25 June 1971 followed by the imposition of President's Rule for the third time since 1968.

In the seventh Assembly Election in 1972, the INC surprisingly won 216 seats while the CPI (M)'s tally went down to only 14 seats from 113 in the last year's election. The CPI (M), alleging widespread terrorization of the overall atmosphere of the state and particularly the areas known to be their strongholds by the INC patronized gangsters and large-scale rigging of the election (Dasgupta 1972), boycotted the assembly for the next five years. Siddhartha Shankar Ray of the

INC became the chief minister of West Bengal on 20 March 1972. During the Siddhartha Shankar Ray regime (1972–1977), 'Massive state repression set in, reaching its peak in the national emergency' (Bhattacharyya 2016, 10). Not only the CPI (M) or the Left parties opposed to the INC, every sort of opposition voices were forcefully silenced in the state. Interestingly, the CPI during this period stood by the INC. It even considered the imposition of national emergency by Mrs Gandhi in June 1975 to be 'necessary and justified' (Varkey 1979, 883) since the repressive resources of the emergency appeared to the CPI to be of full potential to curb Jaya Prakash Narayan's (JP) movement for 'total revolution' in which many of the rightist and reactionary forces of India had participated. Now, almost four decades after this the leaders of the CPI are admitting that supporting the emergency was a great political mistake (*The Hindu* 2015).

In the sixth Lok Sabha Elections in India, held in the month of March 1977, Mrs Indira Gandhi-led INC government at the centre suffered a massive defeat. By and large this was a clear mandate of the people against the national emergency imposed by Mrs Gandhi. The Janata Party came to power with Morarji Desai as the prime minister. Immediately after assuming power the Janata Party-ruled centre imposed President's rule in nine INC-ruled states to dissolve the assemblies there. These states were Uttar Pradesh, Bihar, West Bengal, Orissa, Madhya Pradesh, Panjab, Rajasthan, Haryana and Himachal Pradesh. Subsequently, in the eighth Assembly Election in West Bengal, held in June 1977, the CPI (M)-led LF had a landslide victory winning 231 seats out of the 294 seats in the West Bengal assembly. The CPI (M) alone won 178 seats among these. The tally of the INC went down to a meagre 20 seats. Alike the trend in the sixth Parliamentary election, the state election of West Bengal 1977 too can be regarded as a massive mandate of the electorates of West Bengal against the authoritarian rule of Siddhartha Shankar Roy-led INC government, particularly its forceful suppression of the democratic rights of the people. Jyoti Basu of the CPI (M) became the chief minister of the LF government on 21 June 1977, a post which he held for more than 23 consecutive years until 28 October 2000, when he retired from the position of the chief minister of West Bengal.

THE LF GOVERNMENT AND THE TASKS AT HAND

The LF government had a clear perception of the challenging tasks to rule a state marked by considerable socio-political turmoil coupled with grave economic backwardness. Restoration of democracy and bringing the state back on the path of economic development were the two top priorities of the LF government, which could be revealed from the first message of Jyoti Basu as the CM of West Bengal on 22 June 1977:

> In the past few years, there had been massive attacks on the freedoms and rights of the people of the state and plans were afoot to take them away altogether. I want to assure you on behalf of the Left Front Government that we shall give due priority to the task of restoring and protecting these freedoms and rights.... The economy of the state is in a moribund condition and the people's suffering knows no bounds.... We shall make serious and sincere efforts to tackle these problems (Basu 1977).

To resolve the ongoing 'crises of governability' (Kohli 1997, 353) continuing since 1967, the LF government quickly embarked upon its twin flagship programmes: The land reform policies and the extension of democracy to the grassroots through politically-elected panchayats. These programmes were carefully designed to benefit or provide relief primarily to the middle and lower strata of the rural Bengali society by reforming some aspects of the existing economic and political structure. Such attempts at reform by a Left political coalition, chiefly its spearhead, the CPI (M)—known for its Marxist ideology and revolutionary proclivity, has been termed by many critics as an ideological change or even deviation (to be dealt with later in this chapter) to arrive at a compromise with the system of parliamentary democracy. However, to the newly elected CPI (M)-led LF more important, perhaps, was to extend the base of its legitimacy even further to enhance the viability of Left politics in West Bengal and beyond.

Prior to 1977 West Bengal had been a poor performer among the major Indian states in the economic sphere. As far as the 'net state domestic product (NSDP) per capita at current prices' were concerned, the Planning Commission data reveals that West Bengal ranked 13th

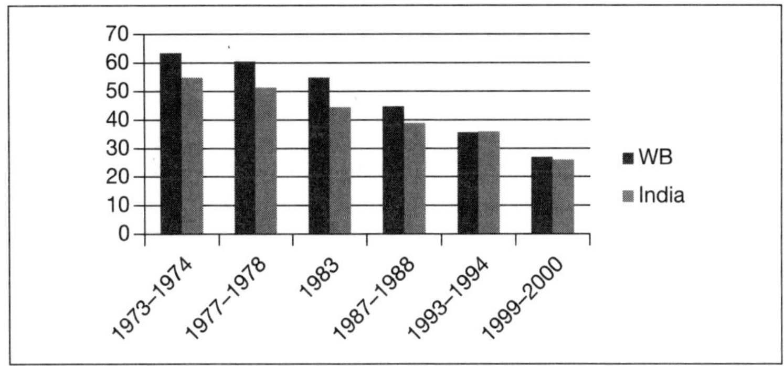

Figure 1.1 *Poverty Level in West Bengal and India during 1973–2000*

Source: http://planningcommission.nic.in/plans/planrel/fiveyr/10th/volume3/10th_vol3.pdf (accessed on 14 October 2018).

and 12th among the 19 major Indian states during the decades of 1960s and 1970s respectively. In the 1990s it progressed considerably to occupy the 6th position along the indicator of 'gross state domestic product per capita at current prices'.[1] West Bengal had been making significant progress in reducing the number of people living below the poverty line since 1973. As the chart (Figure 1.1) represents, the continuous decline in poverty level became quite pronounced since 1983, marking a significant decline in 1993–1994 when it even toppled the national figure.

The decline of poverty in West Bengal as the Planning Commission data indicates, was in a large part due to the significant decline in the level of rural poverty ratio which went down from 73.16 in 1973–1974 to 31.85 in 1999–2000. Such a reduction in rural poverty level can be attributed to the relatively better performance of the agricultural sector of the state during the period. As the same data set reflects, among all the Indian states, West Bengal had the highest rate of agricultural growth of 4.39 per cent per annum during 1980 to 1995, which were respectively 1.27 and 0.57 during 1962–1973 and 1970–1983.

[1] Source: http://planningcommission.nic.in/plans/planrel/fiveyr/10th/volume3/10th_vol3.pdf (accessed on 14 October 2018).

From the above description of facts it is apparent that a distinct and positive turnaround took place in the economic fortunes of West Bengal during the 1980s. Since it was the period when the LF government had been ruling the state, it seems pertinent to focus on the LF's policies and programmes which should have some bearing on this noteworthy achievement. As the economic advancement was achieved primarily through the rural sector, a brief account of the LF's intervention in the rural socio-economic structure and institutions through its much celebrated policies of land reform and decentralization of power to the grassroots is necessary here. Analysis of the policies, their implementations and their possible impacts on the economic institutions and on the existing rural power structure would help us to develop some general understanding about the efficacy of the policies adopted by a state, in this case represented by a democratic Left coalition, in transforming the social and economic lives of the people at large. Moreover, this would also help in perceiving the dynamics of the emerging political processes associated with this change in rural West Bengal. It is expected to throw some light on the LF's subsequent negotiation with the changing nature of politics and economics at the national and international level, beginning in the 1990s through the first decade of the new millennium.

INSTITUTIONAL INTERVENTION BY THE LF

Assuming power in 1977, the CPI (M)-led LF government in West Bengal took no time to initiate a detailed programme for rural development. Such attention to the rural sector was paid probably due to the CPI (M)'s earlier experience of success in dealing with the agrarian question in the two successive UF governments in late 1960s. The major thrust of the programme has been pinpointed by Nielsen (2010, 150) as being:

> Operation Barga (sharecropper): recording the names of sharecroppers and securing them the legal rights they were entitled to; distribution of available ceiling surplus vested land among the rural poor; efforts to detect and vest more ceiling surplus land; giving institutional credit to the recipients of vested land to break the ties of debt and bondage; assigning permanent title to homestead plots in order to prevent eviction of landless

agricultural workers and sharecroppers residing on the landowners' plots as permissive occupiers; restoration of land alienated due to distress sale; and providing irrigation, subsidies, exemption from revenues, and designing food-for-work programmes.

Clearly the programmes mentioned above hint at institutional reforms in the agrarian sector in terms of providing tenurial security and redistribution of ownership of land favouring the disadvantaged segment of the rural society. Since the unequal property relations in the rural society of West Bengal were well entrenched within the upper class dominated rural power structure, the fulfilment of the goals of land reforms was squarely dependent upon a simultaneous effort to shift the power balance towards the lower strata of the rural society. The LF, possibly, on a similar realization, revitalized the Panchayati Raj institution politically. The plan apparently was to interlock land reforms and Panchayati Raj, so that they can provide the necessary reinforcements to each other (Gazdar and Sengupta 1997). Considered against the background of the continual diminishing influence of the landlords in the rural political hierarchy, as a result of the CPI (M)'s rule, this indeed appeared to be feasible (Ibid.).

The expectations were indeed met as the CPI (M)-led LF won the majority of seats in all the three tiers of the panchayats in the 1978 panchayat election in West Bengal. Such democratically elected panchayats were made responsible to supervise, monitor and participate in the implementation of the different land reform measures.

In the late 1960s the CPI (M), as a partner of the UF government, left the task of detecting ceiling surplus land, restoration of benami land and so on to the local initiative of the peasant organizations. More than a legal process, it was a poor and land-starved peasants' prerogative. As the dominant partner of the LF, however, it took a more cautious approach in involving the discourse of legality to the whole issue of identification and redistribution of ceiling surplus land. The Naxalbari uprising of the late 1960s, probably, gave it a real feel of the depth of the inequality prevailing in rural West Bengal. The uprising also revealed the nature of the agrarian discontent along with the revolutionary spirit and preparedness of the marginal and landless peasants to redraw the imbalance, even if it required the path of violence. Hence, the LF government deployed the governmental machinery stretching up to the grass-roots level within the overall framework of land reform laws to make the whole process smooth. In this fashion it attempted to absorb the conflict within the space of the political institutions marked by the intervention of government and the vigilance, monitoring and arbitration of the disciplined political party. There are contestations regarding the efficacy of such an effort of conflict management in the long run or more fundamentally with the perceived differences between the ideological and pragmatic stand of the CPI (M) as a communist party in dealing with the agrarian conflicts. Such debates notwithstanding, the governmental effort of the LF attained considerable success in addressing, or even redressing to some extent, the long neglected issue of institutional inequality in agriculture.

The tenancy reform undertaken by the LF government since 1977 was based on the West Bengal Land Reforms (Amendment) Act 1972, passed by the preceding INC government of the state. The first legal attempt to safeguard the interest of the *bargadars* (sharecroppers) in the state during the post-Independence period, however, was the West Bengal Bargadars Act enacted in 1950. Later, the West Bengal Land Reforms Act, 1955 came into being to plug the loopholes of the 1950 Act. The 1955 Act incorporated the major provisions of the 1950 Act, but it also failed to restrict the large-scale eviction of the sharecroppers by the landlords and the rich peasants. Perhaps, to put a check on this, the Siddhartha Shankar Ray-led INC government came up with the West Bengal Land Reforms (Amendment) Act in 1972. Besides, raising the sharecroppers' share of the produce it also provided them with greater tenurial security. While in the Tebhaga movement of the 1940s, the sharecroppers only demanded enhancement of their share of the produce, this amendment in addition to it also provided them with tenurial security. The West Bengal Acquisition of Homestead Land for Agricultural Labourers, Artisans and Fishermen Act, 1975 was also enacted to provide the ownership of the homestead land to the landless agricultural labourers or sharecroppers or artisans. But the INC government did not make any serious attempt to implement both these laws (Dasgupta 1984).

As the legal framework had already been there, tenancy reform under the LF government, particularly, stressed upon the implementation of the 1972 Act. Among other measures, most importantly, a campaign for recording the sharecroppers known as Operation Barga was launched. This had remained a classic example of implementation of laws with popular participation. The process involved a number of stages. In all these stages, the state bureaucracy was made to act hand in hand with the peasantry, their organizations and the elected members of the panchayats at the local levels.

The result was indeed encouraging. During 1978–1982, about 7.1 lakh sharecroppers were recorded (Chakraborti 2003). As per the *West Bengal Human Development Report 2004*, by 2000 this figure rose to more than 1.6 million. Among the recorded bargadars, the same report mentions, over 30 per cent were SCs and 11 per cent were Scheduled Tribes (STs). Compared to the fact that less than 60,000 sharecroppers got registered during the pre-LF period (Kohli 1987), this should be considered as a remarkable success of the LF government in West Bengal. Implementation of The West Bengal Acquisition of Homestead Land for Agricultural Labourers, Artisans and Fishermen Act, 1975, resulted in title distribution to 5 lakh occupants of such land (Bandyopadhyay 2003; Ramachandran 2001). By bringing in the state bureaucracy close to the people in intimate ties with the peasant organization and elected people's representatives of the villages, the programme had been a unique experience in statecraft.

Another aspect of the distributive reform initiated by the LF government in West Bengal since 1977 was the distribution of government vested (ceiling surplus land) agricultural land to the landless or land-poor segment of the rural population. This programme was based on the provisions of the West Bengal Estate Acquisition Act, 1953, as amended from time to time, particularly those during the post-1977 period ushered in by the LF government. Effort was taken through these amendments to reduce the magnitude of institutional inequality. Of particular importance among these amendments were the ones relating to reasonably lowering the ceiling limit, linking personal cultivation strictly to physical participation in the labour process, necessitating the owners of land to reside in the area for the greater part of the year where the land is situated, entitlement of the sharecropper to receive a formal receipt issued by the landowner on payment of revenue and so on. Apart from its economic goals, these amendments had been significant steps to combat the entrenchment of landed vested interests in different layers of political and social power and to shift the power balance of rural society more and more towards the poor and the underprivileged. As mentioned by Chakraborti (2003), up to March 2002 a total of 10.59 lakh acres of land were distributed among 26.52 lakh beneficiaries. In this aspect also West Bengal's performance in comparison to other states of India had been commanding since it accounted for, '…19.74% of the total land distributed and 46.29% of the total number of beneficiaries covered. Overall, its performance is by far the best in the country' (ibid., 40). The distributive reform was particularly beneficial to the cause of the socially and economically marginalized segment of the population since among the beneficiaries the majority (almost 56%) was composed of the SCs and STs (Government of West Bengal 2004). How this had been instrumental for the LF in developing a concrete electoral constituency among the SCs can be revealed from Figure 1.2 which shows that in every assembly and parliamentary election in West Bengal since 1996 to 2009 the

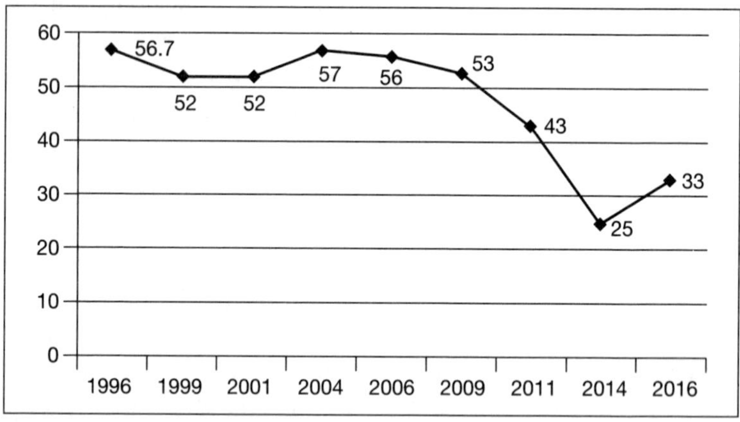

Figure 1.2 *SC Vote Share of the Left Front (1996–2016)*

Source: CSDS Data Unit, NES 1996, 1999, 2004, 2009, 2014 and West Bengal Assembly Election Study 2001, 2006, 2011 and 2016.

SC vote share of the LF never went down below 50 per cent. Although it is showing a decline since the 2011 Assembly Election but signs of recovery are also there.

The distinctive feature of these processes of reforms had been the judicious blending of bureaucratic action with popular participation ensured by the politically elected panchayats under the overall vigilance of a disciplined political party, the CPI (M). Considered in the background of several criticisms launched against the pro-upper class and upper caste bias of Indian bureaucracy, especially at the lower level (Kohli 1987; Varshney 1998), this initiative of the LF government was a unique experiment in expanding the base of democratic governance substantively. The involvement of the panchayats hand in hand with the party in the whole process of tenancy reform and land redistribution added considerable transparency to it. Such a combination attempted to break the perceived nexus between the local-level bureaucrats and the landed vested interests in rural areas. The panchayats, in this way, were successful in taming the local bureaucracy (Kohli 1987). Although, debates may be there regarding the ideological orientation and degree of politicization of the panchayats but there should be little doubt about the extent of democratization of the rural socio-political space brought in by the LF governments' commitment to make the panchayats the primary vehicle of rural democratic governance.

This commitment was explicated by the LF government's efforts to hold the panchayat elections regularly. After assuming state power in 1977, it started to take preparation to hold the panchayat election immediately. In June 1978, after a break of 14 years, the state witnessed direct elections '...to elect 56,000 representatives for 15 zila parishads, 324 panchayat samitis and 3,242 gram panchayats under the West Bengal Panchayat Act, 1973' (Acharya 1993, 1080). Since then the LF government held such elections every five years without considering the overall political climate prevailing in the state and the country, which could've had some determining influence upon the outcome of the elections. The regularity of the panchayat elections was strictly maintained by the LF government, '...even when electoral compulsions dictated otherwise...' (Ghatak and Ghatak 2002, 45).

Such electoral compulsions often proved to be too important for the political parties in some other states of India, such as Kerala, Karnataka, Bihar, Uttar Pradesh and Andhra Pradesh, to go for the panchayat elections. This had been a reality even after the 73rd constitutional amendment of 1992 which made it mandatory for the states to hold panchayat elections after the expiry of five-year term of its three-tier panchayats. Mathew (2001), in this context, cites the instance of the holding of panchayat election by the LF government in West Bengal just following the 1998 Lok Sabha Election in West Bengal where the newly formed TMC had already made significant inroads into some of the LF strongholds.

ACHIEVEMENTS OF THE LF

These interventions by the LF in the institutional sphere of rural West Bengal were marked with considerable success. The LF's attempt in this regard earned the attention of the scholars nationally as well as internationally, perhaps, more for the fillip it provided to the development of the hitherto backward West Bengal economy. Being predominantly an agrarian economy such backwardness had its roots in the agricultural sector. During the three decades preceding the LF rule, West Bengal witnessed a condition of 'agricultural impasse' as argues Boyce (1987). To him the primary technological constraint causing this had been the poor development of the irrigation system. He visualized the nature of agrarian structure characterised by the unequal distribution of wealth and power between the big landlords, rich farmers, moneylenders and the middle to small farmers along with the agricultural labourers as the fundamental institutional impediment for the much needed technological change in the agricultural sphere. The distinction of the LF's intervention primarily lies in its endeavour to reform such institutional inequality through its calculated and cautious attempt to redraw the economic and political balance in favour of the underprivileged.

Not only should the much-celebrated policies of land reform and democratic decentralization of the power to the grassroots be credited for ushering in the pro-poor change in the rural society of West Bengal, the credit must go also to the methodology of implementation of these policies. Land reform laws had been there in India since independence and different states had experienced different rates of implementation while attaining differential levels of success. The unique feature of the LF was that it ensured popular participation in the whole process of implementation of the policies. The idea was to bring the state close to the people not only to make the process transparent and democratic but also to bridge the obvious gaps between policies and practices. Such gaps are natural since social reality is composed of heterogeneous groups having quite diversified needs and aspirations which can render any policy by any government, Left or Right, relatively inappropriate. The difficulty, perhaps, lies with the very ontology of the term 'policy' which is defined to have some definite object(s); the groups or communities which it purports to cater. As the aspirations and dispositions of any social aggregate vary infinitely along the dimensions of time and space, so it is very difficult, if not impossible for any policy to be inclusive enough to incorporate all these diversities within its fold. Perhaps, these explain the increasing importance of the notions of 'participation', 'bottom-up' approach to development, 'decentralised planning' and so on in contemporary development discourse to address or redress the vulnerability ingrained within the top-down policy approach to development. As the World Bank document (2010, 29) argues, 'The poor are the main actors in the fight against poverty; they must be brought to center stage in designing, implementing and monitoring anti-poverty strategies.' Although it glorifies the values of participation by the poor but it also, perhaps, detaches them from the dynamics of their contexts marked by inequalities of different kinds and magnitudes. Poverty cannot be thought of solely in terms of its economic dimensions; it has its own political ramifications. Thus, without a definite political orientation, participation of the poor in the fight against poverty, possibly, bears the risk of getting misdirected, if not appropriated by the vested interests entrenched within the different layers of a stratified society.

Here in lies the crucial role of an organized and disciplined party. In the context of West Bengal, the CPI (M), as a facilitator or a mediator linked the government with the people so that the policymakers at the top have some idea about the complex and often contradictory proclivities existing at the societal level. This allowed the government to incorporate a range of possibilities within the policy discourse. 'Government as practice' as Bhattacharyya (2016) terms this process, '...demands a full recognition of these contradictions, which make the process of governing unwieldy, demanding a dynamic use of tools for working daily through unknown, uncharted and unexpected contingencies' (pp. 28–29). Although the party in charge of the government, in case of West Bengal the parties constituting the LF, particularly its spearhead the CPI (M), often can find such a situation intricate and uncomfortable enough to be negotiated and accommodated ideologically, but from the point of view of governmentalization of the state this certainly opens up 'a field of political transactions' (Chatterjee 1997, 160), a space for dialogue between the government and the people: the celebrated mark of good governance.

INCREASE IN AGRICULTURAL PRODUCTIVITY

The immediate consequence of the LF's strategies of economic and political reforms could be registered in the spurt of the agricultural growth in the 1980s. It has already been mentioned earlier that during this period the growth rate of agriculture in West Bengal was the highest among all the major states of India. Among many other factors, increase in agricultural productivity has been the chief contributor towards the growth in agricultural output (Harris 1993; Sanyal, Biswas and Bardhan 1998).

Such an increase in the productivity in agriculture occurred during a period when the economic sphere of rural West Bengal was experiencing a major institutional intervention by the newly elected LF government of West Bengal. Hence, it is quite natural to consider the latter as having some determining influence upon the former. Derivation of this sort is not conjectural since prior to reform initiative undertaken by the LF government in the late 1970s and early 1980s, the agricultural scenario of West Bengal was indeed dismal. From 1969–1970 to 1981–1982, West Bengal registered an annual compound growth rate in foodgrain production of 0.6 per cent while the national average for the same period was 2.2 per cent (CMIE 1993, quoted in Saha and Swaminathan 1994). It is remarkable that in the next decade, during the period 1981–1982 to 1991–1992, under the LF rule the growth rate scaled to 6.5 per cent per annum—the highest among the 17 major states of India. Many scholars believe that this turnaround was due to the economic reform undertaken by the LF government (Banerjee, Gertler and Ghatak 1998; Gazdar and Sengupta 1999; Ramachandran 2001; Saha and Swaminathan 1994).

Two major dimensions of the land reform laws, namely redistribution of ceiling surplus land to the landless and provision pertaining to security of tenancy rights of the sharecroppers through recording, were indeed instrumental in enhancing the economic freedom of these categories of peasants. The recorded tenants experienced an enhancement in their bargaining power which had a direct impact on the crop share to be paid to the leasers of the lands. Tenurial security removed to a great extent the threat of eviction faced by the bargadars and encouraged them to invest on the land autonomously. As a result of these, agricultural productivity increased significantly. Banerjee, Gertler and Ghatak (1998, 29) argue in this context, 'Our estimates suggest that Operation Barga raised agricultural productivity in West Bengal by 17–18%.'

Besides providing tenurial security to the sharecroppers, Operation Barga also opened the doors of institutional credit to them. The certificates issued to the bargadars during the recording operation, being a legal document in support of their tenancy, could be used to obtain credit from various formal and institutional sources. Needless to mention that availability of credit to the poor peasantry, especially from the institutional sources, has always been a necessary condition for agricultural growth.

Increasing creditworthiness and bargaining power of the poor peasants, the direct offshoots of the land reform measures, had also resulted in 'greater irrigation, higher cropping intensity, greater use of fertilisers and a switch over to higher yielding varieties' which, as consider Gazdar and Sengupta (1999, 72), have contributed positively in raising agricultural productivity. Besides increasing productivity they believe that these factors have also resulted in a simultaneous increase in the demand of labour. Agricultural growth, thus, might be expected to have a positive influence on rural employment also. This is, perhaps, an unacknowledged or less acknowledged impact of land reform on rural economy. As the avowed goal of land reform is to lessen the extent of landlessness in agricultural sector, so it is, perhaps, a natural corollary of the land reform process that there would be lesser availability of agricultural labourers. In such a condition the demand of labour would register an increase leading to a concomitant increase in the rural wages (Bandyopadhyay 2003). This theoretical expectation, however, fails to achieve much support from the ground reality as finds out Chakraborti (2003). The *pattadars* (assignees of vested land), due to the miniscule size of their patta lands (0.39 acres per capita), often could not find full employment in their land, although the case is slightly better for the bargadars. For this, he argues, they were forced to seek employment in others' land or to go for other non-farm employment. Under such a distressed condition the wages, quite naturally, were '...much below the minimum wage rates prescribed by the state government for agricultural labourers' (ibid., 116).

Over and above, land reform policies implemented by the LF government in West Bengal did have a positive association with the increase in agricultural productivity and it helped the once economically laggard state of West Bengal turn out to be one of the fastest growing states in India during the 1980s. Such turnaround might not be enough to eliminate rural poverty and unemployment but it certainly contributed in its decline, which has led Bandyopadhyay (1997, 583) to remark that the '...visible signs of destitution are disappearing from West Bengal's rural area.... A major achievement of the LF government in West Bengal by any standard.'

Harris (1992, 1993), however, seems to disagree with such a positive correlation between reform measures and increase in agricultural productivity. Instead, he attributes the 'quite dramatic spurt in agricultural production' in West Bengal during the 1980s to, '...the growth of boro rice production, based on the development of private shallow tubewell irrigation...' (1992, 219). Moreover, referring to the data about increased fertilizer consumption and that of high yielding varieties (HYVs) as mentioned by Lieten (1990), Harris (1992) contends that the higher growth rate of 'boro' paddy in West Bengal was also due to the availability of HYVs and the declining fertilizer prices. More than removal of structural constraints through land reforms, thus, the productivity spurt in agriculture, he asserts, was due to the state intervention in these directions.

Gazdar and Sengupta (1999), however, seem to challenge Harris' contention relating to the reform independent productivity growth in West Bengal agriculture. They point out to the cases of Bihar and Orissa where also acceleration in the growth rate of agriculture was witnessed during the 1980s. Compared to these states the magnitude of growth was quite high in West Bengal. Since the factors of reduced fertilizer price, availability of HYVs and so on were present in those states as well, the difference in the growth rates of West Bengal and the neighbouring states of Bihar and Orissa might have occurred due to some factors other than those as mentioned by Harris. Sen and Sengupta (1995) through a detailed statistical analysis of the agricultural growth in West Bengal experienced during the 1980s fail to find justifications in favour of Harris' claim. Controlling the factors such as HYVs, fertilizers, irrigated land and the consumption of electricity they came to the conclusion that agrarian and political reforms undertaken by the LF government in West Bengal were the significant factors underpinning the growth in agricultural productivity, which was not the case in Bihar and Orissa. Banerjee, Gertler and Ghatak (2002), adopting a quasi-experimental approach using Bangladesh as a control, where a similar agroclimatic condition, prevalence of tenancy and agricultural technology exist like West Bengal, argue that the rate of growth of agricultural productivity, particularly that of rice, was quite high in West Bengal compared to Bangladesh. They attribute this difference in the growth rate of productivity to the implementation of Operation Barga in West Bengal which was not implemented in Bangladesh. On the basis of their quantitative analysis they, hence, conclude, '...that the tenancy reform programme called Operation Barga explains around 28 percent of the subsequent growth of agricultural productivity' in West Bengal (ibid., 277–278).

Apart from the economic gains, the land reform measures also achieved some other successes which cannot be gauged in quantitative terms. As it happens everywhere, when there is a change or reform in any one of the social institutions, the effect is felt in the entire range of social relationships binding the individuals. Thus, the reform undertaken by the LF government, primarily in the economic and political sphere of rural West Bengal brought in some significant changes in the social life of the rural people. Conferment of ownership right to the landless and providing of security of tenure to the bargadars, besides empowering them economically, also resulted in definite increase in their social prestige. It enhanced their confidence, a necessary condition for a better and healthy social life. The overall social environment geared up to achieve the reform induced values of social equality was an impetus before them to improve their quality of life. The idea of democracy as a matter of everyday practice, in this way, became meaningful to them. The decentralization of power to the grassroots recognized their political agency and enhanced their self-respect by making them active participants of the development process. The LF's measures of rural reconstruction, hence, proved to be instrumental in ushering in '...peace in the countryside since 1981, after a long period of turmoil from the mid-1940s' (Bandyopadhyay 2001, 3902).

POLITICAL WILL OF THE LF: THE KEY TO SUCCESS

If one tries to introspect deeply into the changes brought in by the LF government in the rural areas of West Bengal, a definite political will on the part of its major constituent, the CPI (M), becomes apparent. Through its participation in the two successive UF governments in the late 1960s it came to know about the inequalities and the resultant discontents prevailing in the rural societies. The vulnerability of the peasants' lives was reflected through their desperate attempts to redraw the property relations in rural society on the face of the CPI (M)'s call for direct peoples' initiative in this regard. The situation went to such an extent that the CPI (M), a major constituent of the UF government, had to deploy the state machineries to quell the peasants' uprisings at Naxalbari and other places to prevent the ensuing law and order crisis in the state. This learning was perhaps profound enough to let the CPI (M) realize, under the LF government formed a decade later, that within the limits of constitutional democracy neither the structure of legality nor people's unorganized or unstructured initiative could be the exclusive principle of governance. It should rather be a judicious blending of the two. Hence, the need for pro-poor policies adopted at the level of government and their implementation through various agencies composed of the bureaucracy as well as the people at the grassroots was felt. The politically elected panchayats were conceived as an epitome of such an intertwining of formal legality and popular participation. The role of the CPI (M) as a disciplined and organized party was to closely monitor the entire process to bolster the confidence of the peasants, sharecroppers and landless labourers. This well-orchestrated effort of the LF to intervene in the institutional arrangement of rural society, to sway the economic and political power structure therein towards the underprivileged, had been a unique experiment in extending the reach of democratic governance to the grassroots. Chambers (1992) rightly points out the idiosyncrasy of West Bengal in this regard and comments, 'West Bengal stands out as an example where political ideology committed to the poor, backed by political organization at the grassroots, has led to reforms which have largely eluded the rest of India' (p. 41). Little wonder then that the land reform policies and the decentralization of power to the local levels in this way would turn out to be instrumental in developing the much talked about hegemony of the CPI (M) over the rural electorates of West Bengal.

The West Bengal experience reveals that land reform measures or any other positive pro-poor intervention by a democratic state cannot be considered in administrative terms alone. The issue of political will is also an equally important determinant here. In fact, political will is a necessary sine qua non for pushing forward land reform measures (Bardhan and Mookherjee 2003, 2010). Without a definite political intent of the governing political parties the administrative apparatus of any state cannot be activated to perform the task with a proper spirit. The history of land reform initiatives being undertaken in different states of India since independence provides enough support to this claim. *Report of the Task Force on Agrarian Relations* (Government of India 1973) laments that due to lack of such a political will no tangible progress could be achieved in the field of land reform in India.

As our foregoing discussion suggests, West Bengal (also Kerala as mention Ghatak and Roy 2007) stands, perhaps, an exception to the pan-India pattern. What is noteworthy here is that both these states possess the experience of Left-wing coalition ruling for a relatively long period. Besley and Burgess (2000) considering land reform to be 'intensely political' (p. 411), attribute the failure of land reform measures in most of the states of India to the lack of appropriate political determination exhibited by the tradition of Congress rule therein. Through an analysis of panel data of 16 major Indian states from 1958 to 1992, they contend that in India the Congress party has an overall negative influence on enacting land reform legislations and implementations while the 'hard Left' (ibid.), the CPI (M) and the CPI have a positive one. This might be a pointer to or a plausible explanation of the success of land reform measures in West Bengal and Kerala, compared to its relative failures in other Indian states, which during this period were mostly under the rule of the 'hard Left' parties. Since Congress relied more on the 'vote controlling power of the bosses of rural rotten boroughs' in different states (Warriner 1969, 139), it did not, possibly, implement land reform measures seriously, which could jeopardise the vested interest of this stratum of rural social structure. Often in a number of states the control of the landlord class over many state legislatures, belonging primarily to the Congress party, prevented the latter from implementing the land reform measures adequately (Besley and Burgess 2000; Kohli 1987). In the case of the CPI (M) in West Bengal, in contrast, organized political will was reflected in mobilized forces comprising primarily of the peasants who '...were able to create conditions that brought relative equality as well as redistribution of wealth and power to the countryside' (Ruud 1999, 250). On the basis of evidences gathered from field work in West Bengal, Kohli (1983) assigns the credit for initiating the redistributive reforms to the political characteristics of the CPI (M): its leadership, ideological orientation and the nature of organization. Such political disposition of the CPI (M) was instrumental in performing two important tasks leading to successful implementation, which are, in Kohli's words, '...first, penetration of the countryside without being directly captured by the landed classes; and second, controlled mobilization from "below" to buttress state power as a tool of agrarian reform' (ibid., 784).

The reasons of failure of land reform measures in India, excepting West Bengal and Kerala therefore, more than being bureaucratic are integrally linked with politics, especially the arithmetic of electoral gain or loss. The West Bengal experience suggests that it is not the legislations which matter most, but more important, perhaps, is the overall political environment and it's determining influence on the agencies of implementation. Roy Burman et al. (1974, 52–53) rightly argue in this context that, '...the strategies of land reforms are to be considered, not only in terms of economic and administrative planning but also in terms of political and social planning.'

INSTITUTIONAL INTERVENTION OF THE LF: THE LIMITATIONS

Such political will of the CPI (M), notwithstanding, the score sheet of the LF government in West Bengal after the initial spur somehow failed to exhibit similar encouraging results. This would be perhaps too hasty to say that the political motivation of the ruling CPI (M) to carry on with the pro-poor initiatives got diluted or eroded, but there might be several other reasons responsible for this downturn. This could be due to the factors associated with limited powers of the state governments under the federal political structure of India (as often stressed by the LF, particularly, the CPI [M]), rising expectations, issues relating to routinization preventing the much required innovation in the strategies of implementation, ideological constraints or limitations, along with its alleged transformation and metamorphosis and so on.

To begin with, let us have a brief glimpse of the ground reality as existing there after almost a decade of the initiation of LF's programmes of economic reforms. This can be revealed by the comparative sizes of the population of owner cultivators vis-à-vis the landless labourers. The census reports of 1991 and 2001 reveal that among the working population in agriculture, share of the owner cultivators experienced a significant decline of about 10 per cent (from 53.9% in 1991 to 43.4% in 2001) against a similar increase in the size of the agricultural labourers (from 46.1% in 1991 to 56.6% in 2001) (Bagchi and Das 2005; Banerjee and Roy 2007). Strikingly, this increase was due primarily to the rising numbers of male agricultural labourers (Government of India 2010). Perhaps, more disturbing was the growing proportion of landless rural households which as the NSS data point out, '...increased from 39.6 percent in 1987–1988 to 41.6 percent in 1993–1994 and to as much as 49.8 percent in 1999–2000' (Government of West Bengal 2004, 39). Hence, in spite of the success stories of the land reform measures during the 1980s, at the beginning of the new millennium almost half of the rural households in West Bengal were landless and the rate was indeed fast increasing (Roy 2014).

If one tries to find out the reasons of this increase in the amount of landlessness in rural West Bengal one needs to have a relook at the extent and influence of land redistribution on agriculture. From the account of Gazdar and Sengupta (1997) it can be noticed that up to 1991 a total of 913,389 acres of land were redistributed among 1,993,616 beneficiaries. Thus, a very meagre amount of 0.46 acres of land were distributed to each beneficiary. The figure steadily went down with further land redistribution to only 0.39 acres in 2002 (Chakraborti 2003). The fact of West Bengal with only 1.8 per cent of national ceiling surplus land accounting for almost one-fourth of the land distribution beneficiaries (Lieten 1990) might be encouraging as far as the arithmetic of the success of land reform measures is concerned, but doubts are there regarding its effect in increasing the overall viability of agriculture for the beneficiaries. The 'success' story of land redistribution, as mentioned by Lieten (1990), appears to be confusing since more than 90 per cent and 83 per cent of the pattadars and bargadars respectively were not in a position to find employment in agriculture in their own land throughout the year (Chakraborti 2003).

Moreover, natural increase of population resulting in growth in household size leading to further divisions of it reduced the landownership per household even more. This was especially true for the smaller land-owning families (Bardhan et al. 2014). Such small size of landholding coupled with inadequate availability, if not non-availability, of production inputs certainly was antithetical to the cause of increasing agricultural productivity and sustainability. This was perhaps, evident from the decline in productivity of food grain production from 5.18 per cent a year during 1980–1990 to 1.68 per cent a year during 1990–1995 as recorded by Rawal and Swaminathan (1998). With increasing cost of cultivation, agriculture for the land-poor peasants hence, turned out to be non-profiting and less viable (Sengupta and Kundu 2008). The small amount of holding also acted as a constraint in getting adequate and timely institutional credits. Thus, instead of carrying with non-productive agriculture, many of them considered it imperative to sell off or surrender their land rights to the relatively better off peasants (Chakraborti 2003; Government of India 2010). Distressed sell of land in this way might be a possible reason for the swelling of the volume of landless agricultural labourers in rural West Bengal during 1978 to 1998 (Bardhan et al. 2014).

The increasing volume of landless agricultural labourers made the rural employment scenario more vulnerable. Contrary to the theoretical expectation of Bandyopadhyay (2003) about the positive impact of land reforms on increasing rural wages, the preponderance of agricultural labour in the agricultural economy tended to bring down the wages significantly. Chakraborti (2003) mentions that over 90 per cent of the pattadars and bargadars had to work in the land owned by others where the daily wage was up to ₹65. The fate of the pattadars was even worse since about 70 per cent of them worked with a daily wage of less than ₹30. Clearly, the daily wages of the majority of the agricultural labourers were less than the minimum wages fixed by the government of West Bengal, which were ₹74.33 without meals and 71.3 with meals, as in 2007–2008 (Barua 2010). The growing scope in the rural non-farm employment opportunities during the period had to some extent salvaged the situation. Since much of the increase of employment opportunities in this sector had taken place in the category of 'marginal work', which according to census classification can offer employment for less than 183 days, the concern with gainful employment remained. This perhaps prompted the *West Bengal*

Human Development Report, 2004 (Government of West Bengal 2004, 100) to urge for a much faster rate of growth of job opportunities in non-farm sector, '...in order to absorb the available rural labour force productively.'

The tapering of the agricultural growth and productivity, proliferation of landlessness and the simultaneous growth in the rural non-farm employment in West Bengal after a decade of the initiation of the land reform measures do not depict a healthy state of affairs of the agricultural sector. The foregoing discussion makes it amply clear that the land reform measures undertaken by the LF government in spite of all the hue and cry about moving forward to a more egalitarian rural society might have failed somehow to achieve its desired target. This is also revealed from the fact that within a period of two and half decades of the LF rule 13.23 per cent of the pattadars and 14.37 per cent of the bargadars were alienated from their land, and for almost 22 per cent of the pattadars the mode of alienation was sale while among the dispossessed bargadars 24.14 per cent were evicted (Chakraborti 2003). It is indeed very striking to note that Operation Barga, a programme designed to provide security of tenure to the tenants, saw almost one-fourth of its beneficiaries to be evicted within such a short time period of its initiation. It was perhaps, too early for Lieten (1990) to claim that with the unfolding of the land reform initiative by the LF government, '...the process of depeasantisation (with its implication of proletarianisation and immiserisation) has been halted' (p. 2270). This might well be the initial response of the reform measures which perhaps was not steady enough to continue for a relatively longer period. As witnessed later, the growing alienation of the pattadars especially those with very small landholdings, along with the bargadars from the means of production and their consequent joining the ranks of landless labourers should be considered as a mark of the process of depeasantization resulting into proletarianization of the peasantry.

A probe into the factors responsible for the relative failure of such a well-designed programme promoted by an organized political party with the requisite will to rectify some of the maladies of the rural society, most importantly inequality and poverty, finds its immediate reference into the existing political framework of the country during the time period in concern. Since Independence and also after 1977 when the CPI (M)-led LF came to rule West Bengal, the national government had mostly remained under the control of the Congress party. It has already been mentioned earlier that the latter for its electoral success had always maintained a tacit nexus with the feudal gentry, composed primarily of the landlords and rich peasantry. Moreover, the central government under the control of Congress supported the landlords' lobby within the various spheres of administration (Kohli 1987; Lieten 1990). Thus, it was not possible for the Congress to extend its political will beyond the interests of the rural elites. The primary contradiction of the CPI (M) with the Congress possibly lay in the perceived differences in their respective core constituencies, as the former unlike the latter, had an avowed goal to redraw the power balance of the rural society in favour of the downtrodden. This divergence was fundamental enough to erect stiff obstacles for the CPI (M) to move forward with its pro-poor policies as it, under the principles of federalism, had to operate a state government under the overall policy framework of the national government at the centre. The political rivalry and the ensuing competition between the CPI (M) and the Congress in the state as well as the national plain had been of determining influence over the implementation rates of the reform programmes at the local level (Bardhan and Mookherjee 2010).

Such concerns with the political constraints have been echoed more vociferously by the leaders and activists of the CPI (M). Biplab Dasgupta has at length dealt with the limit of the power of the LF government in West Bengal, arising out of the political differences with the party or coalition ruling the centre. He explains this political limit of the state government with reference to the constitution-granted discretionary powers of the central government, which 'would be used to frustrate the radical legislative measures of the government' (Dasgupta 1984, A–89). Pointing at the then Congress-ruled central government's reluctance to approve the amendment of the Land Reform Act of 1955 brought in by LF government in 1981, he substantiates his argument about the political limitation of the state government. The amendment, it is important to mention here, sought to rectify some of the legal loopholes of the Land Reform Act of 1955. This pertains to its definition of land, which exempted land in religious and charitable trusts and those converted into ponds from its purview by a clause that treats land of every description as 'land'. Needless to mention, that the landlords or rich peasants often made excellent use of these loopholes to evade the ceiling laws in land. Such a significant amendment finally got the Presidential assent only in 1986. Hence, as the ultimate sanction of any law falls under the jurisdiction of the central government, the state government in spite of its positive spirit to implement effectively the land reform measures, was falling short of achieving the desired end. In a similar tune to Dasgupta, Surya Kanta Mishra, the present General Secretary of the West Bengal CPI (M), holds responsible the 'bankrupt anti-people policies pursued by successive bourgeois-landlord Governments in India' for the limited success of the land reform policies in West Bengal (Mishra 2007, 1). Long before in 1977, Jyoti Basu after becoming the chief minister of West Bengal, in a message broadcast from the Calcutta Station of All India Radio, had mentioned about the severe political, constitutional and financial constraints amidst which the state governments in India have to function.

There might be three reasons for the outrage of the CPI (M) against the political constraints created by the Congress-led central government. First, the feeling of absolute discrimination emerging out of the 'limited' economic assistance and public investments provided by the central government to the state, which the state government considered to be far less than its 'proper' entitlement. Second, by putting the blame to the central government, the CPI (M) could justify the limited or incomplete reform initiative undertaken by the LF government. This was helpful in managing the developing frustration among the people at large emerging out of their rising expectations of institutional reform from the Left parties in West Bengal. Thus, it turned out to be an excuse of the LF parties for their relative failure in meeting the people's aspirations. *Kendrer banchana* (discriminatory practices of the Centre) or *kendrer bimatrisulabh achoron* (the stepmotherly attitude of the Centre) were some of these justifications or excuses put forth regularly by the CPI (M) leaders, and rank and file, which penetrated so deeply into the cultural frame of the common Bengali folk, that they often, either ironically or otherwise, used this to imply any sort of discriminatory behaviour in their everyday lives. Third, the 'inadequate' cooperation of the Congress-ruled central government was used by the Left parties as an electoral issue to mobilize the electorates against the Congress party. Hence, the constraints created by the central government under the control of the Congress was of full potential to give the necessary political and electoral mileage to the CPI (M) and other Left parties in West Bengal (Bardhan and Mookherjee 2010).

The political limitation of the LF government, as expressed by the Left parties, particularly the CPI (M), might be a justification but it was perhaps, only a partial explanation of their not so up to the mark performance at agrarian reform. It is true that being in power of a state government in the federal structure of Indian polity, its space for independent policy making and its implementation was restricted. But that restriction also had its limit set by the Constitution. In fact, there are some sectors where the state governments enjoy considerable autonomy. Agriculture is one of these (Kohli 1987).

First and foremost what the CPI (M) could do but didn't was to confer ownership rights of the land to the tenants. Registration of the tenants was definitely a step forward, but to usher in fundamental change in the land relations, movement beyond this was perhaps a sheer necessity. If the tenants were accorded with ownership rights it could improve their creditworthiness even more. By providing better access to other necessary non-land inputs, such improved creditworthiness would ultimately result in further increase in agricultural productivity. The LF government's land reform strategies quite strikingly failed to realize this vital link between enhanced creditworthiness and agricultural productivity. This was evident from the fact that only 14.62 per cent and 20.59 per cent of the pattadars and bargadars respectively were the members of the Primary Agricultural Credit Societies (PACS) in West Bengal as reports Chakraborti (2003). It is apparent from these figures that a bulk of the finance-starved agricultural population was outside the scope of the institutional credit system supplied by the cooperative credit societies, which possibly led them to depend on various sources of non-institutional credit and private money lending system (Khasnabis 1994; Mukarji and Bandyopadhyay 1995) where the interest rates often were 60 per cent per annum or even more (Bandyopadhyay 2003). Certainly, this was one of the reasons for which agriculture proved to be non-viable to a section of the poor tenants, and small and marginal pattadars. The growing incidence of reverse tenancy, as notes Bandyopadhyay (2001) and land alienation of the small-sized pattadars, as discussed earlier, might be fallouts of this.

Conferment of ownership rights to the tenants is a necessary condition to attain the goals of agrarian reforms. This also amounts to the realization of the substance of the term 'security' to the tenants. The recording of sharecroppers under the LF government, as has been discussed earlier, was a result of a definite political will of the CPI (M) and other Left parties. In some other states of India, where the dominant political parties lacked this favourable will, the tenants continue to have unsecured tenancy relations. This variability in the relation between the political will of the ruling parties and the provision of security of tenure, hence, always remains a concern for the tenants. No one perhaps could assure what would be the nature of tenurial security of the recorded tenants in West Bengal if the power relation in the state changes to an unfavourable direction. This has in fact happened in Egypt where President Gamal Abdel Nasser introduced new agrarian relations laws immediately after the 1952 revolution, under which millions of peasants enjoyed quasi-property rights, secure tenancy at fixed rents and other protections which continued for decades. But after the death of Nasser in 1970 things started to change. With the gradual transformation of Egypt into a capitalist market economy under the influence of economic liberalization policies of 1990s, the Egyptian People's Assembly on 1992 reversed the agrarian relations law and adopted a policy that '...raised rents for agricultural land and abolished the provision of the 1952 agrarian reform law that guaranteed agricultural tenants security of tenure on rented land' (Cassandra 1995, 16). If with the downfall of Nasser's socialist ideas the security cover of the tenants could be withdrawn in Egypt, then one cannot be sure that the same would not happen in West Bengal once the LF government is toppled. The Egyptian situation therefore was to be an eye-opener to the CPI (M) for making the bargadars owners of their cultivated land in order to ensure the permanence of the land reform progress (Hanstad and Nielsen 2004).

The LF government under the leadership of the CPI (M), however, did not show the positive intent in this regard. This is in spite of the fact that abolition of any form of tenancy had been an avowed goal first of the CPI and later also of the CPI (M). 'Land to the tiller' had remained an important policy objective of the undivided CPI. After the party split in 1964, the CPI (M) also noted the failure of the 'bourgeois–landlord' dominated Congress government in India since independence in abolishing intermediary rights (CPI [M] 1964). Hence, it bestowed upon the people's democratic government, which would be formed under the leadership of the working class and the peasantry, the task of taking measure to 'abolish landlordism without compensation and give land gratis to the agricultural labourers and poor peasants' (ibid., 38). In 1973 too, the CPI (M) in its 'Resolution on Certain Agrarian Issues' reiterated the same emphasis on conferring ownership rights to the tenants. Interestingly, the CPI (M) under the LF government did not consider the social structure prevailing during the 1980s in West Bengal to be congenial enough to implement this. The unwillingness of the CPI (M) under the LF government to act in this direction was clearly revealed from the opinion of Benoy Krishna Chowdhury, the land reform minister, who apprehended, 'Unless all tenants were recorded...even a casual suggestion to abolish tenancy would trigger a panic among the landowners who would waste no time to evict them' (quoted in Bhattacharyya 2016, 71).

Once again we come across the off-repeated argument of the CPI (M) about the unfavourable socio-political context impeding the progress of land reform initiatives. Khasnabis (1986) acknowledging the limited power of the state government along with the genuine obstacles to implement reform programmes, casts doubt on the potentialities of these constraints in debarring the CPI (M) to adopt more radical steps in granting ownership rights to the tenants. To substantiate his position he cites the example of Kerala, where the same CPI (M) party, '...operating within the confines of the same bourgeois–landlord constitution, and exercising power only at the state level' (ibid., 178) achieved this with remarkable success. The unwillingness of the LF government in West Bengal to convert the tenants into the owners of the land cultivated by them has also been noted by several scholars. Bandyopadhyay (2001) is of the view that with proper legal coverage against eviction this could be achieved smoothly and quickly. This opinion however bears the risk of falling into its own logical trap since enactment of law pertaining to conferment of ownership rights to the tenants is, as was mentioned by the CPI (M) leaders and justified by scholars inclined to it, the jurisdiction of the central government, which happens to be the root cause of the problem. Rather, one should look at the participatory methodology of the implementation of Operation Barga adopted by the CPI (M) itself, which could perhaps be radicalized more to achieve this goal. This seems tenable since the bureaucracy working hand in hand with the political leadership at the local level and the panchayats represented a unique model of governance which attained the seemingly difficult goal of recording the tenants. Chakraborti (2003, 118) argues quite pertinently, 'Given that the local political leadership and the panchayats whose pro-bargadar stance during Operation Barga has been amply demonstrated, will stand by the bargadars, it is unlikely that the owners can indulge in widespread eviction of bargadars.' Conferment of ownership rights to the tenants, much like Operation Barga, should be considered a people's movement within the legal discourse of the state; a movement with a higher level of radicalization. Perhaps, the CPI (M) in its preoccupation with the constitutional constraints failed to underscore the vitality of people's initiative in ushering in institutional transformation. This failure can be attributed to the entrenchment of middle class interest within the CPI (M) since the LF came to power in West Bengal (Bandyopadhyay 2001) or the political will engineered by the instruments of class society to serve the institutions of class society rather than transforming it (Khasnabis 1981). The vulnerability of the pattadars and the bargadars enhanced significantly with the adoption of the neoliberal economic reform strategy by the national government in 1991.

THE NEOLIBERAL TURN

To some scholars the overall decline in the growth rate of West Bengal economy, particularly agriculture, since the mid-1990s had been an offshoot of the neoliberal economic reform measures adopted by the Government of India in 1991 (Bhattacharya and Bhattacharya 2007; Khasnabis 2008–2009). As political and economic practices, neoliberalism also talks about the liberation of individual entrepreneurial freedoms, advocates strong private property rights under the overall context of free markets and free trade with minimal state intervention (Harvey 2005). As a policy, thus, it talks about greater freedom of the market at the cost of limiting the scope of the state. Accepting the International Monetary Fund (IMF) and World Bank dictated Structural Adjustment Programme (SAP), the INC-led Government of India in 1991 espoused the New Economic Policy largely under the neoliberal economic framework that made a strong argument in favour of privatization, agricultural modernization and reform in the labour market. Being predominantly an agriculture-dependent economy the impact of agricultural modernization in India was not very encouraging. Agriculture under the new policy, as argue Bhattacharya and Bhattacharya (2007, 71),

> ...received perhaps the greatest ever shock since independence. The food and fertiliser subsidy was drastically slashed, space for rural credit and priority sector lending was reduced, and land reform as a policy agenda was dropped. The import liberalisation on food, to some extent, aggravated the situation. The PDS was virtually wiped out. The peasantry who now faced very high cost of production, did not get reasonable prices for their crop. The government no longer had any viable mechanism to distribute the surplus foodgrain. It altogether created a great disincentive to produce.

It is clear from the above that the programme of agricultural modernization had deepened the social inequality already prevailing in the agrarian sector. Liberalization policies by neglecting or reducing the scope for public sector investments in agriculture might also jeopardise the future growth rate of agriculture (Gulati and Bathla 2001). By minimizing the state protection of the poor peasantry the reform with the ethics of market fundamentalism, thus had only strengthened the economic standing of the rural propertied classes vis-à-vis the poor peasantry. As a consequence, during the 1990s, the falling growth rate of the primarily agriculture-dependent West Bengal economy became apparent. Another possible reason of the economic decline may be the initial dilemma of the LF government to go for large-scale industrialization under the aegis of global multinational capital following the dictate of the neoliberal economic framework. Although the government of West Bengal finally came up with its new economic policy in 1994 which recognized the key role of the private sector in achieving accelerated growth, the dilemma was apparent in its emphasis on the development and promotion of small-scale industries. The declining growth rate of agriculture coupled with a not so encouraging industrial development made the situation of the peasantry vulnerable. The growing disenchantment of them with the LF government started to generate during the second half of the 1990s, the last phase of Jyoti Basu's chief ministerial tenure.

The parliamentary-Left parties in India are not the only victims of such an ambivalence created by global capitalism operating under the neoliberal framework. Webber (2015) writing on the Latin American Left parties noted the dramatic shift of the Left and the centre-Left parties to the Right during the same period consequent upon the narrowing down of the entire political spectrum due to the onslaught of neoliberal political values. Rather than questioning the logic of neoliberal capital accumulation or organizing protest of the lower stratum of the society against it, the Left parties increasingly came to be entangled with the issues of adopting austerity measures, privatization and liberalization. Social movements, eclipsed by the increasing influence of the internationally financed non-governmental organizations (NGOs), left the path of popular resistance to power inequality and adopted a no-power, depoliticized alternative development approach to attain social change (Petras and Veltmeyer 2009). To be precise, 'Strategic aims of power at the level of the state began to recede from the Left's purview' in Latin America' (Webber 2015, 159).

Not only in Latin America but everywhere in the globe, neoliberal reforms had made the situation difficult to adopt for the electoral

Left parties. The traditional ethos of social democracy held by the mainstream centre-Left and liberal parties had been receiving serious jolt. The unrestrained ascendance of global capitalism led to a striking decline of labour's influence everywhere. Reaganomics and Thatcherism, particularly the ideological slogan of the latter 'There Is No Alternative' (TINA) to neoliberal agenda, had been so powerful that, 'With few exceptions, the governing Left embraced free trade and, most significantly, the general deregulation of economic life...and worked actively to further deregulate capital markets (Centeno and Cohen 2012, 324).

The ambivalent CPI (M) perhaps failed to read the writing on the wall. Unable to acknowledge the political alternative of organizing resistance to neoliberal reforms they took recourse to opportunist and contradictory strategies to maintain electoral power. Banerjee (2008) aptly argues that the CPI (M) has, '...morphed into Janus-like party, with one face as an opposition mouthing rhetoric against the neoliberal model of industrial development at the national level, and the other as a ruling power in three states where they impose the same oppressive model' (p. 12). Bardhan (2005) also criticizes the LF for displaying such duplicity. This double role quite naturally put the credibility of the party and for that matter the whole LF in West Bengal and beyond at stake. For some critiques this is obvious since running a state by any communist party or coalition under the overall capitalist politico-economic structure of the country is itself futile and theoretically contradictory (Banerjee 2008). Rudra (1985) has been arguing in this line since long. There are others who consider it to be a deviation of the Left from its revolutionary ideology (Acharya 1994; Bhaduri 2007; Khasnabis 2008–2009). Whether it was theoretical disagreement or ideological departure, what the CPI (M) and other parliamentary-Left parties failed to perceive, perhaps, was the new meaning Left or Right politics began to assume in the post-1989 period. After the fall of Soviet Union it was possibly irrelevant for the two to diverge on the point of allowing or restricting market freedom. Identifying this to be the central tenet of the third way politics having emancipatory potential for Left politics in the new global order, Giddens (2004) has urged, 'The Left has to get comfortable with the markets...' (p. 34). Rather than seeing the market as the source of all economic problems it has to look at the positive outcomes of markets operated under a 'social and ethical framework' (ibid., 33). The CPI (M) and the LF partners could not 'modernize' them along this line, leaving behind their traditional social democratic outlook.

Apart from its economic dimension, the intricacy of the situation also had its political dimension. Since the end of the 1980s the national level politics in India came to be marked by the growing influence of BJP, possibly at the cost of the dwindling significance of the INC. This had its implication both for the politics of West Bengal and for India as a whole. The CPI (M)-led LF government in West Bengal, in spite of all of its failures in economic ground since the late 1980s, could consolidate its power at the cost of this growing unpopularity and weakness of the INC. This was evident from the seat share of the INC in panchayat elections which went down from 33 per cent in 1983 to 23 per cent in 1988, while the tally of CPI (M) increased from 55 per cent to 66 per cent during the same period (Echeverri-Gent 1992). The picture was not much different in the assembly elections too. At the same time, the traditional opposition between the CPI (M) and the Congress got somehow diluted due to the emergence of the BJP as a significant political force. As the secular democratic forces, it was perhaps imperative for both the INC and the CPI (M) to unite the secular forces to resist political doctrine of Hindutva of the BJP. Thus, on accounts of the growing weakness of the INC and the political responsibility of both the INC and the CPI (M) to resist the rise of the BJP, the traditional oppositional space in West Bengal politics remained quite empty. To occupy this empty space, a number of regional parties sprang up in many states of India. Being a national party it was however not possible for the INC to evoke regional sentiment, in the case of West Bengal, Bengali sentiment to consolidate its political space. Capitalizing on the ambivalence of the CPI (M) and the weakness of the INC the AITC led by Ms. Mamata Banerjee, with a strong anti-CPI (M) orientation, broke away from the INC to appropriate the vacant space of opposition politics of West Bengal in 1998. The relentless opposition of the AITC to the CPI (M) under her leadership ultimately was successful in bringing an end to the 34-year long LF rule in West Bengal in 2011.

Rise and Growth of AITC

Socio-Cultural and Political Economic Dimensions

The declining popularity of the CPI (M), which started since the late 1990s, became prominent in the Assembly election of 2001. In this election the CPI (M) could secure 36.59 per cent of votes against the emerging opposition AITC, which got 30.66 per cent of the votes, as mentions the data of the Election Commission of India. Contesting the first assembly election after its formation in 1998, this was a significant achievement for the AITC. The continual success of the AITC since then had certain important social and political dimensions which deserve the attention of the scholars. As the rise of the AITC was directly related to the gradual decline of the CPI (M), so to understand the nature of the evolving political processes involved with this shift, a critical analysis of the ideological stand of the latter seems important here. This necessarily would have the culture of resistance of the peasantry in Bengal as its reference point, which has been the habitus of Left politics here: both parliamentarian and non-parliamentarian. In order to understand the downfall of the LF and the rise of the AITC, one needs to focus on the CPI (M)'s and the LF's ideological and political dealings with this socio-cultural tradition. There should be little doubt that the LF's initiatives to reform the institutional framework of rural Bengali society were informed by its ideological leaning towards the tradition of peasant resistance against institutional inequality. But the attempt of the LF in this direction, as has already been mentioned earlier, failed to achieve its desired goals in the long run. While the land reform initiatives could not substantively transform the rural production relations, the panchayati raj innovation also could not attain its stated goal of decentralization of institutional power completely, as well. To understand the rise of the AITC, an explanation of the LF's failure on these accounts seems necessary.

DECLINE OF THE LEFT FRONT

Explanation of the declining political significance of the CPI (M), as is being witnessed since the beginning of the present century, should take into account its ideological orientation in a changing perspective. Being a communist party, it involves a critical examination of its class priorities, which should be shaped and guided by the normative and ideological commitments to organize and politicize the working class and the lower-order peasantry for the ultimate goal of proletarian revolution. As a Marxist–Leninist party, its participation in electoral politics and in the state government, under the overall capitalist and landlord-dominated politico-economic structure of India, should be aimed at utilizing the state government as an instrument that helps the proletariat, '...to prove to the backward masses why such parliaments deserve to be done away with' (Lenin 1920, 60). Thus, preparing and organizing the workers and the peasantry along with other segments of the underprivileged masses for class struggle leading to the proletarian revolution are expected to be the key motives of the CPI (M) in taking part in the overall structure of parliamentary democracy in India as well as to rule the state of West Bengal under that framework.

The CPI (M)'s party programme, as adopted in October–November 1964 (in its formative Calcutta Congress), had made certain declarations about the composition of its agrarian class base to form the democratic front to carry forward the people's democratic revolution. This has generated enough confusing understanding about its class character. The declarations, as Pillai (2018, para 7) summarizes it, stated:

> The agricultural labourers and poor peasants who constitute 70 percent of the rural households will be the basic allies of the working class. The middle peasantry are the reliable allies. Due to various factors, by and large, the rich peasants can also be brought to the democratic front and retained as allies for the people's democratic revolution.

The declaration definitely calls for a vertical alignment of agrarian strata in composing the democratic front paying little attention to the class dynamics present in their interrelationships. The programme acknowledged the aspiration of the rich peasants to 'join the ranks of capitalist landlords' (CPI [M] 1964, 45) and their hostility towards the agricultural labourers, on account of the former being the employer of the latter in their farms. Still it made a cause for them to unite with the agricultural labourers in the democratic front since, 'Subjected to the ravages of the market under the grip of the monopolist traders, both foreign and Indian, they come up often against the oppressive policies pursued by the bourgeois-landlord government' (ibid., 45). One can clearly notice hear the absence of a class-based approach pertaining either to the solidarity of the exploited class or to designate the enemy. The reformist agenda of the CPI (M) was apparent here since it tried to amalgamate class with political and other dimensions in designating the potential allies and opponents (Kohli 1983). Instead of forging horizontal unity of the oppressed against the oppressors, the CPI (M)'s emphasis on developing a united rural front across the classes might sound good as a reformist strategy but it would possibly have little influence in promoting the cause of people's democratic revolution, the avowed goal of the party. The drawing of the middle and rich peasants into the revolutionary struggle of the peasantry, hence, bears the risk of 'sabotaging its proletarian character' (Krishnaji 1979, 518). Kohli's (1987) characterization of the CPI (M) and its aims seems appropriate here, as he argues, 'Broad-based political unity aimed at reform is of the essence; revolutionary confrontation with the propertied classes is not really on the agenda' (p. 100).

Over the years and particularly with the increasing entrenchment of the CPI (M) within the culture of electoral politics since 1977, its middle peasant proclivities became more apparent. This was, perhaps, not that much an attempt towards declassing them but to count on their support to have electoral dividends since the rich and middle peasants were numerically significant (Kohli 1987; Williams 2001). Assigning more importance to the middle and rich peasants by the party often amounted to its ignoring the cause of the landless agricultural labourers. Although CPI (M) is credited for the mobilization of the landless for higher wages, the real wages of the landless, as is already mentioned in the previous chapter, were less than the minimum wages determined by the West Bengal government. In fact, the growth rate of the real wages of agricultural labourers in West Bengal during the period 1980–1991 was comparable to Bihar and Orissa (now Odisha) which neither experienced such mobilizations nor underwent any remarkable land reform initiatives (Gazdar and Sengupta 1997). Probably the CPI (M), in spite of its ideological rhetoric to protect the interests of the agricultural proletariats, did not take the movement to increase their wages too seriously to undermine the vested interests of the middle and upper peasantry.

The shift of the CPI (M)'s priorities from the lower-level peasantry to the middle peasants was evident in pre-1977 period itself as the agrarian programme adopted in 1976 designated land redistribution to be an effective 'propaganda slogan' not a 'slogan of action' (Bhattacharyya 1995; Kohli 1983, 786). After 1977 it did not approve its earlier stand of land seizure, recovery of benami land and so on by independent initiative of the peasants and their organizations. It no longer recognized these to be an effective tool for mobilization and politicization of the poor and landless peasantry. Instead, its emphasis shifted towards developing a kind of all peasant unity. To substantiate this Kohli (1983), refers to Pramode Dasgupta, the CPI (M) West Bengal secretary, who in 1979 remarked that to gain the support of all peasantry the party needed to pay attention not only to the land issues but to other issues such as irrigation, seeds and fair prices of agricultural produce. Here one can find the resonance of the most archetypical demands of the rich farmers of western UP, Maharashtra, Karnataka, Tamil Nadu and some other states during the 1970s. Surprisingly, in West Bengal these demands were raised by no other than a communist party with a strong root in the peasant movements of the last two decades against the exploitation of the landlords and the rich farmers. The emphasis on all in peasant unity led the party to, '...abandon political action that would polarize the rich and middle peasants on the one hand and the poor and marginal peasants and landless workers on the other' (Sen Gupta 1982). Such emphasis had indeed been there in the 1964 party programme of the CPI (M), but that was, however debatable it might be, envisioned as a means for organizing the peasantry for the democratic revolution. In the post-1977 period it raised the same issue but with the significant difference being there in its support to the demands of the capitalist farmers, while ignoring the revolutionary agencies of the poor peasantry.

The same middle peasant orientation could be found in the Krishak Sabha (the peasant wing of the CPI [M] and the West Bengal unit of the All-India Kisan Sabha) also. Although linked with the CPI (M), the Krishak Sabha is an autonomous organization which is supposed to represent the interest of all sections of the peasantry. In spite of its emphasis on peasant unity, the Krishak Sabha, possibly for its history of providing leadership to the sharecroppers in the Tebhaga movement in Bengal in 1946–1947, envisioned peasant struggles spearheaded by the poor peasants and agricultural labourers to be one of its cherished goals. In reality, however on both the accounts of its membership and programme, it came to stand by the middle-level peasants (Kohli 1987). Although the Krishak Sabha paid some attention to the land questions and issues of the bargadars, but the thrust definitely had been towards the issues of land taxation, fair prices for agricultural produces and other issues related to the middle and rich peasantry. To consolidate its support among the rich and middle peasants it even advocated lowering of wages of the agricultural labourers, which if necessary could be settled even lower than the basic demands (Bhattacharyya 1995). Little wonder then, that Kohli through an interview in March 1979 with Mehbub Zahedi, a CPI (M) party member, and Sabhapati, Zila Parishad of Burdwan district, came to know that the membership of the Krishak Sabha was significantly skewed towards the middle peasantry. While among its members 60 to 65 per cent were middle peasants, the remaining 30 to 35 per cent were landless peasants and sharecroppers (Kohli 1987). Although the Krishak Sabha claimed that about 75 per cent of its primary members were composed of the agricultural labourers but Bhattacharyya (1995, 2016) found that in the three conferences held by the Krishak Sabha in West Bengal during 1982–1989 the attendance of the agricultural labourers and poor peasants was below 9 per cent and 24 per cent respectively. From these figures it is evident that it was the section of the middle peasantry, which was in control of the Krishak Sabha, disturbing its aspired balance between 'unity' and 'struggle'. The agricultural labourers, who, 'have hardly received any attention' (Rudra 1981, A 61) from the Krishak Sabha, were gradually getting alienated from it. This might be one of the reasons for which they had demanded a separate wing for them within the Krishak Sabha in the early 1980s. The CPI (M) and the Krishak Sabha did not encourage the demand. Rogaly (1998) finds it paradoxical since, '...agricultural employers were also the leaders of the very body that organized strikes by their workforces for wage rises' (p. 2729). The need to form peasant unity across classes, possibly, was too overbearing for the CPI (M) to withstand the issue of peasant struggle: an important avenue for agrarian class struggle.

Such reallocation of class priorities of the CPI (M), perhaps explains its reluctance to take the issues of abolition of landlordism, conferment of ownership rights to the tenants, enhancement of the wages of the agricultural labourers, increasing the financial autonomy of the panchayats and so on, seriously enough to facilitate the institutional transformation of the rural society. Moreover, it also '...lay bare the limitations of reformist measures in a class society' (Khasnabis 1981, A 47). Its emphasis on 'development with redistribution' resulted in the improving economic condition of some sections (especially the middle and rich) of the peasantry, but perhaps it was not good enough to transform the property relations existing in the rural economy. Among the different political parties at the national as well as state level in India, the pro-poor redistributive policies of the CPI (M) definitely stood apart, but apart from rewarding it with exceptional electoral mileage, such policies were of little consequence to carry forward the revolutionary struggle of the exploited peasantry. Possibly, such a realization leads Kohli (1997, 336) to argue that, 'The party is communist in name only and is essentially social democratic in its ideology, social programme and policies.'

As it happens everywhere with the social democratic Left of the centre parties, the CPI (M) also, preoccupied with reformist measures, distanced itself gradually from its earlier traditions of social movements aimed at radical socio-economic transformation. Withdrawing its root in the social movements of the underprivileged, it entrenched itself deeply in the ethos of electoral democracy along with its associated concern with electoral renewal. Leaving aside the path of revolution, the CPI (M) turned out to be a, '…a party of the establishment, too used to seats of power for its own good' (Ruud 1999, 243). Such a change in the ideological orientation and praxis of the party was in congruence with the change in the socio-economic backgrounds of its members. Majority of the members of it comprised urban professionals, land-owning classes, the rural quasi-elite, the educated and well-off sections of the people, the middle peasantry and the city educated but rural-based school teachers, mostly from among the higher castes (Kohli 1987; Ruud 1999). Here the significant absence of the 'landless agricultural laborers, sharecroppers, and the working classes' (Kohli 1987, 103), should be considered as an indication of the changing class character of the CPI (M).

In the 1960s the poor peasants, sharecroppers and landless labourers had been the primary support base of the CPI (M), who considered it to be an organization having the necessary commitment to alter the existing unequal property relation in the rural areas. The radical programmes of the CPI (M) in the two successive UF governments in the middle and late 1960s such as vesting of ceiling surplus land and restoration of benami land indeed were successful in bringing in some changes in the nature of property ownership in the rural areas. In spite of this being quite negligible in quantum, the policies of the CPI (M) under the UF government however were successful in bringing in the rural poor and their independent initiatives to the domains of politics. This was definitely a politics with an entirely new grammar characterized by the overwhelming participation of the underprivileged sections in various political decisions affecting their daily lives under the overall support and guidance of a communist party. Doubts may be there regarding the level of organization and discipline of the activists, but what was certain was their level of consciousness, which might be an incipient form of class consciousness, that informed the entire gamut of such politics. The victory of the LF, primarily the CPI (M), in 1977, besides the overall anti-Congress sentiment prevailing in India at that time, also owed a great deal to the people-centric politics of the CPI (M) in the late 1960s. Its thrust on poor peasants' autonomous agencies in altering the material conditions of their existence being in tune with the historically developed distinct habitus of rebel class-like consciousness, as discussed earlier, provided a favourable moral environment to the CPI (M). Pragmatically, the agrarian programmes adopted and backed by the CPI (M) under the UF governments constituted its chief support base, which proved to be instrumental for it to win the election of 1977. To explain the exceptional continuation of LF rule in West Bengal since 1977 as well as its decline, more attention needs to be paid to the endogenous factors pertaining to its distinct pro-social movement political culture and its subsequent changes during the post-1977 period. Rather than the exogenous ones informed by the national political trend, which seems to be constant for all the political parties at the state level, this seems more relevant.

The major dilemma which the CPI (M) had to confront after coming to power in West Bengal in 1977 was related to its political priorities. Whether it would continue to provide support to the independent initiatives of the underprivileged people to redress the socio-economic inequalities or restrict itself within the limits of institutional politics under the scope of parliamentary democracy. It seems that although the CPI (M), learning from the experience of the second UF government, largely favoured the latter option but it could not, perhaps due to the historical antecedents mentioned earlier, completely leave the former one also. Such unresolved dialectics instead of being disruptive, possibly contributed to the sustenance of the LF rule, since it encouraged continuous innovation of policies and programmes at the level of government along with the ideology and praxis of the directing political party, the CPI (M), as well.

The ambivalence of the CPI (M) was reflected in the nature of land reform initiatives and the effort towards democratic decentralization of power. Land reform remained incomplete and panchayats suffered from inadequate financial and political autonomy. The reasons for the CPI (M) not venturing out to finish such unfinished tasks have been attributed by many to the intrusion of the middle class or middle peasant interests within the leadership and the rank and file of the party. The CPI (M), especially during its rule under the UF governments, was indeed successful to some extent in limiting the economic and political influence of the traditional rural elites composed of the erstwhile landlords and propertied segments of the rural Bengali society. Beneficiaries of such interventions of the 1960s gradually formed the new middle class rural elites, who on account of their newly found agricultural prosperity, enjoyed relatively better socio-economic life chances to capitalize on the emerging non-agricultural opportunities opened up by the LF government. After 1977 with the progress of the land reform, the rank of the middle class elites further swelled up as a segment of the bargadars availed the opportunities of non-agricultural employment while engaging hired labour to cultivate their lands. Among the non-agricultural opportunities created by the LF rule most prominent was that of school teaching. Kanti Biswas, the minister of education of the LF government, reported that since 1977 to 1989 the West Bengal government had 'opened 12,000 schools and appointed 46,000 teachers' (Basu 1989, 220). The newly appointed teachers in most of the cases were CPI (M) party members or sympathizers (Echeverri-Gent 1992).

The CPI (M) rule gave these school teachers the necessary space to establish and extend their political control over the rural society. A majority of them came to man the important positions in the panchayats as well as the local wings of the party organization. Echeverri-Gent (1992) through a survey of 36 gram panchayat pradhans (chairmen) of Midnapore district in West Bengal found that 57 per cent of them were school teachers. Kohli's (1987) survey of 60 gram panchayat members in Burdwan and Midnapore districts also reported almost one-third of them to be school teachers. The survey conducted by the Midnapore district panchayat officer found 42 per cent of all the pradhans to be school teachers, while a similar all West Bengal survey conducted by the Government of West Bengal in 1980 reported 29 per cent school teachers as occupying the post of panchayat pradhan. Strikingly, among the teachers who had become the pradhans of the panchayats a majority happened to be the members of the CPI (M) in sharp contradiction to what could be found in the opposition camp.

These school teachers were the primary constituents of what Bhattacharyya (2009, 2016) terms the CPI (M)'s party-society. Compared to their fathers who had been mostly the middle and small cultivators, they experienced considerable occupational mobility on account of their gaining education. The resultant improvement in their social status placed them in a relatively better position to influence public opinion at the village level. Being mostly the members of the CPI (M) or its supporters and sympathizers, thus, they could extract legitimacy for the LF rule not only from the middle stratum but also perhaps, more importantly from the lower echelons of the rural society. Their educational attainment placed them in a respectable position vis-à-vis the bulk of agricultural labourers since the latter in terms of literacy constitute 'the most deprived occupational group' in West Bengal (Government of West Bengal 2004, 149). Moreover, being educated they could effectively mediate between the government officials and the rural common people either through their capacity as panchayat members or in any other form. This new political elite comprising the educated middle class and middle caste segments of the rural society formed the party-society of the CPI (M), which had been instrumental in extending the hegemony of the ruling CPI (M) considerably.

It is apparent that under the CPI (M)-led LF rule the power balance of the rural society experienced a significant shift from the earlier landed gentry to the middle class composed of the middle peasantry. The new middle class elite of the agrarian society, considering the CPI (M) to be a genuine protector of their interest, invested all their efforts to maintain its rule. The CPI (M) also, being a party primarily of the Bengali Bhadraloks or the middle class, found the middle peasantry as a comfortable base to rely upon and extend its political hold over rural West Bengal. As it is common with the nature of the middle class everywhere, in West Bengal also it supported the status quo and worked for the electoral renewal of the CPI (M). Figure 2.1

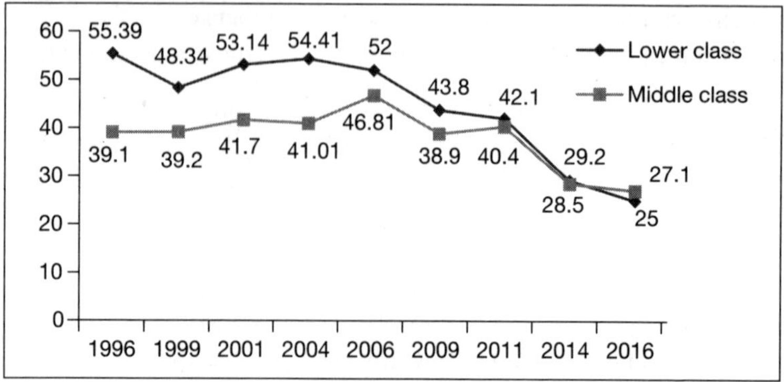

Figure 2.1 *Middle Class and Lower Class Vote Share of the Left Front in Different Elections (Assembly and Parliamentary) from 1996 to 2016*

Source: CSDS Data Unit, NES 1999, 2004, 2009, 2014; and West Bengal Assembly Election Study 1996, 2001, 2006, 2011, 2016.

clearly exhibits the support the LF has enjoyed from the middle class Bengalis since 1996. It however started to decline since the Lok Sabha election of 2009, the election from which the LF's downslide actually began.

Although the LF's vote share of the middle class had slightly declined in 2009 from that of 2004, but the NES data reveal that still it registered a sharp gain of 23 per cent votes among the salaried segment of the electorates between the two elections. This might be a pointer to the growing middle class inclination of the LF developing at that period (Chatterjee and Basu 2014). On the other hand this also serves as the proof of its growing disengagement from the lower social stratum. The chart also shows that the LF's vote share of the poor and lower classes declined from as high as about 55 per cent to 25 per cent during the various elections in West Bengal from 1996 to 2016. It is true that the vote share of the LF declined in both the classes but while for the lower classes its rate of decline was 54.87 per cent, for the middle classes it was 30.69 per cent. Assigning more importance to electoral politics, the CPI (M) began to lose its commitment towards the rural poor and their politics centering on a historically developed culture of resistance. The disjuncture of the CPI (M) from the tradition of class-based peasant mobilization, which created a congenial socio-political and cultural environment in West Bengal for Left politics, was responsible to a great extent for its declining political significance (Chatterjee and Basu 2017; Patnaik 2011; Yadav 2006). The alienation of the poor peasants, sharecroppers and landless labourers from the CPI (M) was an important reason for the declining graph of the LF and the simultaneous rise in the popularity of the AITC since 2004 as depicted by Chatterjee and Basu (2014).

THE CHANGING COMPOSITION OF THE BHADRALOK

Here some reflection is required about the nature and social composition of the Bhadralok, their relation to Left politics in general and its implication for the party competition in West Bengal since the 1990s. Although the urban and rural Bengali societies were different in many respects, but at the beginning of the 20th century they came to converge in at least one aspect: The presence of the common dominant elite. Broomfield (1968) identifies them to be the Bhadralok, referring literally to the respectable people or the gentlemen. Regarding the features of this group of persons he maintains, 'They were distinguished by many aspects of their behavior—their deportment, their speech, their dress, their style of housing, their eating habits, their occupations, and their associations—and quite as fundamentally by their cultural values and their sense of social propriety (p. 5–6)'. They were the chief beneficiaries of the new educational policy and the administrative framework introduced by the British colonialism in Bengal since the first quarter of the 19th century. Being English-educated professionals, they had a stubborn aversion to manual labour and regarded all occupations involving manual labour to be inferior. Their newly achieved educational advantage coupled with the attitude to manual labour to be degrading removed them from agricultural activities, as has been mentioned in the first chapter. This created a structural division within the Bengali society whereby the educated segments of the upper castes regarded them as Bhadraloks or cultured or gentlemen and others in a derogatory sense: the *Chhotoloks* (Roy 2011).

Such attitude to agriculture and any form of manual labour as inferior was the basic distinction between the *bhadra* and the *abhadra* or the respectable and the others, briefly put, the elite and the non-elites or the subalterns. Clearly such aversion to manual labour had been the cardinal feature of the three major upper castes of Bengali Hindu society, namely the Brahmin, the Kayastha and the Baidya. Interestingly, the bulk of the Bhadraloks are drawn so heavily from the three upper castes that the former largely came to be used interchangeably with the latter. Enough room of confusion naturally had been there regarding the relative importance of the factor of their new professions and their caste background for such a stigma to physical labour. From the upper caste bias of the social reform movement of the 19th century Bengal, launched by this segment of the new middle class, as will be detailed in Chapter 4, it can possibly be concluded that the repugnance to manual labour may be attributed to the cultural proscription of the upper caste background of the Bhadralok.

These Bhadraloks in the first half of the 20th century joined hands with the communist movement in Bengal, significantly. A section of the freedom fighters getting frustrated with the line of mendicancy of the Congress under the leadership of Gandhi joined the CPI. It was '...later joined by Bengali intellectuals returning from England, by graduates of the college and universities in Bengal during the 1940s, and eventually by a large section of the urban bhadralok living in and around Calcutta and the West Bengal industrial belt' (Franda 1971, 13). Having a moderate exposure to Marxism, these Bhadraloks got attracted to the tradition of peasant movements in Bengal for their incipient form of class consciousness and began to organize those. Being fed up with the prevailing nationalist discourse of the Congress, which was based on a form of class collaborationist ethos, the subaltern segment composed of the lower-level peasantry came close to the communists to form the Krishak Sabha. The Tebhaga movement of Bengal during the second half of the 1940s had been an outcome of this. After independence too the communist-led Krishak Sabha gave leadership to a number of peasant movements in West Bengal and beyond to achieve various demands of the sharecroppers, poor peasants and landless labourers. Franda (ibid.) is perhaps correct in his assertion that, 'The communist movement is still led by educated, high caste Bengalis from bhadralok families' (p. 14).

The involvement of the intellectuals in the communist movement was also marked by the emergence of a distinct literary tradition, which tried to provide the necessary motivation for the dissemination of the growing class consciousness of the peasantry and the working class throughout the Bengali society. The CPI and later the CPI (M) took active role in it. To widen the reach of the communist movement the CPI since the 1930s formed a number of mass organizations, prominent among these being the Indian People's Theatre Association (IPTA), The Progressive Workers' Workshop and the Mahila Atma Raksha Samiti (an organization of the women). Writers and poets such as Sukanta Bhattacharya, Manik Bandyopadhyay and Samar Sen; music composers such as Salil Chowdhury, Hemanga Biswas, Debabrata Biswas and Hemanta Mukherjee; theatre personalities such as Bijon Bhattacharya, Sambhu Mitra, Sudhi Pradhan and film makers such as Bimal Roy, Ritwik Ghatak and Mrinal Sen came up and got engaged in the project of class awakening of the people through literary and cultural medium. This resulted in the considerable increase in the involvement of the Bhadraloks in revolutionary politics. Gradually, these Bhadraloks came to occupy the political centre stage of West Bengal with the ascendance of the CPI (M) into power in alliance with the BAC in the two successive UF governments in the second half of the 1960s and in the LF government in alliance with some other Left parties in 1977.

With the growing entrenchment of the CPI (M) with constitutional politics its priority tended to shift from its earlier pro-social movement stance to a more pro-election one. As will be dealt with at length later in this chapter, this marked a change in its ideology, composition and aspirations of the leadership as well as the rank and files. Since winning elections became the prime mover of the party, it looked more and more to develop an organization with an effective electoral machinery to serve its need of electoral renewal. This paved the way for the opportunists with corrupt and accumulative tendencies to take entry into the party. In such a situation, the intellectuals who had been working out of their commitment towards social transformation to raise the level of class consciousness of the exploited sections of the society started to desert the party. In this way the earlier traditional Bhadralok or educated middle class in the party were increasingly being replaced by a new middle class Bhadralok with questionable ideological make up appropriate for a communist party. Rogaly (1998) also notes this shift and comments, 'The dominant class in the villages has shifted from bhadralok to chasi' (p. 2731). The chasi or the 'peasant farmer' in Rogaly's terms, were actually the middle peasants to whom the CPI (M) regime had been instrumental to satisfy their own interests. With the shift in the position of the dominant class the economic, political and cultural control also shifted from the earlier rural Bhadraloks to the chasis. Consequent upon this, the party-society of the CPI (M), instrumental for the development of its hegemony, started to disintegrate. With the detachment of the party from the society, the CPI (M) started to lose its moral and ideological base of popular legitimacy. The poor health of the economy in the 1990s added more woe to this. With the gradual disintegration of the party-society the tension between the emerging elites and the subaltern began to surface. In a desperate bid to regain its popular support, the party after an initial hesitation embraced the neoliberal model of development during the late 1990s expecting its fruits to trickle down. Far from chalking out the path to resist the aggression of global capital, the CPI (M) turned into its apologist (Bhattacharyya 2010). The party's commitment towards people's liberation got transformed into a commitment to create a favourable political condition for market liberalization to allow free play of corporate capital. To keep this commitment, the party even did not hesitate to deploy state machinery to violently suppress people's resistance against the onslaught of multinational capital. This had happened in Singur, Nandigram and some other places in West Bengal in the second half of the first decade of the current century.

RISE OF THE AITC: IDEOLOGICAL/ SOCIO-CULTURAL FACTORS

All these resulted in the growing disenchantment of the subaltern with the Party since the late 1990s. Obviously this created enough space for

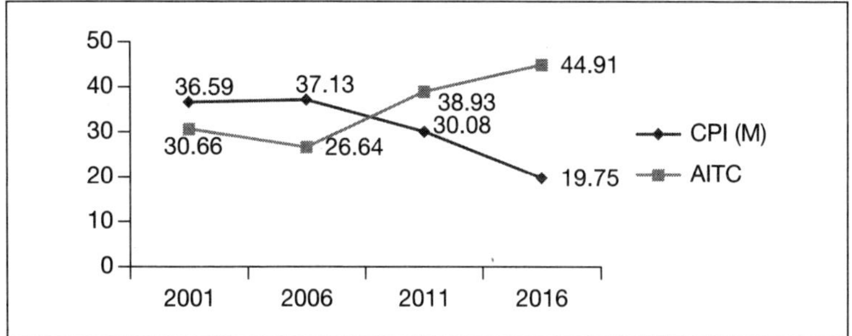

Figure 2.2 *Performance (in per cent) of the AITC and the CPI (M) in West Bengal Assembly Elections from 2001 to 2016*

Source: The Election Commission of India.

the opposition AITC to expand its political influence over the lower stratum of the Bengali society and thereby occupy a distinct position in the West Bengal political scene. The AITC's continuously enhancing electoral support base in West Bengal and the simultaneous weakening of the same for the CPI (M) in various Assembly elections in West Bengal since 2001—the first Assembly election the former fought—to 2016 can be seen from Figure 2.2.

Not only in the Assembly elections, the trend can also be traced in the parliamentary elections as well. According to the data released by the Election Commission of India, the CPI (M)'s vote share has declined to 22.96 per cent in 2014 Lok Sabha election from 35.41 per cent which it could achieve in 1998. During the same period the AITC's vote share has gone up from 24.43 per cent to 39.79 per cent.

This was the time when the 'subaltern' in the form of the 'local' or 'grassroots' was gaining strategic importance from the discourse of participatory development propagated by the international agencies such as the United Nations and the World Bank. In the contemporary neoliberal development regime, grassroots empowerment through participation has emerged as keywords and process to attain the goals of development and governance. The logic of empowerment under neoliberalism, 'seeks to enable grassroots actors…' (Sharma 2008, xvi). This emphasis on the agency of the people at the grassroots however has been depoliticizing since it does not make any reference to the existing political economic inequalities at the societal level. This 'new politics' as Harris (2011, 91) puts it, which is considered by many to be more participatory than representative democracy, however, brings an ominous signal for ideology-based politics in general and Left politics in particular. The importance being attached to the terms grassroots actors, local people, indigenous people, participation and so on has been pushing the class-based ideology and praxis of the Left to the point of near redundancy. In the late 1990s when the lower stratum of the Bengali society, especially the rural subalterns, apprehending greater marginalization was getting detached from Left politics, such an emphasis on the role of the grassroots helped the anti-Left forces. Particularly, it assisted the AITC, both symbolically and materially, to create and consolidate its own niche in the political domain of West Bengal.

Symbolically, the Bengali word 'trinamool' literally meaning the 'grassroots', helped the AITC to find a space in the contemporary discourse of global politics. Its election symbol, signifying the 'grassroots' (two saplings on the grass), tries to portray it as a party of, for and by the subalterns. Samaddar (2016) does not hesitate to term AITC as a subaltern party. The AITC supremo, Ms. Mamata Banerjee, has been acquiring gradually the shape of a charismatic leader with considerable mass following, yet another mark of the 'new politics' (Harris 2011), as well as the hallmark of subaltern politics. Materially, the gaining importance of the subaltern in the discourse of contemporary global politics helped the avowedly pro-subaltern AITC to build up its constituency among them. It was instrumental for the AITC to get hold of the imagination, aspirations, crises and growing frustration of the lower stratum of the rural society, who found themselves marginalized under the Left rule. The electoral success achieved by the AITC, since its formation in 1998, has so far been primarily built upon the wholehearted support of the subaltern section of rural Bengal. Moreover, the name 'All India Trinamool Congress' also stands for a rejection of the elitist orientation of the INC, the party from which Mamata Banerjee broke away to form her new outfit. Since the 1980s Mamata Banerjee, under the INC, had been fighting relentlessly against the CPI (M). But due to the growing weakness of the INC in the state as well as at the national level since mid-1980s, and its mutual obligation of national politics, as mentioned earlier, its high command showed a somehow reluctant attitude to carry forward the anti-CPI (M) struggle too far. As a mass leader, having intimate connection to the grassroots, Miss Banerjee could feel the simmering discontent growing against the CPI (M) since then. As a result, to fight out the CPI (M), her sole political opponent at that time, she broke away from the INC but, interestingly named the party as 'Trinamool Congress'. Hence, the very name might also be suggestive of her protest against the elitist orientation of the INC.

The rise of the AITC, thus, was a corollary of the concurrent ideological detachment of the CPI (M) from its earlier revolutionary stand. Its failure to nurture the cultural capital, historically developed out of the rebel class consciousness of the peasantry, added to its weakness as a revolutionary party. There is little wonder that in the CSDS-West Bengal Assembly Election Study 2011, one-third of the sampled electorates did not consider the CPI (M) to be a revolutionary party against an almost equal number who did.[1] The growing middle class priorities of the CPI (M), replacing the old Bhadraloks had resulted in the loosening grip of the party-society: an important base of its political legitimacy. The new middle class continuously sought electoral renewal of the party to maintain their power advantage probably at the cost of the growing alienation of the party from the subaltern mass composed of the poor sections of the Bengali society. Since the late 1980s and early 1990s questions began to arise within the party itself and beyond about the viability of participating in parliamentary democracy as a tactical means to progress towards the goal of people's democratic revolution. Apprehension about the means displacing the goal, that is, whether or how far the participation in electoral democracy for the purpose of electoral renewal was becoming the exclusive goal of the CPI (M) rather than revolution was in the air. It is pertinent here to quote the view of the CPI (M) Central Committee itself in this regard,

[1] Source: CSDS Data Unit.

> Parliamentarism is a reformist outlook that confines the Party's activities to electoral work and the illusion that the Party's advance can be ensured mainly through fighting elections. This leads to the neglect of the work of organizing mass movements, Party building and conducting the ideological struggle. If the focus had been on strengthening the independent role of the Party and building the Left and democratic Front (which is a class based alliance, not an electoral alliance), then what we see in practice today of concentrating on electoral tactics, seeking to build an electoral understanding with bourgeois parties and projection of an alternative which is only electoral in nature could have been avoided. (CPI [M] 2015a, 22)

Although the ideological deviation started in the early 1990s, it took almost 25 years for the CPI (M) to realize the detrimental impact of becoming excessively parliamentarian. The concern of the CPI (M) Central Committee about parliamentarism makes explicit its ambivalent attitude towards electoral participation. The inability of the CPI (M) to take a resolute stance about electoral participation or entering into electoral understanding with the bourgeois parties was revealed in the West Bengal Assembly election 2016, where it formed an electoral alliance with the Congress party. Strikingly, this alliance was built just after a year of the CPI (M)'s 21st Party Congress at Hyderabad held in January 2015, where the Central Committee in the Draft Political Resolutions, declared quite unequivocally that, 'The Party will have no understanding or electoral alliance with the Congress' (CPI [M] 2015b, 38). Such dilemma of the CPI (M) about concentrating on electoral politics possibly is rooted in its own heritage of being a party of mass movement for the underprivileged. With the increasing control of the middle class, it was turning out to be difficult for the CPI (M) to do justice to this heritage. The complexity of the situation lay in the fact that it was also not possible for it to expose complete detachment from the tradition of mass protests either. This ideological dilemma, pertaining to the nature of the CPI (M) as a party of reform, or of movement at the grassroots, had its influence upon the policy priorities of the LF government.

RISE AND GROWTH OF THE AITC: POLITICAL-ECONOMIC FACTORS

The CPI (M)'s overwhelming proclivity to maintain its power base through elections in a competitive framework of party competition, somehow pulled back by its own image of a 'social movement party' (Heller 2001, 155), had certain serious implications for the political economy of West Bengal. The issue will be dealt here from the vantage point of political culture since political economy or the social and political bases of economic systems cannot be comprehended without the necessary reference to the values, ideas and political conduct, in sum, the political culture prevailing among the people at the level of society at a given point of time. In a similar tune, Ruud (1999) refers to the norms governing political behaviour as political culture. These norms determine '...the role of contacts and networks, what people expect to gain from engagement in politics, all those elements that constitute the microfoundations of a functioning polity' (ibid., 237). Hence, political culture is indicative of the overall political atmosphere: its trends and dynamics, with the specificities built around the dimensions of time and space. The goals and strategies of different political parties often are instrumental in shaping these norms which in turn also are shaped and reshaped by it. Apart from directing it, political parties also reflect the sentiment and aspirations of the people on the basis of which political institutions under a democratic polity, specifically the state, interact with the people through their policies and programmes. Viewed through this angle, political culture largely is a guide to the state that determines the nature and objectives of its policies as well as the means of implementation. In the context of West Bengal the influence of the ruling CPI (M) on the norms of political behaviour deserves some brief comments here. This is specifically important since it was allegedly undergoing transformation in its core values since the 1990s.

Any discussion about the influence of political parties on political culture must highlight their political conducts. It should focus on the macro level consisting of their policies and programmes and on the micro level of execution where they interact with the people. For the present purpose we will concentrate on the post-1990 CPI (M) in West Bengal. This was the period when the above-mentioned dilemma of the CPI (M) got more pronounced. With the gains of the land reform and panchayati raj innovations tapering off, this period posed serious challenge to the CPI (M) as far as the continuation of its rule was concerned.

With the CPI (M) becoming more and more entrenched in the electoral politics, its policies and schemes increasingly came to be scrutinized through the critical points of winning and losing elections. As is common in electoral competition, parties often frame their policy approach to attract the electorates in order to count on their support in the elections to win it. The case of the CPI (M), being a party to usher in people's democratic revolution, should have been different from other parties operating in the electoral arena. Its policies and programmes should have the goal of preparing the masses for the revolution, instead of the opportunistic electoral calculations. But as elections became a prominent goal to the CPI (M), allegations of opportunism have also been raised against it as well.

Critiques find the imprint of such opportunism in the two flagship programmes of the LF government, namely land reforms and democratic decentralization of institutional power to the grassroots. Kohli, while according credit to the CPI (M)'s pro-poor political will, believes that its pro-poor initiatives were '...aimed at securing political position by improving the conditions of the lower classes' (1987, 95). Thus, the thrust of the reform programmes of the CPI (M)-led LF government had been a factor of its effort to build up an electoral constituency. In a similar tune Bardhan and Mookherjee (2010) also argue that the land reform initiatives of the Left parties, the CPI (M) in particular, was to have an electoral majority in the rural areas. The implementation of the reform measures slackened once the LF was able to control a majority of the local governments. They attribute the CPI (M)'s reluctance to carry the tenancy reform measures to the point of conferring ownership rights to the tenants, to the growing dominance of the middle class peasants in the party. Granting land titles to the landless would lead towards their economic empowerment, which in turn, would reduce their willingness to work for low wages in the lands of the middle owners. Thus, to secure the electoral support of the middle peasantry, the CPI (M) compromised the class interests of the landless and poor peasants. Both the explanations of Kohli, and Bardhan and Mookherjee seem to follow the economic logic of political action as put forward by Downs (1957), who in stressing the role of electoral opportunism in policy formulation and implementation argues, 'Political parties in a democracy formulate policy strictly as a means of gaining votes' (ibid., 137).

Similar criticisms have been raised about the panchayat system as well. Sengupta (1981), referring to the manner in which panchayats are organized as distributive agencies, considers this to be an extension of parliamentarism to the grassroots. Instead of making the panchayat the site for political mobilization of the rural, mostly the poor people, against the upper classes, the LF government has converted it into an arena for electoral contests. For this he casts doubt about the efficacy of the panchayats in offering an alternative strategy of people-centric model of rural development to those of the moribund bourgeoisie. In a similar vein Webster (1992b), in spite of considering the panchayati raj as a bold and innovative strategy of the LF, appears to be apprehensive about the increasing trend of bureaucratization of the panchayats with the sole political goal of electoral renewal of the CPI (M). He doubts if the panchayats are actually offering a radical and pro-poor programme of rural development at all or is it basically playing the role of an organ to strengthen the party's electoral position in the rural societies.

The point which Sengupta and Webster are making perhaps has some relation to the overshadowing of the autonomous space of the panchayats by the partisan aspiration of the Left parties, principally the CPI (M). Decentralization of power ontologically implies the holding and independent exercise of power by the people at the grassroots to redress the traditional power inequality. The control of the CPI (M) over the panchayats, as argue the critiques, had detached them from this primary goal and converted them as agencies to garner electoral support for the party. Acharya (1994), and Mukherji and Ghosh

(2010) note the incompatibility of the principle of democratic centralism of the CPI (M) and the ethos of democratic decentralization upon which the panchayats are founded, as the primary reason for this. As a principle of democratic centralism entails that deliberations at the lower tiers of the party over policies would move up to the central level where the final decisions would be taken. The final decisions once taken should be binding on all, the lower levels had to follow the decisions and execute them. If any lapses are there in the execution, the lower levels are answerable for those. As the CPI (M) is organized around this principle of democratic centralism, so it was rather difficult for it to allow the autonomous space for the practice of decentralization in the form of self-rule to the panchayats under its exclusive control. So, it was rather obvious that the entry of parliamentarism induced vices of electoral opportunism at the party level, which would be found in the operations at the local level panchayats also. That parliamentarism is giving birth to electoral opportunism at the party level is accepted by the Central Committee of the CPI (M) also. In its *Report on Organization* adopted by the Plenum on Organization at Kolkata in 2015, the Central Committee of the party declares:

> The reluctance to take up social issues like dalit oppression and conduct struggles is due to the opportunist fear that it may harm the electoral prospects by antagonizing dominant caste groups. Similarly the class orientation towards the poor peasant-agricultural workers and taking up their issues for struggle is glossed over in order to advance electoral prospects by not disturbing the dominant sections. (CPI [M] 2015c, 30)

Such opportunist trend of the CPI (M) at the policy level informed the implementation process at the micro level too. The reluctance to organize struggle for the dalits, the poor peasant and agricultural workers, as noted by the Central Committee document quoted above, serves the proof of this. At the local level the cardinal norms of political behaviour to which the party members became acclimatized was to maintain the power of the party by winning elections at all levels. The imperative to winning elections had led the party to expand its membership base as much as possible. Chatterjee (1997, 154) remarks in this context, 'It was reported three years ago that some 80 percent of the nearly one hundred thousand members of the party in West Bengal had joined it after the Left Front came to power in 1977....' These new members' exclusive political purpose for joining the party, as he argues, was to win elections. The party also, in return, satisfied their rising class aspirations by offering them salaried jobs, primarily as school teachers. Survey data of the CSDS, as mentioned earlier, has also confirmed this by pointing out the increase in LF's electoral support among the salaried portions of the middle class during the first decade of the new century. The entry of the opportunist members in large numbers coupled with the party's increasing electoral orientation made the situation intolerable to a section of ideologically sensitive members who considered the party as a vehicle to carry forward the goal of revolution. Any challenge to the party leadership raised by these members on ideological level was punished severely through suspension and expulsion from the party. A large number of these committed members in such a disgusting condition either started to resign from the party or did not renew their party membership any more. The new entrants, although increased the size of the party quantitatively, contributed very little in the qualitative improvement of the party in respect of organizing the people in social movements leading to social transformation. On the contrary, there was effort on their part to become powerful enough to satisfy their personal ambition (Echeverri-Gent 1992), starting with the local level rising up even to the higher ones, utilizing their position in the party. Obviously this led to factionalism within the party. Factionalism of this sort was obviously not over differences in political and tactical line of the party, rather to the differential access and share of the 'rewards' associated with power (Chatterjee 1997). The party which occupied a much revered place in the popular imagination of Bengali populace in the 1960s and 1970s for its commitment to organize people's resistance against exploitation and oppression, degraded to the extent of various charges of corruption being levelled by the people since the early 1990s (Echeverri-Gent 1992). The CSDS West Bengal Assembly Election Study 2011 also makes this explicit where almost 57 per cent of the respondents report that there is a lot of corruption in the party.

COLONIZATION OF THE LOCALITY

The encroachment of opportunist interests within the CPI (M) had influenced the norms of political behaviour significantly. The leaders and party members began to posit themselves as the party itself having the sole authority of institutional power. At the micro level this resulted in transforming the image of the party, or for that matter the leaders as the primary agency to decide over the beneficiaries of the fruits of various governmental welfare schemes and programmes meant for the poor and downtrodden. This brought in a necessary change in the political conduct of the ordinary people too, who came to be engaged in politics only to get close to the leaders with the expectation to receive the necessary governmental assistance. Webster (2009) has aptly described it as 'crony democracy' where '...the interests of CPI (M) party members have come to override more principled considerations of popular control, equity and poverty reduction' (p. 84). Such mediation of governmentality by the party gave rise to what may be termed colonization of the locality. This is a situation where local government-controlled welfare benefits and developmental assistance reach the people through the direction, regulation and overall guidance of the dominant party. Colonization of the locality as was done by the CPI (M) in West Bengal since 1990s implied a situation where, as argues Williams and Nandigama (2018, 10):

> All requests for help were mediated through the local party high command: official forums for deciding on the distribution of benefits—such as village open meetings and the village development committees—were therefore used to 'consult' the public, but decision-making power was held by the panchayat leader, and particularly the local party bosses.

More than the mere blurring of the party–government relationship, it entailed a complete engulfment of the local governmental sphere by the party. Among others, it was quite clearly visible among the school teachers upon which the CPI (M) had considerable influence. Ruud (1999) finds out that among the school teachers those who happened to be the CPI (M) party members were, 'excused from their normal working hours if they spent the time in political meetings or other 'politically relevant work' (p. 250) of the party. The School Inspectors

(SI) couldn't help lamenting over it. The present researchers had an opportunity to meet one teacher of an undergraduate college in Paschim Medinipur district who refused to submit a leave application to the principal of the college on account of his absence on a specific day. When the principal asked him to submit the same he replied that he had submitted it where it was to be submitted, referring indirectly to the CPI (M) party officials of the level to which he was a member. What he wanted to imply was that the principal perhaps had no moral authority to demand the application from him. Rather than the service conditions fixed by the government, the incidence proves that the government employees who double as CPI (M) members considered themselves to be governed by the rules and norms of the party exclusively.

Colonization of the locality by the party had created a condition where even the rights and entitlements of the citizens came to be defined and shaped by the party. In West Bengal, the decentralization of power to the grassroots rather than attaining the goals of empowerment of the grassroots, actually helped the local level CPI (M) leaders to appropriate the governmental power at the micro level. The relatively better educational, economic and social positions of the CPI (M) party members vis-à-vis the common rural people had been instrumental for the former to extend their domination over the latter. In the formal democratic space of the panchayat public meetings, where the marginalized people were expected to express their needs and problems, the poor villagers primarily the poorer scheduled caste people, as reports Webster (1992a), spoke out very rarely. It was very difficult for them to even believe that they can speak anything at the same platform where the CPI (M) members, comprising the teachers and others belonging mostly to the middle and upper castes are present (ibid.). Moreover, people preferred to remain silent in these meetings also because of the fear psychosis emanating from the threat of coercion by the CPI (M) cadres. While speaking if they articulate their concerns and criticize any function of the panchayats that might be counted as a criticism, even opposition to the party, which the newly emerging political culture of the CPI (M), developing since the early 1990s, was not habituated to tolerate. Colonization of the locality by the CPI (M) therefore by impeding the faculty of free thinking and expression of the poor rural folk had led to their growing dependence on the party to receive the benefits of different governmental welfare schemes to which they were indeed rightfully entitled. The bottom-up approach of participatory development possibly fails to bear its fruits in a situation overtly controlled by the top-down political ethos of centralized political party, in this case: the CPI (M).

The overwhelming control of the CPI (M) on the public life of the society took very little time to extend its scope further to bring the private lives of the families within its command. The grass-roots level workers of the CPI (M) in the conduct of their everyday politics got close enough to the people to appear as the moral guardians not only in the more impersonal public sphere but also in their private domains of intra and inter familial relationships. In his discussion on CPI (M)'s party-society, Bhattacharyya (2009, 60) has noted this and argues that, 'It was not uncommon to solicit a party's intervention in most intimate and private affairs.' Although to him this 'specific form of sociability' was helpful in extending the electoral advantage of the party but that was certainly at the cost of the much celebrated notion of individual liberty. The respondents of the CSDS conducted West Bengal Assembly Election Study 2011 also confirm this, as 41.3 per cent of them reported that party workers interfere in their personal matters against 30.2 per cent who did not feel so. The surveillance and control of the party over individuals' lives was so deep that it was often not possible for them to take decisions about their private affairs either on their own or by taking recourse to any agency other than the party, since that would be considered as a disregard or challenge to the party authority. Hence, the everyday lives of the Bengalis, especially the rural folk were plated with many incidences where the party workers regularly intervened in their personal or familial matters. Property disputes within the family, matters related to love affairs and 'proper' selection of marital partners (the Rizwanur Rahman suicide in 2007 as mention Chatterjee and Basu [2014] is a case in point) are common among these. Williams and Nandigama (2018) in their study in Birbhum district of West Bengal come to know about an incidence where the support of the party was sought to proceed even with a divorce. The enclosure of the private sphere by the party and its conversion into a 'party-politicised space' (ibid., 5) obstructed the process of socialization and hindered the personality development of the individuals with the necessary awareness about the social and political trends and currents of the period in concern.

In such a condition, the much-talked about agency of the rural poor people of West Bengal for collective mobilization to protest against exploitation by the upper class, as was evident in the 1960s and 1970s, began to wane since the early 1990s. The sharecroppers, landless labourers who rose to revolt many times in the history of pre-independent Bengal and post-independent West Bengal moved far away from the arena of social movements. The CPI (M) also, on account of its growing middle class inclination, gradually distanced itself from the politics of collective mobilization of the lower stratum of the agrarian society. By this one should not think that the conflicts between the classes of rural society were not there. Conflicts were certainly there but these were contained and managed effectively by the local cadres of the CPI (M), who were allowed the necessary power and leeway to deal with these (Rogaly 1998). The local leaders with the support of the party higher echelons coupled with their detailed knowledge of the local people, colonized the locality to the extent that they were successful in settling wages of the agricultural labourers to an even lower level than the basic demands. The agricultural labourers rather than protesting seemed to accept this and continued to vote to the ruling LF parties, particularly the CPI (M). Thus, the flexibility in fixing the class-based priorities and the thrust on class collaborationist policies had replaced the need for social movements aiming at social transformation.

It would possibly be a mistake to say that the CPI (M) had completely disowned its own heritage of being a social movement party. As a political party, located largely in the habitus of social movements, as has been mentioned earlier, it would also be risky for the CPI (M) to expose complete detachment from the social movements. This realization led them to stick to the social movement rhetoric perhaps to earn electoral dividends. This was evident from a number of 'political-organizational reports' and 'political resolutions' adopted at different party congresses even after 1990. In all these the party urged to organize struggle, against globalization and the impact of neoliberal economic reforms. The praxis of the party did not seem to match with its statement of ideological path. This was strikingly revealed in the cases of Singur and Nandigram where the party openly advocated and invited multinational capital while adopting political resolution to resist the same in the party congresses.

Further research is required to ascertain whether the particular political culture created by the LF since the beginning of the 1990s had any direct relation to the declining tone of the West Bengal economy being witnessed since then. The early success of the LF's agrarian programme began to fade away as the agricultural growth rate registered a steep decline from 16 per cent during the period 1990–1991 to 1995–1996 to 9 per cent during 1995–1996 to 2000–2001 (Banerjee et al. 2002, 4213). In comparison to the 1980s, the annual growth rate of revenues of West Bengal went down during the decade of 1990s. The rate was not only less than the national average; it was also less than that of Bihar (ibid.). Like agriculture, growth rate of industrial output also declined from 9.8 per cent in 1980–1981 to 5.1 per cent in 1995–1996 (ibid.) and further dipped to 4.6 per cent in 2008–2009 as reports Khasnabis (2008–2009). During 1984 to 2001 number of industries in West Bengal grew from 5,369 to 6,091 only, while in India it grew from 97,000 to 1,31,000 (Guruswamy, Sharma and Mohanty 2005). The picture of industrial employment also was not encouraging either. During the period 1984–2001, employment in the organized industrial sector declined about 50 per cent (ibid.), while in organized private sector it went down to 7.99 lakhs in 1997 from 10.84 lakhs in 1980 (Banerjee et al. 2002). Some of the important development indicators such as health, education, school enrolment of girl students, level of infrastructure available for primary education and overall Human Development Index, as mentions Bhattacharyya (2016), West Bengal showed very little improvement during the first two decades of LF rule. Gazdar and Sengupta (1999) are also of the opinion that the agricultural growth-led poverty reduction here did not translate into similar gains in health and educational outcomes.

Although we are not in a position to say that this steady decline of the West Bengal economy since the early 1990s was a direct offshoot of the emerging Left political conduct during the same period, but as our preceding discussion reveals, the LF also did not take positive steps to check this. The land redistribution movement and its gains could be sustained by a follow-up move to cooperativization. Certain basic cooperative efforts to pool draft power, implements and the facilities of cooperative credit to the small landholders and bargadars were also absent (Sengupta 1981; Chakraborti 2003). Possibly, the Left parties had failed to recognize that movement towards coopertivization of production activities could be an effective means of class struggle as well (Sengupta 1981). Little attempt was undertaken to consolidate the small holdings of the pattadars to remove the economic constraints associated with agriculture in small plots. Bargadars were recorded to provide tenurial security but the LF government did not consider it necessary to take initiatives to confer ownership rights of land to them. Hence, the land reform efforts remained incomplete. Panchayats, rather than becoming a platform of participatory governance, turned out to be partisan due to which it could not provide the much required impetus to independent initiatives of the rural people. Since the 1990s, the panchayats became engrossed in routine work only, losing much of its early enthusiasm (Mukarji and Bandyopadhyay 1995). For the lack of required innovation, it could not lead the LF's redistributive reform efforts to touch newer and even higher levels. All these might have some relation to the CPI (M)'s changing class priorities. Its growing middle class orientation since the early 1990s led to its alienation from the '"basic classes" that it is supposed to struggle for, namely, the workers, peasants, agricultural labourers, and the rural poor' (Patnaik 2011, 12). Distancing itself from the praxis of revolutionary social movements to transcend capitalism, the CPI (M) gradually got used to a class collaborationist strategy. Rather than organizing struggle to reduce or eliminate socio-economic inequality, such policy metamorphosis of the CPI (M) left the issue unaddressed, amounting to its further sharpening. If the spurt in economic growth of the 1970 and 1980s could be attributed to the CPI (M)'s ideological and practical opposition to social inequality since the second half of the 1960s, the economic downfall of the 1990s would have some relation to the changes in these aspects occurring in the same period as well.

NEOLIBERAL CHALLENGE

The neoliberal reform measures accepted by the Government of India in 1991, however, complicated the situation even more, particularly for the electoral Left parties. Not only in agriculture in other aspects of the economy as well, the neoliberal reform, as a strategy to 'activate global process of capital accumulation' (Petras and Veltmeyer 2009), had been instrumental in widening the disparity between the classes. It therefore becomes imperative to the communist parties to resist the onslaught of such a policy of economic reform. Alike its counterparts throughout the world, the CPI (M) also quite unequivocally had taken political resolution to organize struggle against neoliberal economic policies as one of its key tasks (CPI [M] 2005). It was really a challenge before the CPI (M) to maintain such ideological commitment under the overall structure of parliamentary democracy, where the party had certain genuine stake. The ideological deviation of the CPI (M), continuing since the mid-1990s, however had prevented it to do justice to its avowed ideological goal. The resultant dilemma had its toll on the political fortune of the CPI (M). In West Bengal, even after ruling for record 34 years it could neither provide any alternative nor did it show any positive intent to resist the rapid forward march of neoliberal development.

Perhaps, the alienation of the CPI (M) from the basic classes, as mention Patnaik (2011), and its growing middle class priorities were the primary reasons for this. These two intertwined factors detached the party from its earlier tradition of social movements to such an extent that it was perhaps not possible for it to organize any protest movement against neoliberalism. This was in spite of the fact that on a number of occasions the Central Committee of the CPI (M) recognized the role of neoliberalism in augmenting inequality and gave the call to fight against it. Though some sections of the middle class might have found a chance to improve their economic fortune through the liberalized market economy, but for the bulk of the poor, composed mostly of the unskilled industrial workers, small and marginal peasantry and the landless labourers, the policy of deregulation of the economy and elimination of state protection could have devastating consequences. But while the CPI (M) was unable to launch resistance movements against neoliberalism, it was also not forthright in embracing the economic reforms implied by this either. To satisfy the aspirations of its newly emerging middle class constituency, the CPI (M) could not perhaps take the risk of losing its traditional core constituency, who amidst all the ideological shift of the party continued to provide electoral support to it so far.

Caught in the duality of electoral politics and social movements, the LF government in West Bengal under the chief ministry of Jyoti Basu, finally recognizing the importance of private capital in providing accelerated growth, came up with the new industrial policy in 1994. Notably, it welcomed private sector investment for industrial development. The same policy also underscored the need of foreign technology and investment. The ambivalence of the CPI (M) was reflected in the considerable emphasis the said policy placed on the development of the small-scale enterprises. Instead of taking measures to remove over-regulation, improve infrastructure facilities and develop skills of the workforce, the three factors need to be taken care of for industrial growth in West Bengal as found out by a joint study of the World Bank and the CII (Banerjee et al. 2002), the LF's thrust on the development of small-scale industries did not seriously contribute to the progress of industrial fortune of West Bengal. Instead of moving steadily towards large-scale industrialization initiatives to resist the significant decline in the growth rate of industrial output and employment opportunities, such emphasis on the small-scale industries resulted in making West Bengal by the end of 1990s, '...a small-scale production-dominated economy, most of these units were unregistered, thereby posing serious issues regarding social security of those who were employed'

(Raychaudhuri and Basu 2007, 21). Since these units are not registered under the Factories Act, 1948, the workers there are largely outside the scope of the legal provisions like Minimum Wages Act or provision of social security schemes and so on. To protect their rights, the workers of these units cannot also find the established trade unions since these are engaged mostly in the organized sector. With the withdrawal of state patronage on account of economic reforms of the 1990s (Government of India 2010) their vulnerability had increased manifold. Thus, the proliferation of these workers in West Bengal during the 1990s was not at all a healthy sign for industrial development. Such a weak industrial performance of the LF government marked by the declining growth rate of organized industrial sector coupled with the deplorable conditions of the unorganized sector were the important factors providing the necessary impetus to the people to search for a political alternative in the form of the AITC.

That the LF was realizing this was evident from its various steps to make the investment environment of the state favourable to the investors. This was clear from the statement of Mr Buddhadeb Bhattacharya, who became the chief minister of West Bengal in 2000 after the retirement of Mr Jyoti Basu from the post. During his visit to Singapore and Indonesia aimed at attracting foreign direct investments (FDI) in West Bengal he argued, as reports Suryanarayana (2005, para 4 and 6),

> You see, communists. We can't speak anymore about old dogmas. The world is changing. We are also changing. Look at China. The situation is completely different if you compare it to [what existed] before 1978. The Chinese realise that their position in the world has changed. So, they changed their policies accordingly. Deng Xiaoping used to say: 'We learn truth from the facts, not from books.' We learned from our experiences in India and abroad. ...We have to formulate new policies...globalisation is a must...nobody can halt this process...we will take advantage of this situation.

The statement could not hide the feeling of ambivalence of Bhattacharya towards inviting foreign capital for industrialization of West Bengal. However, realizing the potential of FDI in creating employment opportunities through industrialization, he justified his position by relegating to 'old dogmas' the traditional ideological contradiction between the communists and capitalists centering on the conflict between labour and capital. The change in the ideological orientation of the CPI (M), as we are talking about, was explicit from the statement of Bhattacharya. The CPI (M)'s embracing of transnational capital might have some determined influence on the alienation of the urban and rural proletariat from the party. This created an opportunity for the AITC to develop its support base among them. The shift in the ideology of the CPI (M), however, was successful in drawing huge investments by the Tata Motors in Singur and Salim Group's proposed chemical hub at Nandigram. But the question remains whether industrialization can be conceived as a policy matter imposed from top as a political decision or as a process of culture change signifying the transition of an economy from a less advanced technique of production to a relatively advanced one. The unfolding of the events at Singur and Nandigram along with its political impacts in the second half of the first decade of the present century added some more substance to the debate.

Social Movements and Democratic Politics in Contemporary West Bengal

The Cases of Singur and Nandigram

The comfortable victories of the CPI (M) and its alliance partners in the Lok Sabha Election of 2004 and the Assembly Election of 2006 boosted the confidence of the LF government to jump on the bandwagon of massive industrialization under private transnational capital as a preferred way to development. We have already discussed the change in the ideological standpoint of the CPI (M), facilitating its move towards this direction. We have also seen the manner in which the then chief minister of West Bengal Mr Buddhadeb Bhattacharya invited capitalists to set up industries in West Bengal much before the West Bengal Assembly Election 2006. He was trying earnestly to convince the industrialists that West Bengal was the most preferred site for industries to develop. To convince them further, he even gave the assurance that as the dominant party, the CPI (M), had been taking every attempt to change the mindset of the workers, so that the latter can shrug off their long held 'dogmas' about the traditional opposition between labour and capital (Suryanarayana 2005), and stay away from the path of labour militancy. Bhattarcharya's statement about changing the mindset of the industrial workers should be read against the background that West Bengal happened to be the state where the extent of labour militancy under the CPI (M)-led trade unions, particularly in the form of strikes, was highest among all the Indian states (Mukherji 2009). This was one of the important reasons which allegedly made the state a less attractive destination for capital investment for industries. The new direction in which the LF government wanted to move was amply depicted by the slogan 'Agriculture is our foundation, industry is our future' popularized during the run-up to the Assembly election of 2006.

The victory of the CPI (M) and the LF in the 2006 Assembly Election in West Bengal was considered by them to be the manifestation of people's support toward their proposed industrialization drive. But the CPI (M) perhaps overestimated the correlation. For a party which convincingly won nine consecutive Lok Sabha elections and six assembly elections prior to 2006, winning the Assembly Election in 2006 could well be an outcome of routine effect. The hegemony which the CPI (M) successfully built up in rural West Bengal, by establishing what Bhattacharyya (2004) terms 'Permanent Incumbency', could well result in winning another election. In fact, winning an election in such a situation by the CPI (M) was a foregone conclusion (Banerjee 2006). Hence, the victory of the CPI (M) might not have any direct relation with the proposed industrialization drive, which the party seemed to conceive. But the story of the election result of 2006 had its other part as well, which the party perhaps overlooked if not underestimated. After its meteoric rise in the Assembly Election of 2001, the AITC, in the two subsequent elections, namely the general election in 2004 and the Assembly Election in 2006, secured 21.04 per cent and 26.64 per cent votes respectively. The performance of the AITC was significant enough to prove its viability as the chief face of opposition politics in West Bengal. Moreover, except the general election of 2004, the combined vote share of the AITC and the INC in the Assembly Elections of 2001 and 2006 was greater than that of the CPI (M). From the vote share of the CPI (M) vis-à-vis the opposition, it is evident that the former had to depend on the other partners of the LF primarily, the CPI, the RSP and the Forward Bloc, to remain in power in West Bengal. In spite of this, the difference in vote share of the LF and that of the combined opposition was not high enough. Given the opposition camp led by the firebrand leader Mamata Banerjee, whose single point agenda happened to be the ouster the CPI (M) from the power of West Bengal, such a difference at any point of time might turn out to be uncomfortable, indeed.

We will first have a cursory look at the events which took place in connection with the land acquisition process in Singur and Nandigram. It all started on 18 May 2006, just a few days after the LF was voted to power in West Bengal, when Mr Ratan Tata, the then Chairman of the TATA group, announced that a small car project was to be set up in Singur, in Hugli district of West Bengal. A few days later, from 25 May, agitations began there against the state government's proposal to acquire 997 acres of farmland. The villagers immediately formed an informal platform named Singur Krishi Jomi Raksha Committee (Singur save agricultural land committee; SKJRC) to voice their collective protest. The then opposition leader Mamata Banerjee entered the scene on 25 September; the very same day, the police beat up the protesters and Banerjee alleged that she herself was manhandled. On 2 December the work of fencing the acquired 997 acres of land started amidst protest by the villagers. In the ensued police action a large number of villagers were injured, some of them critically. From 4 December Banerjee began an indefinite hunger strike protesting the land acquisition issue that she ended 25 days later on 29 December, upon the request of the then Prime Minister Dr Manmohan Singh and the then President of India, Dr A. P. J. Abdul Kalam. Tata Motors started the construction of the factory from 21 January 2007 when women torched the factory fencing and on 9 March Tata Motors finally got possession of the land. Three days later, on 12 March, a protesting farmer committed suicide, the earliest of a row of suicides. On 16 March a fierce mob attacked the factory, and on 25 March it was reported that five of the factory guards were injured in another attack, and frequent attacks followed henceforth. On 10 January 2008 Tata Motors unveiled the Nano at New Delhi Auto Expo, and the protesters burnt down its replica in Singur on the very same day. On 18 January the Calcutta High Court delivered its judgement in favour of the state government regarding land acquisition. On 15 February Tata Motors announced that the Nano would be launched by October the same year. Meanwhile, with an unexpected gain in panchayat elections, winning a majority in the Singur Panchayat, TMC began to make its comeback from 21 May. On 27 June protesters broke into the Tata Motors factory. Between 18 to 20 August a series of events followed—the then Chief Minister, Buddhadeb Bhattacharya invited Mamata Banerjee for talks, where Banerjee claimed that at least 400 acres of land have to be returned to the (unwilling) farmers who received no compensation in lieu of their land which has been acquired for the automobile project. They failed to come to terms, and the talks failed. Meanwhile, on 22 August Ratan Tata made the earliest warning to relocate the Nano production out of Singur if violence continued. Tata Motors had by that time begun to receive invitations from other states to relocate the factory. On 2 September Tata Motors announced the suspension of work at Singur, on the logic that alternate sites were being explored. A section of the peasant protestors, perhaps being gradually convinced about the economic benefits of the project, formed the Nano Bachao Committee (save the Nano committee) on 2 October 2008. On 3 October Ratan Tata declared that Tata Motors would pull out of Singur, and finally on 7 October Tata Motors confirmed the relocation of the Nano project at Sanand in Gujarat, abandoning the Singur factory.

The Nandigram problem began with the issuing of a notice on 28 December 2006 by the Haldia Development Authority (HDA), identifying 27 mouzas of land in Nandigram and 2 mouzas of land in Khejuri, comprising 25,000 acres of land for acquisition, to set up a chemical hub by the Indonesia based Salim group. On 3 January 2007 when the anti-land acquisition protesters sought clarifications regarding the notice at the panchayat office, they were manhandled by the police and a police van caught fire, which could either be an accident or a deliberate action on the part of the masses. This was the beginning of violence in Nandigram. In the next couple of days the people of Nandigram put up roadblocks and made the interior parts inaccessible by police and administration. On 5 January 2007, several opposition parties such as the AITC, Congress, Socialist Unity Centre of India came together to form the Bhumi Uchhed Pratirodh Committee (BUPC). On January 7 armed CPI (M) cadre allegedly hurled bombs and fired bullets in Nandigram, killing at least five people. The infuriated masses set on fire a CPI (M) camp at Baratole, at Khejuri block and burnt down the house of Shankar Samanta, a local CPI (M) leader, killing him. Even though Mr Binoy Konar, a CPI (M) State Secretariat Member, warned the protesters gravely, the local administration held a peace meeting after the 7 January violence, with both the members of the ruling LF and the opposition, where it was settled that all parties would cooperate with the administration to restore peace and order in Nandigram. The dug up roads were proposed to be rebuilt and police camps were to be set up again wherever required. The then chief minister of West Bengal, Mr Buddhadeb Bhattacharya declaring that it was a mistake of the HDA to issue such a notice, asked it to be torn down and affirmed that in further dealings with the issue, the interests of everybody concerned would be kept in mind. However, violence continued between CPI (M) cadre and BUPC on a regular basis. On 7 February a police sub-inspector was killed and West Bengal Home Secretary, Mr Prasad Ranjan Roy declared that in view of the prevailing violence the administration would have to think differently about the police action in the villages in Nandigram, where police action was restricted so far. On February 12 the then chief minister assured that no land would be taken from those unwilling to give it. However, the very next day, the CPI (M) MP from Haldia of the Purba Medinipur district, Mr Lakshman Seth said that the land mentioned in the 'notice' issued by the HDA 'would be acquired'. On 10 March the district magistrate summoned a meeting of all the political parties which was boycotted by the opposition on grounds that the earlier proposals were not fulfilled. On 14 March, police gathered around Nandigram on grounds to reconnect it with the mainstream. On being held up by protesters, they fired after a number of warnings, killing 14 of the protesters and injuring many. On the next day the Calcutta High Court called for a special inquiry of the incidence by the CBI. On 19 March the state government issued written notice declaring withdrawal of the special economic zone from Nandigram. The BUPC, with utter disbelief, kept up its blockade of the area till 11 November when allegedly the CPI (M) cadres 'liberated' the area or *gram dakhal* ('capture of the village' as say the villagers).

With the deployment of CRPF and their camps in Nandigram the overt violence came to an end.

From the above accounts of the disputes regarding land acquisition for industry a number of distinctive features of these movements become apparent. These were not the peculiar characteristics of the protest movements in Singur and Nandigram exclusively, but in other similar events during the same period in West Bengal and beyond we came across these. First was the nature of the protest. Everywhere the affected villagers spontaneously reacted to the issue of land acquisition for industrialization and urbanization. Following Blumer's (1946) typology of social movements this can be termed as a 'general social movement' since it lacked proper formal organization, established or recognized leadership with formal guidance and control. From the standpoint of Hobsbawm (1971), these can be termed as rural movements although critiques tend to differ from Hobsbawm's characterization of these movements to have less developed class consciousness, hence 'archaic' or pre-political in nature. The tradition of peasant movements in Bengal also contradicts Hobsbawm's point of view since it amply demonstrates the existence of class solidarities in a variable degree along with other relevant dimensions among the exploited and oppressed peasantry.

Second, in most of these resistance movements the presence of women in significant numbers among the protestors with their active participation had been remarkable. In the context of Singur movement, Banerjee (2006, 4718) notes,

> Whenever the government officials tried to enter the villages to serve the notifications to the farmers for acquiring land, the women appeared in spontaneous resistance with brooms and sticks in their hands after alerting others by blowing conch shells.

The history of peasant movements in West Bengal as well as India provides enough examples of the noteworthy participation of women. This was especially pronounced in those movements where the adivasis, the dalits and other socio-economically weaker segments of the population participated significantly. That the women participated in the anti-land acquisition movements actively could be discerned by the fact of their victimization. In the context of Singur movement the women protestors, as mentions the *Interim Report of the Citizens' Committee on Singur and Nandigram* on 29 January 2007, '...were beaten up by male policemen, filthy language was used....' The National Confederation of Human Rights Organizations (NCHRO 2006) mentions on 5 December 2006 that during the Singur protest, 'The female arrestees at Chandannagar police station alleged that they were manhandled, beaten, molested and sexually abused by the male policemen at the time of arrest and while being transported to the police station.' The women protesting land acquisition did exhibit a well-developed consciousness about the goal of the movements and the difficulties involved in attaining it. In the context of Nandigram, the Muslim women surrounding the members of the Citizen's Committee expressed their obstinacy, 'Jami amra chharbuni' (we will not leave our lands). They continued with the same vigour, 'Even if we lose our sons and husbands, we will fight on, how many policemen can they send, there are more of us' (South Asia Citizens Web 2007).

Finally, the informal nature of the organization formed to carry forward the movements. In Singur, as has been already mentioned, the anti-land acquisition protestors formed the SKJRC, while those supporting the Tata Motors factory at Singur formed the Nano Bachao Committee. In Nandigram we come across BUPC (committee to resist eviction from land) formed by the village people to resist the proposed land acquisition drive. Similarly in Raiganj in Uttar Dinajpur district of West Bengal, peasants organized themselves under the Krishi Jomi Bachao Committee (committee to save the farmland) in January 2007 to resist land acquisition for a proposed army training camp there (Nielsen 2018). Nielsen also mentions about the Jami Bachao Vasstu Bachao Committee (committee to save land and homes) in Mahishadal, in Purba Medinipur district of West Bengal, Panskura Jomi Suraksha Sangram Committee (action committee to secure land) in Panskura of the same district, Krishi Jomi Raksha Committee (committee to save farm land) in Kharagpur of Paschim Medinipur district, Krishi Jomi Jiban o Jibika Raksha Committee (committee to protect farmland, live and livelihood) in Andal of Burdwan district and many others, which were formed to oppose acquisition of agricultural land. All these organizations were informal people's forums to resist the land acquisition drive of the LF government in West Bengal formed during the second half of the first decade of the 21st century. They lacked the formal organizational structure of an organized political party. These were also without a definite and recognized leadership pattern. Another distinctive feature of these organizations was there rootedness in the locality. This was important not only to wage localized wars against land acquisition but also to address effectively the issue of cultural aspiration of the local people, which under the economic onslaught of multinational capital might face the threat of jeopardy. Formal political organizations perhaps for their institutional nature and wider scope and network of activities, fail to touch upon the cultural distinctiveness of particular communities embedded in their respective localities. Unlike the established political parties, these were the autonomous political spaces facilitating the cause of everyday peasant resistance at the micro level against the accumulative drive of capital, national as well as global, operating under the neoliberal framework.

These features of the anti-land acquisition movements exhibit close resemblance to collective mobilization of the subalterns. Their spontaneity, gender neutrality as was apparent from the wider participation of the women and informal or loosely patterned localized organizations mark these off from the more institutionalized politics of the elites. These bring them close to the political idioms of the subalterns, which relied '...more on the traditional organization of kinship and territoriality or on class associations depending on the level of the consciousness of the people involved' (Guha 1988, 40). These marks of subalternity, which find their ready reference among the classical peasant movements associated with the manifold aspects of politics, economics and culture of agriculture, were also present in the popular movements against land acquisition at Singur, Nandigram and elsewhere. This ultimately leads to the portrayal of the movements having the conflict core in the fundamental contradiction between agriculture and industry.

Undeniably, acquisition of agricultural land for industries of scale, as has been done by the LF government, created the necessary space for the opposition to mobilize the peasantry. This was quite evident in Singur, Nandigram and some other places. Since the process of land acquisition in spite of all the protests was completed at Singur, so it would be a classic example to analyse its impact upon the evolving nature of political contradiction in West Bengal during the first decade of the present century. At the surface level this contradiction appears to have emanated from the tension between industry and agriculture emerging out of the transitional drive of a predominantly agrarian economy to industrialize itself. But from the NES 2009 data set of the CSDS, as shown by Chatterjee and Basu (2014), we get a different picture. It reveals that among the respondents of the study who have heard the demands made by the protesting farmers in Singur, 71 per cent and 68 per cent engaged in agriculture and non-agricultural professions respectively, consider these to be justified. The overwhelming support of the electorates, attached either to agricultural or non-agricultural professions, towards the farmers' demands at Singur might be a pointer to the fact that rather than the industry versus agriculture contradiction, the Singur agitation had turned out to be, '...a social issue that involved the pertinent questions of liberty, autonomy of the citizens and the permissible limits of state control of the social space (Chatterjee and Basu 2014, 298). Such a position finds support in the West Bengal Assembly Election Study 2011 (Table 3.1).

The table clearly reveals the disapproval of the electorates to the LF government's management of the Singur and Nandigram agitations. It would thus be very naïve to believe that the movements against

Table 3.1 *Electorates' Awareness about Singur and Nandigram Movements and Their Assessments of LF Government's Handling of These*

		If Heard, How Did LF Govt. Handle It?	
Incidence	*Heard about It*	*Handled Well*	*Handled Poorly*
Singur agitation	77	25	51
Nandigram violence	80	25	51

Source: CSDS Data Unit, NES 2009.

Note: All figures are in % and rounded off; rest 'No Opinion'.

land acquisition for industries in Singur, Nandigram and some other places in West Bengal were the signals of people's overall sentiment against industrialization. Far from this, the people of West Bengal were really looking for the economic opportunities thrown up by the large-scale industries. The survey data of the NES 2014 provides ample evidence to this.

During the survey when people were asked to express their opinion about the statement: 'Shifting of the TATA nano project to Gujarat from Singur is a bad news for West Bengal's economic growth', almost 81 per cent of the electorates agreed with the statement against only 19 per cent who disagreed with it. In a similar statement placed before them during the course of the CSDS post-poll survey of the West Bengal Assembly Election 2016, almost 87 per cent of the respondents agreed that the shifting of the Tata's Nano car project from Bengal is a huge loss to the common people of the state.

Mukherji and Ghosh (2010) mention at least three pertinent issues to prove that the primary contradiction was not between agriculture and industry as such. First, agricultural lands were also acquired in some projects for industrialization and urbanization at Rajarhat, Howrah, Siliguri and in some other places almost during the same period where no such movement against land acquisition took place. Second, in Singur there was a spontaneous uprising by the peasantry cutting across political affiliations from the very first day when a team of Tata Motors along with some government officials visited the proposed project site. Interestingly, with the passage of time a section of this protesting peasantry could realize the developmental potentials of the project, who formed the Nano Bachao Committee (save the Nano committee). The Nano Bachao Committee was also composed of the peasants representing both the ruling CPI (M) and its primary opposition: the AITC. Had the contradiction between industry and agriculture been the primary one, the same peasants who once opposed the industry could not perhaps come forward to save it. Finally, they found that there was a definite declining tone in the appeals of the mobilizations led by Mamata Banerjee in Singur over time. Probably, the contradiction between industry and agriculture as she along with other forces of opposition were emphasizing to be the primary one was not in tune with the basic issue which was at work among the protesting peasants. On the basis of these three reasons they conclude,

> [I]f the government had designed a compensation package that could ensure the reproduction of livelihoods, particularly of the poor and marginalized, at existing or better levels, this acute dislocating situation would probably not have arisen. (Mukherji and Ghosh 2010, 208)

The present authors also had come across several inhabitants of Singur, after interacting with whom it was revealed that the whole issue reached to such an alarming extent for two reasons: the issue of compensation package and returning the land of the unwilling peasants. In both the issues they felt that the insensitivity shown by the LF government had complicated the entire land acquisition process and had marred the prospect of the set up of the industry. In fact, in the opinion of the inhabitants these two issues were interrelated. If the government could enhance the compensation package, it would have been more attractive to the landowners, which in turn would reduce the number of unwilling peasants considerably. Furthermore, had the government shown some positive intent to return the land of the unwilling peasants, the anti-land acquisition movement would weaken significantly. By making the whole process democratic and pro-people, this could brighten the image of the government or for that matter the CPI (M) to a great extent. Without doing any of these, the government, displaying its stubbornness and arrogance only complicated the issue further.

The compensation offered to landowners in Singur was ₹8.7 lakhs and ₹12.8 lakhs per acre for single-cropped (Sali land) and double-cropped (Suna land) land, respectively. The registered bargadars (sharecroppers) were to receive 25 per cent of this value (Chandra 2008; Das 2016; Government of West Bengal 2007), while the unregistered ones no compensation at all (Ghatak et al. 2013; Mohanty 2007). Perhaps, these were not enough to satisfy the aspirations of the displaced people. It has also been alleged that the compensation rate offered by the government was even lower than the existing market price of land (Chandra 2008; Chatterjee and Basu 2014; Ghatak et al. 2013). Furthermore, fixing the rate of compensation at any period of time must take into cognizance the factor of inflationary pressure of the economy which can really disrupt the entire calculation of rate of compensation at any point of time in the future. The factor of land being an avenue of future earnings is also important here. Little wonder then, the farming land is considered by the farmers to be the most effective security cover and the best safety net. In fixing the market price of land in Singur, perhaps these critical dimensions pertaining to security and safety of the peasantry were not paid adequate attention. Das (2016) interviewed an AITC leader of Singur in 2009, who during the course of the interview expressed that the opposition to land acquisition would not have crystallized had the government increased the rate of compensation. Interestingly, the leader also mentioned, 'I saw many agitators convincing the farmers that the government would give in and raise prices if they could just hold on a little longer' (ibid., 12). Chandra (2008) also finds out the discontents of the bargadars regarding compensation to be an important factor of the Singur movement when he says, 'Actually, the state awarded too little to the bargadar (₹25) and too much to the landowner (₹100). It is no wonder that the bargadars were quite agitated' (p. 45).

Hence, it appears that the whole issue pertaining to the 'adequate' compensation of acquired land turned out to be the fundamental concern of the peasantry. Dispute centering on the proper compensation of the industrialization- and urbanization-induced displaced population of the rural communities has remained the central question not only in Singur, Nandigram and other areas of West Bengal, but also in India and other countries in Asia and sub-Saharan Africa (Ghatak et al. 2013). Displacement of rural communities from land has always been integrally connected with the process of industrialization itself, but the problem possibly is becoming more acute in the contemporary period with the unfolding of the neoliberal model of development that visualizes large-scale industrialization to be the most preferred route to attain its goals. The push towards industries of scale is so strong that the questions of the productivity and fertility of the land to be acquired, let alone the dependence of the cultivators on it for livelihood, are increasingly failing to find the proper focus in the neoliberal development discourse. Obviously, the issues pertaining to rehabilitation or compensation of the displaced people would find very little attention in it. The striking feature of West Bengal is that here a Left government, which had paid serious heed to all these concerns pertaining to agriculture and the peasantry during the first two decades of its rule since 1977, was turning out to be the apologist of such a model with enough potential to germinate the process of depeasantization.

Apart from the economic aspects, the issue of compensation has some other angles as well, notably social-psychological and legal-administrative ones. From the social-psychological standpoint, the most intricate issue perhaps was related to the supposed exchange relationship between agricultural land and compensation against its acquisition primarily for non-agricultural purposes. The moot question here is whether agricultural land after all can be compensated monetarily? (Chatterjee and Basu 2014). This leads us to consideration of the exchange value of the land, the conception of which differs from the buyer or the agency acquiring the land to the farmers. For the former land has great exchange value as a productive force, while for the latter it is not only full of use value but also it possesses some extra-economic properties which can hardly be conceived economically. Quinn and Halfacre (2014, 118) rightly point it out as they contend, 'Land is more than a place to grow crops; farms are locations with history, symbolic meaning, and repositories of emotion.' Land to the farmers, therefore, is more than the mere calculus of profit and loss. It is the anchor of their social and cultural existence. The very identities of the farmers, cultivators and the peasantry are shaped through their cultural, spiritual and shared emotional attachment to land. Such an emotional attachment to land becomes more pronounced in the case of ancestral inherited land. Here land acts as the symbolic means to be connected to the ancestors. It also becomes a moral and ethical responsibility of the current owner of the inherited land to pass it intact to the upcoming generations. The effort at transition from agriculture to industry, not only in Singur and Nandigram in West Bengal but everywhere, has to face this predicament concerning the difference in the ontological implication of land. The problem of 'modern' mercantile economy is that without paying sufficient and substantive attention to the dilemma it tries to resolve the whole issue of acquisition of agricultural land merely through monetary compensation.

From the legal and administrative point of view it must be mentioned that the entire land acquisition drive in Singur was guided by the dated colonial Land Acquisition Act of 1894. This Act has been termed by many critiques to be 'draconian' for its insensitiveness to the cause of the farmers in acquiring their land for 'public purposes'. It has, critiques argue, little protection for the landowners and the issue of their adequate compensation was to be arbitrarily decided by the government. In its rush to carry out the land acquisition in Singur at the aegis of this colonial act, the LF government perhaps failed to do justice to the term 'public purpose'. The government in order to circumvent the mandatory requirements of Part–VII of the Land Acquisition Act of 1894, which deals with the matter of acquisition for companies, sought to disguise it as acquisition of land for public purposes to be dealt under Part–II of the said Act. Possibly to make the acquisition process hassle free and quick, the government took recourse to this, since it allows considerable freedom to the government in acquiring the land (as argues Justice Gowda in the historic Supreme Court verdict on the Singur Land Acquisition case on 31 August 2016). Although Justice Mishra differed from Justice Gowda in his opinion about the implication of the term 'public purpose', but both the judges concurred on declaring the land acquisition at Singur by the LF government to be illegal. The legal battle set apart, it is indeed very striking to note that a venture of the multinational Tata Motors Ltd. is considered as a public purpose by no other than a Left government in West Bengal. The issues of employment generation and socio-economic development of the area resulting from the setup of the industry, as advocated by the Government of West Bengal, perhaps, were not enough to make the purpose public.

To wrap up the land acquisition process quickly through compensation, and on account of the conviction on the part of the CPI (M) that its rate was 'well over one and a half times the prevailing market prices' (Editorial 2006), the LF government possibly failed to notice the intricate issues involved with the nature of compensation offered. Primarily, this was related to the various dimensions related to the determination of the compensation package. Although the government incorporated a special provision of value-addition on the ground of accessibility of a plot with different type-class of roads, the compensation paid by the government was almost uniform (Ghatak et al. 2013). Apart from awarding differential rates to the mono-crop or multi-crop lands, it did not actually take into account the relative locational advantages and disadvantages of the acquired lands. It is common sense that the piece of land close to the rail, road network, public hospitals and other places of public utilities compared to the ones far off from these cannot have the same valuation (Chandra 2008; Chatterjee and Basu 2014). Apart from the physical distance in the physical space, people also occupy a cultural space in the community where the calculation of distance follows a symbolic logic of proximity, which cannot possibly be measured quantitatively, and therefore cannot be compensated monetarily too. For this, rehabilitation of community has become a highly contentious issue in the contemporary development discourse.

Moreover, the nature of dependence of the owner on her/his land is also a variable that needs to be addressed by the administrators in the determination of compensation package. It is known that a total of 12,000 people were to receive compensation for less than 1000 acres of land to be acquired from five villages of Singur block of Hugli district, namely Gopalnagar, Sinher Bheri, Beraberi, Khaser Bheri and Baje Melia. Going by simple arithmetic one can say that given the small amount of land per titleholder (on an average 0.08 acre per capita) a large number of them had to depend on other non-agricultural activities to earn livelihood. This is also corroborated by the Census 2011 data of Hugli district. It reveals that among the total workforce of the five villages mentioned above only about 16 per cent and 14 per cent are cultivators and agricultural labourers respectively. So, for near about 70 per cent of the total workforce, agriculture is not the primary occupation. What follows from these is the variable nature of dependence of the persons on land. The dependence of the segment of population for which agriculture is the primary source of livelihood cannot be the same for those who profess other non-agricultural pursuits. For the latter, apart from the asset value of land it also serves as a channel to accumulation and profit since they possibly lease out it to the sharecroppers. Unlike the former, acquisition of land in no way threatens their livelihood options. Hence, these two groups should not be treated equally while determining the compensation package. In Singur the government calculated the market price of land purely as property having asset value. It would have been better had the government incorporated the livelihood dimension of land providing security to the owners in arriving at the compensation formula. This could also be a preferred option as far as the principle of natural justice was concerned. Instead of following this, the LF government stuck to its formula of uniform compensation, which ultimately came to be, '...biased in favour of non-cultivating absentee landowners, and grossly unfair to the actual cultivators, bargadars and agricultural labourers' (Chandra 2008, 49). The resultant feeling of relative deprivation of the cultivators, the agricultural labourers and the sharecroppers, particularly the unregistered ones, might be a possible reason for them to move to the forefront of the anti-land acquisition movement at Singur under the Krishi Jomi Raksha Committee at the beginning and later the AITC.

Finally, compensation was also related to the important factor of legal ownership of the acquired land. For the majority of the rural people of India, ownership of land is still customarily understood. There exists considerable confusion among them regarding the legal and wonted connotation of ownership of land. Under such condition monetary compensation based on the exclusive criteria of legal ownership can fuel misunderstanding and bickering at the levels of neighbourhood and community. Such confusion, resulting into claim of multiple ownership of a single piece of land, often turns out to be a serious concern. This was witnessed in Singur when the process of giving compensation to acquired land was initiated. While the owners of land started to collect the compensation cheques after verification of their land deeds, it was discovered that compensation had also been received by some who do not have the legal entitlements. This happened particularly with those lands which have been sold to others but not mutated (Mukherji and Ghosh 2010, 210). Here it is to be kept in mind that transferred but unmutated land still shows the name of the earlier owner in the transfer deed. It is only through mutation of the property the name of the new owner is updated in the land records of the government. There had been quite a good number of such types of land in Singur which was sold to others but not mutated. Normally this created a complex situation where there were multiple claimants for the same land. The government however failed to address such complexities with the proper degree of sensitivity deserved by those.

Not only in the instance of Singur, such insensitivity of the government was evident in other places also where it attempted to acquire land for mega industrialization projects. This is striking since the LF government was spearheaded by the CPI (M): A party known for its close touch with the people, especially the poorer segment of it. It is interesting to note that it was the same party which, through the land reform initiatives, had been instrumental in making the hitherto landless peasants owners of some amount of land, was now trying to displace them even forcibly, as alleged. The CPI (M) had to pay a big price for such a volte-face in its orientation. It allowed the much wanted political space to the opposition led by the AITC to significantly encroach into the rural support base of the CPI (M). The way violence erupted at Nandigram, which claimed several lives coupled with its 'hyper-real' telecast in the media were terrible indeed. Allegations about the involvement of the CPI (M) cadres of the local level in the whole affair were in the air. The situation gradually went out of the control of the state government. The inability of the state government in maintaining law and order at Nandigram irked not only the opposition parties but also a sizeable section of the traditional Left supporters. There was an overall disapproval of the role of the CPI (M) in Nandigram incident which can be gauged from Table 3.2.

A close look at the table reveals that not only the AITC and the INC supporters who happen to be the opposition of the CPI (M), but also a sizeable proportion of the CPI (M) supporters and those of its other Left partners have also considered the role of the CPI (M) there, to be unjustified. This criticism of the Left supporters about the role of the CPI (M) in Nandigram might be a pointer to the diminishing political influence of the CPI (M) in particular and Left parties in general. This

Table 3.2 *Opinion (in %) on Role of CPI (M) in Nandigram*

Political Party	*Justified*	*Unjustified*	*No Opinion*
CPI (M)	53	30	17
AIFB	47	28	25
RSP	47	37	16
CPI	50	28	22
AITC	24	61	15
INC	23	62	15

Source: CSDS Data Unit, NES 2009 adopted from Chatterjee and Basu (2014, 298).

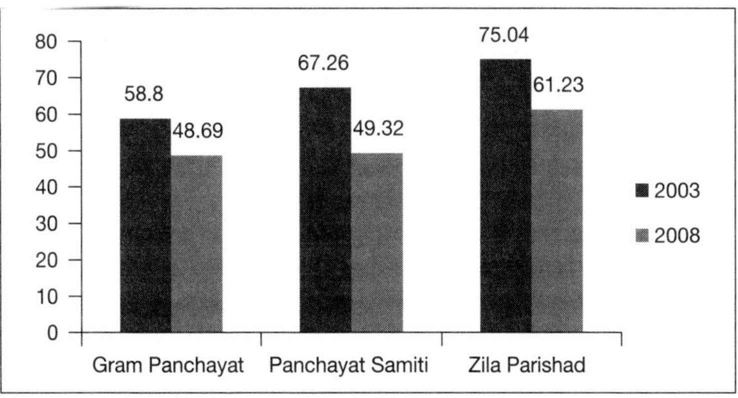

Figure 3.1 *Percentage of Seats Won by the CPI (M) in the Panchayat Elections 2003 and 2008*

Source: Compiled from the data of West Bengal State Election Commission.

was also reflected in the results of the Panchayat Elections of 2008 as depicts Figure 3.1.

The effect was there in the outcome of the Lok Sabha Elections of 2009 as well. Quite noteworthy were the comparative figures of the performance of the CPI (M) and the AITC in the two successive Lok Sabha Elections of 2004 and 2009. While the AITC registered a spectacular rise in its seat share from 1 to 19, the CPI (M)'s share of the seats went down from 26 to 9 between the two elections. Continuing the trend, in the Assembly Election of 2011, the AITC was successful in bringing an end to the 34-years long LF rule in West Bengal. This turnaround in the electoral fortune of the LF, the CPI (M) in particular, and the AITC should have its reference to the LF's newly found economic thrust since 2006 to go for large-scale industries necessitating huge amount of land to be acquired.

It is evident from the election results mentioned above that the much talked about LF's hegemony over the electorates of West Bengal, especially belonging to the rural areas, was effectively challenged by the AITC. The discontent of the rural populace against the LF's insensitive drive towards land acquisition helped in the crystallization of the AITC as a counter-hegemonic force. The AITC, under the leadership of Mamata Bannerjee, stood by the agitating peasants in Singur, Nandigram, Bhangar and elsewhere. Giving moral support and active leadership to the anti-land acquisition movements, the AITC won the much desired confidence of the rural electorates, instrumental to develop its counter-hegemony.

Mamta Bannerjee's rigid anti-CPI (M) stance also contributed to her emergence as the icon of the anti-CPI (M) struggle in West Bengal. Given the poor investment climate in West Bengal (Banerjee et al. 2002), her stiff resistance to land acquisition for mega industrial projects was also resulting in her being labelled to be anti-industrial, hence, anti-development. Not only her political adversaries such as the CPI (M) and other Left parties but also a number of economists were questioning her position vis-à-vis development. To answer her critiques, she quickly improvised her posture to direct all her opposition to the 'forcible' acquisition process. This was primarily aimed to project her investment-friendly image to the private investors while attributing the cause of her opposition to the overconfidence and anti-people policies of the CPI (M)-led LF government (Nielsen 2010). This was evident from her stubborn stance to return the 400 acres of land to the peasants who were not willing (*anichhuk*) to sell their land for the project against compensation. However anti-development her position might appear to be, this was successful in projecting her to be pro-people especially, pro-poor people that proved to be of immense importance to the AITC for making considerable inroads in rural Bengal, the erstwhile citadel of Left politics. That the AITC had successfully encroached into it was proved by the result of the panchayat election in 2008. The significant turning away of the farmers from the Left to the non-Left coalition in the 2009 Lok Sabha Election compared to that of the 2004, as mention Chatterjee and Basu (2014) on the basis of the NES 2009 database, was also a reflection of this.

It is however not enough to hold the ideological deviation of the CPI (M) responsible for this. More important is to track the percolation of this down to the network of the party's well-knit cadre-based organization, which was instrumental for its consecutive electoral victories. During the 1990s, when the CPI (M) was gradually getting detached from the tradition of social movements, its electoral successes gradually led to a kind of fetishization of its organization. Being extremely powerful, the party organization encroached into every aspect of public and private life of the people. As the governmental space of the democratic state largely came under partisan control, a political crisis concerning the fundamental issue of the legitimacy of the state was cropping up. At the same time a moral crisis was generating since the all-powerful party organization allowed very little autonomous space to be enjoyed by the community. This was leading to a situation where the CPI (M) was gradually getting detached from its political agenda. The organization was close to the people, but as unequal partners, 'managing', 'controlling' and 'guiding' their activities. Although it was successful in rewarding CPI (M) with a number of electoral victories, but since it was achieved without a substantive political ethos, question about its sustainability had always been there.

The organization fetish created a 'myth of invincibility' (Mukherji and Ghosh 2010, 208), which led the ruling CPI (M) to sustain itself exclusively on its cadre-based organization. The habit of winning elections led the party leadership in believing the myth to be a reality. With the increasing relegation of the questions of politics and ideology to the backstage, such invincibility was translated into arrogance. The arrogance was evident when Mr Buddhadeb Bhattacharya, the then chief minister of West Bengal, commented during the Singur agitation against land acquisition, '*amra* 235 *ora* 35' (we are 235, they are 35). Clearly by 'amra 235' (we are 235) he referred to the number of seats won by the LF out of a total of 294 seats in the West Bengal Assembly Election 2006, and by 'ora 35' (they are 35) to the seats won by the AITC. What he wanted to imply perhaps was that as the LF had won so many seats against very few of the opposition, so there was no point in giving any heed to their voices against land acquisition for the Tata Nano project at Singur. His emphasis on 235 versus 35 was indeed an arrogant attempt to understand social reality through electoral outcome solely, ignoring the significance of people's initiatives as expressed through their social movements at the grassroots. This, as Table 3.3 shows, had its obvious reflection in his declining popularity as the chief minister in contrast to the opposition leader Mamata Banerjee during the course of the 2006 and 2011 Assembly Elections in West Bengal.

Moreover, Bhattacharya's attitude was also a reflection of the overshadowing of the governmental space of the state by the ruling party or coalition. This was evident from the fact that being a chief minister, he was referring to the electoral strength of his party or coalition as a justification for the action of the government. As a chief minister and as a veteran politician, he must have known that no state in a democracy can be run by such partisan logic. Rather than trying to develop broad-based people's consensus for the land acquisition for industry in Singur, he visualized the entire course of people's resistance as a ploy of the opposition AITC to malign the image of his party and the government. Such a realization perhaps led him to quell it through the crude use of force by the government machinery acting in congruence with the party machinery. The intellectuals, human rights activists and other members of the civil society who protested such takeover of the governmental sphere by the ruling party and stood by the displaced

Table 3.3 *Popularity of Major Political Leaders as CM Choice 2006 and 2011*

Popularity of Major Political Leaders as CM Choice	*2006*	*2011*
Buddhadeb Bhattacharya	45	31
Mamata Banerjee	23	44

Source: CSDS Data Unit, West Bengal Assembly Election Study 2006 and 2011.
Note: All figures are in per cent.

people at Singur were also branded by the CPI (M) as either anti-Left or ultra-Left having tacit understanding with the AITC. The overwhelming control of the government and its various organs by the CPI (M) made it arrogant enough to misjudge the fundamental nature of democratic mobilization of the people which often cuts across, at least initially, the institutional boundaries of established political parties. The presence of both the CPI (M) and AITC members and supporters in SKJRC, Nano Bachao Committee at Singur and BUPC in Nandigram serves the proof here.

Invasion of the governmental sphere of the state by the ruling party or coalition, as was witnessed in the case of CPI (M) in West Bengal during the LF rule followed the analytical reasoning of the notion of the 'Shadow State' formulated by Harris-White (2003). By 'shadow state' she implies the existence of a parallel informal state run by private intermediaries having strong connection and a relation of dependence with the bureaucrats of the official state. By 'intermediaries' Harris-White implies the '...private armies enforcing black or corrupt contracts, intermediaries, technical fixers, gatekeepers, adjudicators of disputes, confidants, contractors and consultants' (ibid., 89). Das (2016) refers to them as the 'alternative bureaucracy', which operates under the shadow of the state. The shadow state with its functionaries, namely the alternative bureaucracy, coexist with the formal state. It is simply because the intermediaries cannot sustain them without the patronage of the formal bureaucracy, and the bureaucrats of the official state may find a channel of personal gain in these intermediaries. Thus, the actual size of the operating state is much larger than the official state because it takes into its orbit the shadow state also. In functional terms it is the shadow operators who gradually come to takeover and perform the basic functions of the state. With the increasing degree of operation of the shadow state, the formal state suffers from legitimacy crisis emerging out of the charges of inaction and corruption on the part of its officials.

Much like Chatterjee's (2004) notion of political society, the intermediaries working under the shadow state try to cater to the various survival needs of the marginalized population. They arrange for squatter housing, water, electricity and so on. They provide protection to the marginalized, adjudicate various disputes and also provide certain basic services. But unlike the political society, which through its mediation between the governmental state and the population to be governed opens up a space for dialogue essential for the latter to achieve their perceived entitlements through bargaining with the former, the shadow state is fundamentally rooted in illegality and corrupt practices. In this sense it comes close to what Chatterjee (2009, 44) calls 'the political management of illegalities'. The intermediaries active in the shadow state by weakening the legitimacy of the official state, make the population dependent on them for their survival. Here one can find the parallelism between the shadow state and the slipping of the governmental authority to the cadre-based organization of the CPI (M) under the LF regime in West Bengal. It is apparent that with the ideological deviation of the CPI (M) since the 1990s, the cadres came to play a number of roles performed by the shadow state operators as mentioned by Harris-White (2003). Gradually it resulted in growing dependence of the poor and the marginalized electorates, mostly of the rural areas on them. With the passage of time, as the imperative to win elections became more pressing for the CPI (M), these cadres also came to enjoy privileged positions within the party on account of their grip over the electorates. In this way, they came to enjoy enormous institutional power of the state in exchange of the assurance of electoral renewal of the ruling party. The governmental bureaucracy, thus, either turned out to be ornamental or proved to be secondary, while the alternative bureaucracy became highly active, so much so that the day-to-day governmental activities came to depend on it. Das (2016) remarks quite aptly, 'Much along the lines of the shadow state, West Bengal witnessed the increasing importance of political managers/workers/cadres during the Left rule, and true power, especially in the countryside, rested squarely with them' (p. 5).

This was revealed in the entire incidence of land acquisition in Singur. That the government totally relied on the party machinery of the CPI (M) was evident on a number of accounts. As an example, here we will discuss the contentious issue regarding the fertility of the land acquired. The CPI (M) sources claim that, '...of this land that has been acquired, over 90 per cent is mono-crop land. Less than 10 per cent of this land belongs to the more than one crop category' (Editorial 2006). Even the then Chief Minister Mr Buddhadeb Bhattacharya in an interview on CNN IBN channel on 25 February 2007 expressed the same, although he admitted that the report on the basis of which he was claiming this may not be up-to-date. But in the *Interim Report of the Citizens' Committee on Singur and Nandigram* dated 29 January 2007 headed by Professor Sumit Sarkar and some other intellectuals with a Left orientation, we come to know about the opinion of 50 to 60 villagers of Singur who had reported that most of the acquired land was multi-crop. On this basis, Sarkar (2007), refuting the claim that the most of the acquired lands were infertile and mono crop, came to the conclusion that these were extremely fertile and multi-crop. In the same interview when Mr Bhattacharya was told that the Left intellectuals had arrived at this finding about the character of the land acquired through repeated visits to the affected villages and through conversation with the villagers therein, he asserted, 'I know these farmers better than them particularly, and my colleagues are working there, my party, my peasants' organization, they know better than these people' (Bhattacharya 2007). Clearly, the reliance of the chief minister appeared to be more on his party colleagues than the official bureaucracy under his command. From a Foucauldian perspective, this should be regarded as a glaring example of how the organs of a ruling party enjoying considerable institutional power of the state formed and shaped knowledge about the fertility of the land and thereby produced a discourse that informed state policy and provided justification for the action of the state apparatus. It is evident from Bhattacharya's reliance on the information received through party workers at the local level, that during the CPI (M) rule in West Bengal a 'regime of truth' (Foucault 1984, 74) was created where the knowledge produced and sustained by the party machinery was counted to be true and reliable, which in its turn used to induce such exercise of power by the party. The production of truth or knowledge about the reality of the social conditions was so inextricably linked with the exercise of power by the party managers at various levels, that no other knowledge appeared to be qualified enough to be regarded as truth.

That the local party managers had poured in incorrect information about the fertility of the acquired land to the top level can be revealed from Sinha (2008), to whom the acquired land was highly fertile to the extent that, '...if cultivated with care, virtually every bit of its land is a veritable gold mine' (para 3). Chandra (2008) argues that the government has done a blunder '...by offering highly fertile land in Singur' (p. 49) to Tata Motors Ltd. Banerjee (2006) on the basis of the statistical information collected from *Statistical Handbook of West Bengal*, 2004 (Govt. of West Bengal, 2004a), and *District Statistical Handbook of Hugli*, 2004 (Govt. of West Bengal, 2004b), concludes that land of the acquired villages was fertile enough. Although the yield rate for rice was slightly less than the state average, but the same for potato was higher than the state average. This is also a pointer to the fact that to the state government, under the control of the CPI (M), only information received through party channel was reliable. It was accepted so uncritically that the need of its verification with other reports, even the technical ones, did not arise.

Allegation of this nature pertaining to the government's partisan interest to protect the interest of the local party workers had been there with respect to the demarcation of the factory site as well. It was alleged that there had been a deliberate attempt on the part of the authority to, '...undermine the opposition stronghold by marking plots owned by TMC supporters for acquisition while leaving CPI (M) loyalists' land untouched, thus resulting in a zigzag shape instead of a conventional quadrangular area for the site' (Das 2016, 9). For Nirupam Sen, the then industries minister of West Bengal, such a zigzag shape was due to the effort on part of the authority to ensure that fertile portion of the land along with homestead ones were excluded from the acquisition as far as possible (Chattopadhyay 2006). But the present authors, through interaction with the inhabitants of Singur came to know that such zigzagging was due to the skipping of lands of some local-level influential CPI (M) workers keeping into mind the enhanced price they might get out of those once the factory starts regular production.

Such reliance of the government on the local leaders of the ruling party could be revealed in the process of acquiring consent of the landowners and in the important issue of negotiating the compensation package with them. While the government claims that the compensation package had been worked out after detailed consultations with the local population (Editorial 2006), the reality seemed to be different. In Singur and Nandigram there was no panchayat meeting, no party spokesman talked with the people regarding the land acquisition (South Asia Citizens Web 2007). The villagers came to know about the acquisition from newspapers and the notice displayed in the Block Development Office. The party convened a meeting with all the farmers at Singur, but not to discuss with them about the acquisition and compensation package. It was to convey the decisions already taken regarding these to the farmers (Das 2016). The same was true about the negotiation camps. While no government official was present, the party workers in these camps tried to 'encourage' the local people to surrender their land and receive the compensation quickly. Such 'encouragement' however did not preclude violence or the threat of violence which happens to be a strategic resource at the disposal of the party workers at the local level for building consensus (Chatterjee 2009). How effective was the threat of violence can be learnt from Balai Das, once an active CPI (M) cadre at Singur but gradually got detached from it since he refused to sell his land for the project. In an interview with Das (2016, 11) he maintained,

> I was a CPI (M) supporter, a regular in party meetings and demonstrations. But I realised that only if one abides by what the leaders say, one can survive and be rewarded, but otherwise the party will coerce you into submission, even by brute force if necessary. That is what has happened to us because we refused to sell our land.

Sumit Sarkar and the other members of the Citizen's Committee during their visit to Singur found the evidence of application of force as the protestors were beaten up particularly on the nights of 25 September and 2 December 2006. Most interestingly, the Committee came to know that although the police was there, it was the CPI (M) cadres who 'did the major part of the beating up' (Sarkar 2007, para 4).

It is not sure whether this form of political transaction was the symptom of the dissolution of the party-society about which Bhattacharyya (2009) is talking about. If one considers the ontological make-up of the party-society, an attempt to develop hegemony of the party over the rural electorates would come up as a major constituent of it. The CPI (M) leaders at the local level, with the attributes of 'simple lifestyle, moral virtue, close familiarity with and easy access to people...' (Chatterjee 2009, 44), had been the chief architects to build up such a massive support base of the CPI (M) rule among the rural electorates. This was a moment of hegemony in the typical Gramscian formulation which tries to develop consensus within the context of civil society in support of a rule that exercises power without taking recourse to violence and coercion. But since the 1990s, the change in the ideology and praxis of the CPI (M), on account of the changing economic and political conditions at the state, national and the international level, gradually opened it up to new members more inclined to maintain the electoral domination of the party with doubtful ideological and political commitment. Replacing the earlier cultural leadership of the party marked by the presence of educated persons mostly the school teachers, the brokers, promoters and middlemen now came to compose the party leadership at the local level. More than politics, to them joining the party was a means to attain the goal of maintaining and consolidating their economic interest. Naturally they were more inclined to the electoral renewal of the CPI (M). Obviously, the issue of consensus building, that too for a rule of the communist party, a process requiring a great deal of political maturity, perhaps was beyond their capability. They considered election to be an end in itself, not as a means to achieve the much cherished goals of democracy. It is little wonder that in their bid to win the elections, these new entrants to the CPI (M) will not hesitate to apply the strategy of violence or threat of violence over the electorate.

Evidently, this hints at a diminishing, if not vanishing, influence of the CPI (M)'s party-society. In such a situation, more than consensus the logic of domination and coercion came to be the prime mover of rule. Growing detachment of the party from the political dynamics of the society created a situation where the party appeared to be an instrument to carry out the interest of its members without bothering about legitimacy. Violence became a means to achieve it, which by its very nature, would have little concern towards civil liberties and democratic rights. Autonomy of the community and liberty of the individuals were under serious threat of relinquishment. The party became the sole custodian of the locality and its constituents determining all aspects of their lives. This was witnessed in Singur where no consultation, as alleged, with the villagers took place before the acquisition of fertile land, on which almost one-third of the affected villagers' livelihood was dependent. The compensation package was also unilaterally determined by the party allowing little or no room for negotiation. The coercive image of the party in this way brought the entire locality under its fold. The CPI (M) itself turned upside down its much-celebrated programme of the decentralization of power to the grassroots. In the local space autonomy was replaced by subjugation; participation was replaced by intimidation; people's independent initiatives were replaced by party dictates to give birth to the condition of colonization of the locality. The more it grew in scope and penetrated deep into the localities the more the influence of the part-society dwindled. This in its turn downsized the base of legitimacy of the CPI (M), leading to its ultimate downfall.

Politics of Identity

The distance of the CPI (M) with its ideological constituents, namely the industrial workers and the peasantry, began to crop up during the dying phase of Jyoti Basu's chief ministerial tenure in the second half of the 1990s. It tended to increase when Buddhadeb Bhattacharya became the chief minister in the early 2000s only to reach its zenith during the second half of the first decade of the new millennium, as exemplified by the incidences at Singur and Nandigram. It was the period when the LF government in West Bengal, rather than carrying forward its much talked about pro-poor policies such as the land reforms and the decentralization of institutional power to an even higher level, turned its focus to the neoliberal model of development whose anti-poor impacts were being increasingly felt in most of the developing countries throughout the globe.

This would be a mistake to say that the CPI (M)-led LF government was the only communist coalition having compromised with the global aggression of capital. Everywhere, in every continent, the electoral Left had to shift towards the Right (Webber 2015) and contributed towards the global accumulation of capital through dispossession, as argues David Harvey (2009). As an example of this, he cites the instance of Nandigram (Harvey 2018) and from the events at Singur we can see how a state having, 'monopoly of violence and definitions of legality' (Harvey 2009, 74) promotes or facilitates this process of accumulation by dispossessing the people from their land and resources. This is perhaps a pointer to the declining tone of traditional class struggle represented by the trade unions, peasant associations and the political parties emerging out of these. Such weakness of class as a mobilization principle notwithstanding, resistance to neoliberal capital accumulation has been taking place in some other forms, mostly resembling the shape of 'new social movements' (NSM). Detached from the sphere of traditional institutional politics, these movements represent a new politics that emphasizes issues of equality, participation, human rights and so on (Habermas 1981; Offe 1985). With their locus in the non-institutional domain of the civil society, these movements are instrumental in the development of collective identity of the participants. Besides the resistance of the rural folk at Singur and Nandigram, we come across a number of such identity assertions during the same time in West Bengal. Setting aside the question of class, these movements based on the identities of caste, religion, region and ethnicity have raised important questions regarding the future direction of struggle against neoliberal economic and political agenda.

In the context of post-1990 West Bengal, the political ascendance of identity can be approached from a number of related standpoints. First, since the mid-1990s, the gradual detachment of the CPI (M) from its traditional support base signalled an overall decline in the importance of class in the arena of constitutional politics. Given the conceptual opposition between class and identity (Burgmann 2005), such a retreat of class provided a congenial environment for the maturation of identity politics based on caste, religion, ethnicity and so on. Second, the growing disillusion of the rural poor from the CPI (M) also enfeebled the party-society, which had contributed positively to the long sustenance of the CPI (M) in the state power of West Bengal. With the poor rural folk getting alienated, the intimate link between the party and the society was getting ruptured. As a result the CPI (M) rule was failing to acquire the legitimacy necessary to maintain its hegemony. In such a situation it was perhaps natural for the people to go for alternative channels to negotiate with the institutional political sphere. 'Such substitutes can be alternative political parties, or caste and religious associations, or a combination of both' (Bhattacharyya 2010, 56). Hence, the disintegration of party-society could be a potential reason for the growing relevance of identity politics. Finally, the cultural logic of market fundamentalism under neoliberalism, with its stress on freedom and individual independence with limited government prevents, 'class fissure from developing into class divides' (Wrenn 2014, 507). This actually disempowers the poor by restricting further the scope of their class-based mobilizations. To get empowered, this segment of the population might take recourse to identity politics. In the particular context of West Bengal, hence, it seems important to explore the identity assertion of different communities contingent upon the complex interplay of all these processes. Although subsumed under the term identity-based mobilizations, in West Bengal there have been considerable differences in the nature and respective goals of the identity-based movements. Broadly two distinct trends can be discerned in these movements. First, is the Dalit identity assertion and second is the aspiration of the regional identities. These have been dealt with in two separate sections here.

SECTION I: DALIT IDENTITY ASSERTION

West Bengal, with a SC population of 23.51 per cent of its total population, ranks third, only after Punjab and Himachal Pradesh as far as the size of the Dalits or the SC population is concerned (Census of India 2011a). In spite of such a significant presence of the SCs in the total population, the articulation of Dalit interest in formal politics of West Bengal is a recent phenomenon. The newly found relevance of caste in the institutional political sphere of West Bengal, although limited in scope compared to what can be found in other Indian states, merits the attention of the scholars since the distinct cultural history of West Bengal allows little space for caste-based aspirations to be articulated at the level of formal politics.

The 19th Century Social Reform Movements of Bengal and the Question of Caste

The reform movements of 19th century Bengal had the primary objective of rectifying certain evil practices and superstitions prevailing within the fold of Hinduism. Well known as Bengal Renaissance, these movements were influenced by the western liberal doctrine brought into this part of India by the British colonizers through the medium of English education. Historically one can trace the root of civil society in Bengal in these movements, which in due course contributed significantly to the rise and growth of Indian nationalism. The chief architects of the reform movements had been personalities such as Raja Rammohan Roy, Henry Louis Vivian Derozio, Pandit Iswar Chandra Vidyasagar and many others. Although reform of Hindu religious practices had remained their central concern, but in one way or the other they had to confront the question of caste since at the level of the everyday life, all such practices are carried and mediated through the institution of caste. In fact, the issue of caste appeared to be the major dilemma before the 19th century reformers. Imbued with the idea of liberty, these enlightened social reformers opposed the social reality of caste division and discrimination but their effort, far from being uniform, had been marked by serious disjuncture. It is important to focus on the waves of 19th century reform movements in Bengal, keeping into consideration this subtle but important gaps created by the question of caste.

Rammohan Roy was not only the initiator but also the central figure of the 19th century reform movements of Bengal. He relentlessly undertook every effort to establish the worship of the Supreme Being in spirit as opposed to the prevailing idolatry of the land. More importantly he translated some of the Shastras of the Hindu religion such as Vedanta, Cena and Isho Upanishads, Katha and Mandukya Upanishads into Bengali and English and in some cases in Hindi also to prove the purity of its monotheistic doctrines against the corrupt practice of idolatry. He established the Brahmo Samaj: the society of the worshippers of the One True God in 1830 to give his reform effort an organizational shape. Parallel to religious reform, his valiant effort resulted in the abolition of the inhuman practice of suttee when Lord Bentinck's decree formally banned it in 1829.

Rammohan's exposure to English education, as he himself had repeatedly argued, was the key to the development of such liberal and rationalist outlook in his worldview. This is also apparent from his untiring effort to introduce, spread and extend the scope of English education among his countrymen. He quite vociferously denounced the knowledge imparted through Sanskrit education given by the Hindu Pandits at that period. For the overall development of rational outlook of his countrymen through the contact with the Europeans, he steadily advocated and supported the demand for European settlement in India. In spite of severe criticism launched against him by the orthodox Hindus and the orientalists, he considered the plan of the British government to impart western education to the natives of India as a blessing for which the natives should remain grateful to the English rulers (Sharp 1920).

Being an outright rationalist, it was rather natural for Rammohan to oppose the caste system and its associated forms of inequality. Interestingly, he did not embark upon the movement path to fight against caste discrimination. Biswas (1964) thinks that, perhaps, on the realization that it was too early to fight against a system like caste, quite an elaborate system of social stratification affecting almost every aspect of life and culture of the Hindu population, Rammohan refrained from it. Not only during Rammohan's period, Debendranath Tagore, who took charge of the Brahmo Samaj in 1843 after Rammohan's death in 1833, also maintained a similar opposition to caste discrimination (Tagore 1876, 115). He also resolved to act against it rather slowly in a gradual fashion so that the feeling of caste prejudice could be eradicated from the inner core of the Hindu mind fundamentally.

The dilemma concerning the method or means to be adopted to fight caste distinction, in this way, continued to haunt the Brahmo Samaj since its inception. It however took a decisive turn with the assuming of the leadership of the Brahmo Samaj by Keshab Chandra Sen in 1862. Along with his adherence to the declared goal of the Samaj to fight against the evil practices of Hindu religion, he had been equally vocal and active against any form of caste discrimination from his very first day at the Brahmo Samaj. Sen quite radically opposed the wearing of the sacred Brahmanical thread (*poita*) by the Brahmos (Slater 1884). He even considered caste to be a monster 'that has for centuries eaten into the vitals of India' (Sen 1904, 401–402). The Brahmo Samaj under Sen also advocated quite strongly for inter-caste marriage. His strong anti-caste disposition annoyed the older and more conservative members of the Samaj. Subsequently the disagreement reached such a height, that Sen along with the progressive liberals under his command, ultimately left the Samaj to form a new society, named the

'Bharatvarshiya Brahmo Samaj' (The Brahmo Samaj of India) in 1866. The second schism within the Brahmo movement giving birth to the Sadharan Brahmo Samaj in 1878 occurred out of the controversy of Keshab Chandra Sen's controversial contemplation of the marriage of his eldest daughter at the age of 13 years. The aversion to caste system of the Sadharan Brahmo Samaj, could be traced from the lecture delivered on caste division by Pandit Sivanath Sastri, a prominent member of it, on 24 July 1884. In this lecture he particularly pointed out the evil effects of caste system on the social, economic, cultural and political lives of the people of India. From the standpoints of history, anthropology and sociology this lecture stands out to be a masterpiece on the dynamics of caste-based social stratification in India.

That the society in Bengal in the 19th century was undergoing a wave of renaissance had been evident from other instances outside the influence of Brahmoism, as well. A number of movements of varying scales under the leadership and influence of some enlightened personalities took place in this period through which people expressed their longing for the liberal and rational principles of life replacing the orthodoxies of religion, caste and similar social institutions. Among these the Young Bengal Movement led by Henry Louis Vivian Derozio (1809–1831), a teacher of English literature and history of the Hindu College, Calcutta (later Presidency College) and his students, and the effort of Pandit Ishwar Chandra Bandyopadhyaya, also known as Vidyasagar, were significant. These radical movements questioned and attacked the Brahmanical foundation of Hinduism. Together with the effort of the Brahmo Samaj all these movements can be considered to be a representation of the anti-caste proclivities present in the then Bengali society.

From the above account of the main currents of the reform movements in 19th century Bengal, certain features of it can be derived. First, the urban and educated middle class segment of the Bengali population led and participated in it. Second, the question of caste, either covertly or overtly, not only featured in it but also posed great challenge to it. The possibility of reforming Hindu religion and its practices, with or without calling into question the prevalent system of caste discrimination, time and again came into the forefront. Finally, was the facilitating influence of western liberal values and ideals as brought into this part of the country by the British colonizers.

The features of the reform movements also reveal that although they were successful in setting up a tradition of protest against the evil practices of Hinduism, their appeal was restricted to a tiny segment composed of the urban, primarily English-educated middle class. The upper caste background of the middle class also limited the movements to within the orbit of Bengali Bhadraloks. The vast majority of the rural Bengali population, mostly the illiterate peasants of the lower castes, remained largely outside the influence of the reform movements. Interestingly, most of the leaders and the rank and file of the reform movements remained reluctant and often opposed the various movements of the peasantry at that time against the exploitation of the British ruler and zamindar (landlord) combine. Perhaps, both the middle class and the zamindars, being the creations of the colonial Permanent Settlement Regulations Act of 1793, did have a genuine interest in the continuation of the British rule.

Seen from the lenses of class structure of the then Bengali society, these two genres of social movement represented quite different tendencies and objectives. Despite the divergences, these two traditions of movements however seemed to converge (though perhaps, with different reasons) in their respective attitude towards caste-related issues. If caste division was an obstacle to the middle class to achieve their modernist aspirations of liberty and individuality, for the peasantry, caste could hardly be relevant since their material condition of living and the experience of composite exploitation by the colonizers and the zamindars transcended every limit of caste boundary and distinctions.

The Tradition of Peasant Movements in 19th Century Bengal

After receiving the *Dewani* (administrative power) of Bengal, Bihar and Orissa in 1765 the British East India Company started a detailed process of land settlement with the ultimate aim of collecting land revenue in a systematic manner. It resulted in a substantive increase in the amount of land revenue to be collected from the peasantry. The level of increase can be gauged from the enhancement of revenue of Bengal and Bihar from ₹1.23 crores in 1764 to ₹2.20 crores in 1765 (Dasgupta 1982). Obviously, such an increase in the amount of land revenue intensified the exploitation of the peasantry many times. Such exploitation of the peasantry coupled with natural disaster and crop failure resulted in the Bengal famine of 1770–1771 which claimed the lives of almost one-third of the entire population of Bengal province (Gough 1974; Hunter 1868). The Fakir–Sanyasi rebellion, a direct offshoot of the famine, was directed against the British East India Company and the landlords loyal to them. It was led conjointly by the Muslim fakirs and Hindu *sanyasis* and joined by thousands of exploited peasantry from both the religious denominations. Not only the Fakir–Sanyasi rebellion, the beginning and continuation of the colonial exploitation in Bengal gave birth to a series of peasant uprisings during the second half of the 18th century and almost the entire span of the 19th century. Among these the major ones, as far as their scale and impact were concerned, were the Rangpur uprising of 1783, the Wahabi movement in Bengal (1831), the Faraizi uprising (1838–1847), Santhal Insurrection (1855–1857), the Indigo Rebellion (1859–1861), Pabna Bidroha (1873) and so on.

In most of these instances the peasants revolted to oppose the heavy demand of land revenue imposed on them by the landlords. In the case of Indigo rebellion, however, it was directed against the oppression of the Indigo planters, including a section of the landlords, who forced them to go for indigo plantation. As the landlords got the necessary administrative and political patronage of the colonial rulers, these rebellions ultimately acquired the shape of a political struggle against the colonial rule.

Such unison of the landlords and the colonial rulers was primarily oriented towards extracting the agricultural surplus from the peasants. What happened in England, in the form of 'enclosure' movement during the turn of the 18th century, also took place here in the second half of the 18th century. The landlords, bolstered by the colonial redefinition of property as not only private but also exclusive, began to challenge all sorts of customary tenures including those of the community and village control of land use. This transformation of the property relation in the rural societies was the first attempt to link Indian agriculture with global capitalism.

In spite of the apparent similarity of the British and the Indian experiences, there had been substantive differences between the two. It pertains to the fact that the Indian process, in contrast to England, was directed by the motive of British imperialism to appropriate her natural and human resources as much as possible. Thus, while in 17th century England 'enclosure' being accompanied by a thrust for 'improvement' ushered in the British Agricultural Revolution by enhancing agricultural productivity through greater use of technology and farming techniques, the Indian peasantry continued with their pre-modern agricultural implements and techniques. Neither the colonizers nor the landlords under their control ever took serious interest in increasing the overall health of Indian agriculture. Their sole goal was to earn profit from agriculture to the highest extent, which given the backwardness of Indian agriculture, entailed a severe exploitation of the peasantry as a whole.

The exploitation unleashed by the colonizers and the landlords had as its objects the various categories of peasants such as the tenants, sharecroppers and landless labourers, irrespective of their caste, religion, ethnicity and other socio-cultural boundaries. To resist, the peasant movements also developed a horizontal unity of the peasants across these dimensions. As British colonialism made its inroad in India through Bengal during the 18th century, so peasant mobilizations in Bengal had revealed this trend quite prominently.

The horizontal unity of the exploited peasantry could be noticed in their rebel consciousness. The imprint of this was apparent in the careful selection of the enemies against whom to rebel and the comrades—unity with whom was instrumental for the success of rebellion. As far as the enemies are concerned, the sarkar, sahukar and zamindar were the obvious targets since this triumvirate was composed of the principal oppressors of the peasantry. But peasants took utmost care to expand their range of operations against those persons or segments also who had been the local faces or representatives of one or any combinations of the three groups forming the triumvirate. In almost all the cases of such designation, class consideration prevailed over caste, religious, ethnic and other considerations. This was evident in the case of adivasi peasants as well, where the adivasis in their struggle against the non-adivasi landlords, moneylenders and colonial rulers, spared the poor segment of the non-adivasi peasantry and artisans. In the Santhal Insurrection of 1855–1857 some of the poor non-adivasi occupation groups, especially belonging to the lower castes, also participated with the adivasis in no less significant manner to bring an end to the exploitation they all were subjected to (Chaudhury 1979; Guha 1999).

The predominance of class orientation in identifying the foes and the friends was most evident in those peasant uprisings which originally began with a goal of religious purification (primarily of Islam as in the cases of Wahabi and Faraizi uprisings in 19th century Bengal) but ultimately acquired the shape of social and political movements against the oppression of the landlords and colonial authority. Since a considerable portion of the peasant population in eastern Bengal was Muslim and the bulk of the landlords were Hindus (Hunter 1876; Roy 1966), there was enough possibility for these movements to follow the religious path in determining the enemies overshadowing that of the class. But the rebel consciousness among the peasantry was matured enough to go beyond the narrow limits of religiosity to develop an overall unity and solidarity of the oppressed peasantry. This is clearly evident from Hunter's (1876, 64) account of the Wahabi movement in Bengal (1831):

> Any form of Dissent, whether religious or political, is perilous to vested rights. Now the Indian Wahabis are extreme Dissenters in both respects; Anabaptists, Fifth Monarchy men, so to speak, touching matters of faith; Communists and Red Republicans in politics.... In the peasant rising around Calcutta in 1831, they broke into the houses of Musalman and Hindu landholders with perfect impartiality. Indeed, the Muhammadan proprietors had rather the worst of it....

In Smith (1943) also we come across a similar assertion about the class content of the Wahabi movement in Bengal. He finds out that the movement was not one of the lower class Muslims against the lower class Hindus. To him the movement did not, '...divert lower class Muslims from economic issues to a false solidarity with their "communal" friends but class enemies' (ibid., 189). The movement besides giving a call to the Muslims to come out of their superstitious practices also attempted to forge the unity of the oppressed against the exploitation of the landlord and the colonizers. A similar trend could be found in the context of the Faraizi movement (1838–1847) led by Dudu Miyan in Faridpur of eastern Bengal (now in Bangladesh) as well. Initially a religious movement to preach 'Faraizi' principle, soon it acquired the character of a political movement against the landlords and Indigo planters. In the 'no-tax' campaign of the movement, thousands of peasants from both the Hindu and Muslim religious denominations used to participate enthusiastically against the landlords and the troops of the East India Company (Roy 1966). Although not primarily a religious movement like the Wahabi and the Faraizi uprisings, the Pabna Bidroha (1873) also witnessed a remarkable solidarity of the peasantry across caste and religious dimensions. In Pabna district of eastern Bengal (now in Bangladesh), notes Guha (1999), the percentage of Hindus was less than 10 per cent of the total population, but a majority of either the landlords or the rural gentry dependent upon them were Hindus. On the contrary, the rest of the population were peasants and nearly 70 per cent of them were Muslims. Given this population composition, religiosity did play a role in uniting the peasantry, mostly the Muslims against the Hindu majority landlords, but, 'Clearly it was the anti-landlord aims and operations of the peasants' league that gave the movement its basic identity' (ibid., 172).

In all the rebellions mentioned above and many more, the peasantry focused their attention exclusively to the exploitation of the landlords, moneylenders and the colonizers and mobilized collectively to bring an end to this. The peasantry, being a collectivity with 'low classness' as mentions Shanin (1966), remarkably exhibited the maturation of class consciousness as reflected in their effort to move beyond the levels of caste and religion to organize more like a class of oppressed people to wage political struggle against the oppressors. The penetration of capitalist motive of surplus extraction from the peasantry violating the subsistence ethic had inflicted serious damage to their notion of social justice and reciprocity. To be precise, colonialism in this way had undermined the 'moral economy of the peasantry' (Scott 1976, vii). In this situation there was little option left for the peasants but to revolt against the landlords, moneylenders and their political patron: the colonizers. The awareness of the peasantry regarding the difficulty and risk involved in resisting such a firmly entrenched power led them to develop a unity of the oppressed. There had been effort from the ruling classes to break this solidarity of the oppressed peasantry through the manipulation of cultural differences among them, but the peasantry had time and again proved their capabilities of waging class struggle across the lines of cultural divergences to redress their common grievances (Gough 1974). This emphasis on the class-like solidarity of the oppressed, although localized and unorganized in form, has led Chaudhury (1979, 538) to argue that 'The peasant movements of our period, however, were, rarely organized on caste lines....'

Thus, the two steams of social movements in Bengal: the reform movements and the peasant movements, operating more or less in the same historical context marked by the origin and development of colonial rule in India, diminished the influence of caste as a principle of social and political organization. At this juncture it has to be kept into consideration that British imperialism in India, particularly in Bengal, had represented itself differently, even contradictorily, to the different segments of its population. To the emerging enlightened segment of the middle class, it appeared to be a means of attaining the goal of bourgeoisie liberal values in the form of freedom and liberty of the individuals, negating the bond of conservatism of the feudal social structure. To the peasantry colonialism was nothing but a rule oriented to extract their surplus in a systematic fashion. Putting off the garb of bourgeoisie liberalism, colonialism in order to plunder the agrarian wealth produced by the peasants, went on to reproduce feudalism, as was manifested from its administrative steps to create a new class of landlords and moneylenders. There was little wonder that from the earlier days of British rule in India, the peasantry engaged themselves in the most protracted struggle with the alien rulers and their allies to safeguard their existence. Through the revolts against colonial power, the peasants expressed their aspirations for '...a more democratic and egalitarian society' (Gough 1974, 1403) and a consciousness that transcended successfully the identity of caste, religion and so on.

It is indeed very astonishing that the enlightened segment of the middle class, busy in organizing 'progressive' movements to bring the Hindu society of Bengal and India out of the clutches of superstition, idolatry, suttee, polygamy, caste discrimination and so on, failed to notice the progressive potentials of the peasant mobilizations of the same time. In the situation of any feudal society getting transformed into a capitalist one, the former is expected to lead the latter. Far from this, the enlightened middle class came to even oppose the movements of the peasantry, as was evident from Raja Rammohan Roy's and Dwarakanath Tagore's opposition to the Indigo rebellion (Natarajan 1979; Sarkar 1914), and Bankimchandra Chatterjee's similar attitude to the peasant rebellion in general (Chatterjee 1872). Under the overarching influence of colonial modernity, as revealed from their longing for the modern principles of individual liberty informed by the power of colonial discourse, they turned out to be the obvious support base of the colonial project among the Indians.

The very ontology of the notion of colonial modernity, however, speaks about its anti-liberal spirit since the cherished value of individuality cannot be attained under the context of colonial domination. Thus, the fight of the reformers to eradicate caste system along with other social evils of Hinduism, right from the beginning, was marked by a dilemma set by the limits of colonial modernity. First, their reliance upon the colonizers as a moral and ideological force to oppose the inhuman practices of caste discrimination was not very firmly grounded. Colonialism, far from meeting their expectations, perhaps, invented caste (Dirks 1989), made caste more visible, 'pervasive' and 'totalizing' compared to the earlier periods (Dirks 2001, 13). The colonial power/knowledge constructed caste as something antithetical to progress and modernity, which served the very justification for colonial rule in India. By projecting European modernity vis-à-vis the invented caste-centric traditionalism of India, it attracted the imagination of the enlightened Bengali middle class through its promise of modernity. It was, however, a 'limiting condition of coloniality' (ibid., 10), since the promise of progress or modernity was a promise which was not to be kept.

Second, the leaders of the reform movements, under the influence of colonial modernity, perhaps failed to grasp the sociological reality of caste as a social fact, which, as says Durkheim (1982), has to be studied in its relation to other social facts. They went on to oppose various issues of gender discrimination such as suttee, prohibitions on widow remarriage, negative attitude to women's education, polygamy and child marriage without a consideration of the fact that these were the products of a larger politics informed by the mutual reinforcement of caste and patriarchy. The question of caste thus remained the primary source of ambivalence of the reform movements. The several schisms within the Brahmo Samaj movement had been the reflections of its indeterminate stance towards the caste system.

Finally, the limiting influence of colonial modernity. It resulted in the construction of a universalized hierarchical caste structure with the Brahmins at the top denying any variation across time and space. This had narrowed the scope of the 19th century reform movements within the orbit of the upper caste itself. The issues addressed by the reformers such as suttee, polygamy and prohibition on widow remarriage which were found to be affecting the upper castes, primarily the Brahmins more than others (Chakrabarty 2000; Mani 1987, 1998; Nandy 1975) had restricted the spread of the movement across the different cross-sections of the society. To prove that the evil and superstitious practices of the then Hindus did not enjoy the support of the Hindu religion and its scriptures, they constantly referred to the Hindu Shastras, which also provided the religious support to the hierarchy of caste system based on the notions of purity and pollution. The pro-reform intellectuals' quest for the sacred texts also received the colonial, hence 'modern' patronage. These texts with all its upper caste, particularly Brahmanical bias, used to be the guide to the colonizers in their attempts at inventing caste as the dominant mode of social relations in India (Dirks 2001). Thus, influenced by the upper caste tendencies of colonial modernity it was perhaps not possible for these reformers to develop a strong ideological critique and protest movements against the caste system, although they realized the need for the same. This was perhaps enough to alienate the lower castes or the subaltern from the tradition of reform movements. They regarded the same Shastras along with the hierarchical caste system sanctified by these as the root causes of the caste discrimination to which they were subjected.

The Subaltern Response

From the foregoing discussion it is amply clear that the reform movements of the Bhadraloks, were unable to convert it into a general social movement (Blumer 1946) encompassing different cross-sections of the Bengali society. The subaltern on the contrary, since the pre-colonial time, was engaged in opposing the elitist social structure represented either by the Hindu or the Muslims. Opposition to caste discrimination along with other forms of elite domination was an integral part of their everyday life events and experiences.

The subaltern consciousness about caste in pre-colonial Bengal can best be understood through the practices of popular religion by the minor sects. Ramakanta Chakraborty (1996) has mentioned about 56 such heterodox sects which were quite popular in Bengal. Most of these sects are classified as Vaishnava or semi-Vaishnava having a differential degree of influence of Sahajiya Vaishnavism also known to be the Sahajiya movement of Bengal led by Chaitanya (1486–1533). Although detailed discussion of the movement of the Sahajiya cult is out of the scope of the present exercise, but it is worthwhile to mention that its influence in developing a strong critique of Hindu caste system in Bengal had been paramount. Its anti-upper caste tendencies can be gauged from the opposition to Sanskrit, primarily a language of the upper castes, rejection of the role of the Brahmins as ritual intermediaries between man and God, and through its most radical rejection of caste as a system (Dimock 1966).

What is evident is the effort of the Sahajiyas to reject thoroughly the elitist cultural substance of institutional Hinduism and its associated Brahmanical model of caste stratification. Turner (1977, 158) identifies such a failure 'to recognize hierarchical structural distinctions' to be the typical feature of Sahajiya and of Vaishnavism as a whole. During the 19th century the Baul sect in Bengal, influenced heavily by Sahajiya Vaishnavism and Sufism also revealed the same trend. The *adiguru* (first guru) of the Baul Sect, Lalan Fakir (1774–1890) had composed several songs which revile caste, sectarian religion and some external rituals of both Hinduism and Islam such as puja and *namaz* (Salomon 1991). It is apparent that the rejection of caste hierarchy by the Vaishnavs, Bauls and other minor sects might be a representation of the overall anti-caste feelings of the subalterns.

It seems obvious that with the advent of colonial rule and the associated ideology of colonial modernity, which encoded caste hierarchy as a mechanism to facilitate colonial power/knowledge, it was the subaltern people who came forward to oppose such 'cultural technologies' of colonial rule (Dirks 2001, 9). Thus, it was rather natural for the peasants under colonialism, whom Chakrabarty (2000) refers to be the subalterns, to transcend their respective caste boundaries to develop a horizontal unity to resist the exploitation of the triumvirate composed of the zamindars, moneylenders and the colonial rulers. The historically-developed subaltern consciousness reflecting the rejection of elite cultural ethos, therefore, was the habitus (Bourdieu 1977) of the caste-independent nature of the peasant movements. By integrating their past experiences of subalternity with their current reality of exploitation, it infused substantive meaning and provided a sort of moral justification to the act of rebellion. The internalization of such a habitus resulted into the development of the rebel consciousness among the peasants.

Movement against caste discrimination, hence, was embedded in the peasants' overall protest against colonial conquest. The historicism involved in colonial historiography either ignores altogether or designates these, following the lead of Hobsbawm (1971), to be 'prepolitical', which Guha (1999) and other subaltern critics reject. In contrast to the reform movements of the upper caste Bhadraloks, who could not reject the caste hierarchy, the politics of the peasantry or the subaltern was fundamentally egalitarian where caste or similar type of structural hierarchical distinctions had very limited appeal. As the upper castes were and still are the minorities in Bengali society (Chatterjee 2016; Roy 1952), such a distinctive politics of the subaltern composed of the majority Bengali population is expected to have much wider cultural implication.

In the 20th century with the introduction of institutional politics in the shape of organized political parties, the peasantry of Bengal had also become part of it. Their distinct habitus, inclined more towards class-like solidarity than caste, had been of particular importance to the communist parties. In a number of communist-led movements in Bengal such as the Tebhaga uprising, Naxalbari uprising and so on the peasants were the prime movers. They were also the chief constituents of the formidable party-society of the CPI (M) under whose leadership the world's longest elected Left government had ruled West Bengal from 1977 to 2011. Besides the communist parties, the caste-neutral disposition of the peasantry had led all the other political parties in West Bengal to stay away from caste-based articulation of politics. This was also witnessed in the recent mass movements of the peasantry at Singur, Nandigram, Lalgarh and in some other places.

In a marked difference with such a caste-independent political tradition, West Bengal has been witnessing a growing involvement of caste in politics since the beginning of the 21st century. This is evident from the constantly increasing number of assembly constituencies being contested by the Bahujan Samaj Party (BSP), a party well known for its inclination towards caste-based politics, in the West Bengal assembly elections since 1996 to 2016. Although the BSP has so far failed to win a single assembly seat and its vote share has remained very scanty, the number of seats contested by it rose from 48 in 1996 to 161 in 2016, as mentions the Election Commission of India. Along with the BSP, the recent politicization of the Namasudras of south Bengal could also be a pointer to the articulation of caste priorities in institutional politics.

THE NAMASUDRA IDENTITY

The Namasudra caste, a SC community in West Bengal, belonging to the Matua cult constitutes 3.84 per cent of the total population of

West Bengal. As reports the Census of India (2011b), the Namasudras numerically are the second largest SC community here next to the Rajbanshis. As far as the SC population of the state is concerned, the Namasudras constitute 16.33 per cent of the total SC population of the state. Although they are found to be present in almost all the districts of West Bengal, numerically they are concentrated in three districts of West Bengal, namely Nadia, Jalpaiguri and North 24 Parganas where they represent 17.48 per cent, 8.81 per cent and 8.56 per cent of the total population of the districts respectively. Namasudras compose the significant core of the SC communities in the districts of Nadia and North 24 Parganas, the two southeastern districts where they constitute almost 58 and 39 per cent of the total SC population respectively (Census of India 2011b). These two districts in the recent time have been the primary areas of mobilization of the Namasudras.

The movement of the Namasudras, an untouchable caste, to uplift their social and economic status dates back to the second half of the 19th century. They were earlier known as Chandals, who according to Manu are the 'lowest of men' (Buhler 1886, 404) born out of the illicit union between a Brahmin woman and a Sudra man. This is enough to perceive the magnitude of caste discrimination this group was subjected to by the upper castes. They primarily inhabited the low-lying swamp area of East Bengal, presently Bangladesh. Earlier they used to profess the occupations fishing and boating. With the expansion of cultivation in these areas of eastern Bengal, the Namasudras, through rapid reclamation of the marshy land, transformed into an agricultural community.

The relatively improving economic standing of the Namasudras or at least a segment of it through agriculture and later on by producing cash crops, primarily jute, they wanted to redress the caste discrimination inflicted upon them by the upper caste Hindu Bhadraloks. When their claim to higher social status was resisted by the upper castes, the Namasudras started to defy the authority of the higher castes and this gave rise to the Namasudra protest movement in 1872. Gradually this protest movement took the shape of an organized movement for social upliftment with the growth of the Vaishnavite sect, Matua, comprising the Namasudras. Initiated by Harichand Thakur (1811/12–1887), the Matua sect led to greater cohesion and solidarity among the Namasudras. As a liberal form of Vaishnavism, the Matua rejected the notion of caste distinctions, collective religious worshipping and advocated gender equality. Later under the leadership of Harichand's son Guruchand, the sect attaining doctrinal cohesion consolidated its organizational solidarity further by bringing in the relatively better off and the common Namasudras under a single organizational set-up.

Here it is to be noted that not the Matua sect alone, a number of such sects being influenced by the Bhakti Movement of Sri Chaitanya since the 16th century had contributed to the emergence of a distinct popular religion in Bengal which thoroughly opposed the practice of caste distinctions of Hinduism. Mention can be made here about the Sahajiya Vaishnava tradition, the Baul sect, the Fakirs most prominently represented by Lalan Shah, the Kartabhaja sect, Sahebdhani sect, the Balahadi or Balarami sect and many others as discussed by Chakraborty (1996), which had been instrumental in disseminating a distinct caste and gender neutral approach to social life. The Matua sect although exhibiting the same principle was distinct since it was associated with the social upliftment movement of the Namasudra caste. It was also distinct for its avowed liberal and material outlook which can be discerned from Guruchand's emphasis on work ethics 'Hate kam, mukhe nam' (doing worldly duties while chanting His holy name) (Bandyopadhyay 2004, 97). Preaching this ethic Guruchand actually urged every Namasudra to become a respectable person by earning money through educating themselves (Bandyopadhyay, 1989). Such stress upon respectability resulted in a sanskritizing drive on the part of the Namasudras. Since moving upward in the caste ladder is the only option to earn social prestige in the structure of caste-based social stratification of Hindu society, so the Namasudra movement gradually incorporated this goal within its fold.

The first glimpse of this could be traced in their demand to be named 'Namasudra' rejecting the earlier 'Chandal' which was a derogatory term. The Census of 1911 labelled them as Namasudras. In 1907 Guruchand Thakur submitted a memorandum to the then governor of Bengal demanding the status of Brahmins for the Namasudras (Bandyopadhyay 2011).

In spite of the strong motivation of Namasudras to be regarded as upper castes, it was paradoxical indeed that they consciously refused to participate in the anti-partition movement of 1905–1911 and the ensuing Swadeshi agitation on the ground that these were primarily led by the upper caste Hindu Bhadraloks. They also opposed the movements as these were launched against the British rule. The Namasudras in many occasions like this supported the British colonizers as the latter were systematically allowing certain concessions to the Namasudras. Through these patronages the British was quite successful in alienating the Namasudras from the stream of anti-colonial nationalist movements of the early 20th century. To oppose the nationalists, they even got closer to the Muslims who according to them were equally despised by the Hindu upper caste elites. Thus, three distinct trends emerged in the Dalit politics represented by the Namasudras during the beginning of the 20th century: Alienation from the nationalist politics of primarily the Hindu upper castes, tie-up with the Muslims for their supposed opposition to the domination of the Hindu elites composed primarily of the upper caste gentry and keeping firm allegiance to the dominant colonial elites. Together with the emerging peasant middle class among the Muslims, the Namasudras and other SC communities posed serious challenge to the political and economic dominance of the Bhadraloks in Bengal during 1930s and 1940s. The unity of the Dalits and Muslims in Bengal took a concrete shape in 1945 with the foundation of the Bengal provincial branch of Dr B. R. Ambedkar's Scheduled Caste Federation by the Namasudra leader Jogendra Nath Mandal in alliance with the Muslim League. He considered that the political alliance of the Dalit and Muslim peasantry would effectively serve the interest of the former.

But the politics concerning the partition of India on account of independence in 1947 raised certain complex issues before the Dalits that had certain definite implications for their relationship with the nationalists and the Muslims. Specifically, the question regarding the proposed plan of partitioning India, whereby the undivided Muslim majority of Bengal joined Pakistan, assumed immense political significance. Almost the entire Hindu political opinion from Shyama Prasad Mukherjee-led Hindu Mahasabha to almost all the factions of Congress to the Communists were unanimous in demanding the partition of Bengal with the Hindu majority western districts including Calcutta joining the Indian Union. The Muslims under the Muslim League opposed the partition of Bengal and argued for the undivided Bengal joining Pakistan. The nationalists, comprised primarily of the upper caste Hindus finding their future to be insecure in the Muslim majority Pakistan, stood by the demand of partition of Bengal. The SC communities, particularly the Namasudras of eastern Bengal and the Rajbanshis of north Bengal experienced serious divergences of opinion within their respective communities since partition of Bengal would lead to a spatial dislocation of the two communities into two countries. Fissures developed among the Dalits with one section under the influence of the Hindu Mahasabha and the Congress supported the partition of Bengal, while the other one belonging to the Scheduled Caste Federation opposed it. The autonomous space of Dalit identity politics in this way shrunk considerably on account of the encroachment of communal politics that marked the partition of India during 1947. The partition of Bengal which ultimately came into effect with the independence of India did not help the Dalit cause. Contrary to the vision and the demands of the Dalits, the Namasudra dominated districts of Bakarganj, Faridpur, Jessore and Khulna and the Rajbansi dominated Dinajpur and Rangpur remained in East Pakistan. Weakening the prospect of future Dalit mobilization in West Bengal considerably, the partition of Bengal hence consolidated the political dominance of the upper caste Hindu Bhadraloks.

In the ensuing Partition-induced migration the upper caste Hindus along with some middle class Namasudras migrated to India soon after the Partition. The majority of the Namasudra peasantry could not migrate then since they lacked the economic resource for it and for the assurance given to them by the Muslim League ministry that their interest would be protected in East Pakistan. But with the growing Islamization of Pakistan polity (Bandyopadhyay and Basu Ray Chaudhury 2014) witnessed since 1950, the forced migration of the Namasudras started. This also led Jogendra Nath Mandal, the labour and law minister of the Liaquat Ali Khan Ministry of Pakistan, to resign and then migrate to India. The poor Namasudra migrants settled in various refugee camps of the border districts of North 24 Parganas and Nadia, and most importantly in Thakurnagar of North 24 Parganas, where P. R. Thakur, the grandson of Guruchand Thakur established a colony for the Namasudra refugees. This was, 'the first Dalit refugee colony in India started by an independent Dalit initiative' (ibid., 13). Gradually P. R.Thakur became the religious 'guru' of the Matua Mahasangha at Thakurnagar, originally founded by his great grandfather Harichand Thakur. An ardent Gandhian, P. R. Thakur envisioned Thakurnagar, a place 63 km. away from Kolkata, to be a cultural centre of the Dalit Namasudra refugees.

Partition gave the displaced poor SC migrants the 'refugee' identity in India by relegating their 'Dalit' identity to the backstage. This was evident from their slogan, '*Amra kara? Bastuhara*' (Who are we? Refugees). The slogan became very popular during the refugee movement of the 1950s and 1960s. More than caste the issues about rehabilitation of the refugees became their central concern. Demands about proper settlement and rehabilitation imparted among the refugees a new language—the language of unity. Gradually the localized protest of the refugees located at different camps and squatter settlements came under the umbrella organizations such as the United Central Refugee Council (UCRC) or the Sara Bangla Bastuhara Samiti[1] (SBBS). The steady influx of refugees, primarily Namasudras from East Pakistan during the 1950s and 1960s attracted the attention of the political parties of different ideological standpoints to develop vote banks among them. The CPI came to control the UCRC while the centrist Praja Socialist Party, tried to organize them under the SBBS. Gradually, the CPI-led UCRC became the primary organization of the refugees' contingent upon the CPI's demand to the government to recognize the refugee colonies as part of its larger demand of abolition of landlordism. Till 1977 the Matua refugees remained with the Congress and afterwards switched over to the LF during its rule. They maintained their overall non-political stand and continued to support the LF till 2009.

[1] All Bengal Refugee Association.

The political climate in West Bengal tended towards change in 2009 when the hegemony of the ruling LF came to be challenged by the counter-hegemonic force represented by the AITC. The seriousness of the AITC challenge was actually revealed in the Panchayat Election of 2008 itself where the CPM fared poorly amongst the SC, especially Matua-dominated North 24 Parganas. It was even worse in the Gaighata subdivision of the district where Thakurnagar, the headquarters of the Matua sect is situated. Of the 39 panchayat samiti seats here, the CPM could win only two (*Indian Express* 2009a). In the Lok Sabha Election of 2009, as reveals the Election Commission of India, all the LF candidates in the two districts of Nadia and North 24 Parganas were defeated by the AITC. Among the 49 assembly segments of these seven parliamentary constituencies the LF could win only in 6. Amidst the overall declining trend of the LF during the period, its outright defeat in the Matua heartland and the simultaneous rise of the AITC there might have some relation to the frustration of the Matuas over the LF and the cultivation of their community sentiment by the AITC chief Mamata Banerjee.

The growing feeling of frustration of the Matuas with the Left parties leading to the former's withdrawal of support to the latter requires some further attention. Sinharay (2013) has attempted to analyse it from the standpoint of the disintegration of the party-society, which according to Bhattacharyya (2009, 2011) opens up the possibilities of identity politics to increase its significance. This is because party-society as a special form of sociability in rural West Bengal makes the political party as the only channel of public transaction displacing the other ones based on religion, ethnicity, caste and so on. Thus, it follows logically that with the dissolution of the party-society these dimensions of social bond would get more importance. But, to apply this model to the case of the Matuas, certain cautions should be taken. First, it is to be noted that despite the influence of the party-society of the CPI (M), which essentially focuses on class-based issues of the poor peasantry; the Matuas continued to carry forward the cause of their identity construction and maintenance. In fact, Thakurnagar became the epitome of the Matua identity, contributing to the cultural and religious construction of the sect. How far or to what extent their continued electoral support to the CPI (M) was due to the political influence of the latter is an open question. It could well be the fact that the CPI (M)'s ideological neglect of the caste issues might have allowed this closed community to practice its caste-based and sectarian rituals without much political interference. Then it should also be taken into consideration that the Matuas being international refugees, the issues of the Matuas have some important anchorage in international relations involving the two countries, India and Bangladesh. The discourses and counter discourses of security and sovereignty of these two nation states have serious implications for the determination of the citizenship status of the Matuas, which necessarily transcend the operational sphere of the state government of West Bengal and the ruling party. The Act and rules framed by the central government about the refugees and their citizenship status, thus, are binding on the state governments. This was evident from the statement made in 2003 by the then chief minister of West Bengal Buddhadeb Bhattacharya about the refugee issue as cited by Banerjee (2003, 864), '...on the question of dealing with illegal infiltrators from Bangladesh, our state government is in agreement with the government of India that whenever such infiltration is detected, the foreign nationals should be pushed back forthwith'. This was enough to frustrate the Matuas and other poor segments of the SCs, a large chunk of whom out of sheer economic insecurity and uncertainty had to migrate to India from East Pakistan without valid documents, hence, were 'illegal'. In fact, repealing The Citizenship (Amendment) Act, 2003, enacted by the then National Democratic Alliane (NDA)-led central government, which considers all refugees who have migrated to India after 1971 as illegal, was an important demand of the All India Matua Mahasangha. In this context, Bhattacharya's statement was enough to hurt the sentiments and citizenship aspirations of the Matuas, which perhaps more than the dissolution of the party-society, could have led them to turn away from the CPI (M) and the LF. This allowed the opposition AITC, led by Mamata Banerjee, the necessary space to penetrate among the Matuas.

In order to woo the Matua community Ms Banerjee, in her capacity as the union Railway Minister in 2009, declared a number of projects in Bongaon, Thakurnagar and in the adjacent areas. That she was successful in her effort had been revealed by the fact that in 2009 she was offered life membership of the Matua Mahasangha and declared to be its 'chief patron' in 2010 by Boro Ma Mrs Binapani Devi, the widow of P. R. Thakur, and the revered mother of the Matua sect.

Being alarmed by Mamata Banerjee's effort to win the support of the Matuas, the CPI (M), Congress, BJP and other parties also put their effort at the same direction. It was quite surprising to see the CPI (M) joining the path of gaining the support of a caste community because Jyoti Basu, its respected leader, on his capacity as the chief minister of West Bengal, once remarked before the Mandal Commission in 1980 that in West Bengal 'there were only two castes: the rich and the poor!' (Ghosh 2001, 5). The prominence and strength gained by the Matua identity in the electoral arena of the democratic polity of India, perhaps, had been powerful enough to dislodge the CPI (M) from such an avowed class-centric ideological position. Moving away from its ideological standing the CPI (M)-led LF government, to counterbalance Mamata Banerjee's largesse on the Matuas, started a scholarship in Harichand Thakur's name, came up with the assurance to build a college in his name and earmarked land to set up a research centre (Bose 2011). But the Matuas, accusing the LF for not delivering on its promises, continued to support the AITC, which along with other factors was also an important reason for the ultimate debacle of the LF in 2011. The overwhelming supports of the Namasudras to the AITC vis-à-vis the LF in different elections, state as well as national, from 2009 to 2016, can be revealed from Figure 4.1.

During the run-up to the Assembly Election of 2011 and after eventually winning it, Mamata Banerjee took every effort to consolidate the AITC's Matua support base. In the 2011 Assembly Election itself, Manjul Krishna Thakur, the youngest son of Mrs Binapani Devi, won the Gaighata assembly seat on the AITC ticket and was appointed as the minister of state for Refugee Relief and Rehabilitation in the AITC government in West Bengal. In the Lok Sabha Election of 2014, Kapil Krishna Thakur, the eldest son of Mrs Binapani Devi, won the Bongaon parliamentary constituency on behalf of the AITC. Due to the untimely demise of Kapil Krishna Thakur, the Bangaon constituency went to

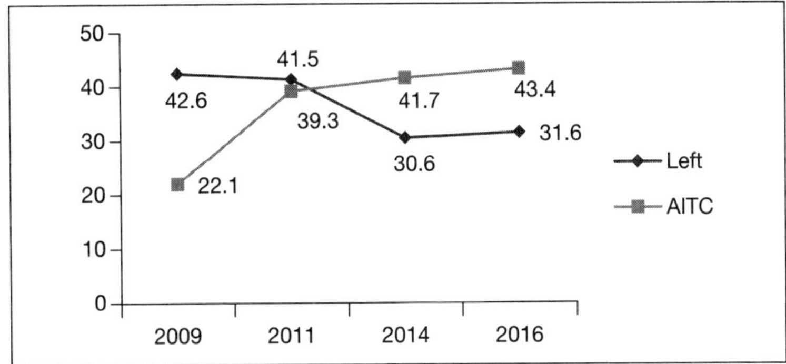

Figure 4.1 *Comparative Vote Shares of the AITC and the LF among the Namasudras (2009–2016)*

Source: CSDS Data Unit, NES 2009 and 2014; West Bengal Assembly Election Study 2011 and 2016.

by-election in February 2015, where the widow of Kapil Krishna Thakur, Mrs Mamatabala Thakur was fielded by the AITC as its candidate. In an interesting turn of events, Manjul Krishna Thakur resigned from the ministry and left the AITC to join the BJP along with his son Subrata Thakur before the by-election. Subrata Thakur contested the by-election on the BJP ticket only to be defeated by Mamatabala Thakur of the AITC. The much-revered Thakur family of Thakurnagar, the citadel of Matua culture and religion, thus, got divided on political line.

The issue of the politicization of the Matuas can be approached from two angles. On the one hand, it can be seen as an extension of the sphere of institutional politics to pay 'due' attention to caste discrimination, while as a means of their collective bargaining with the democratic state by forming a pressure group, on the other. The expansion of the institutional politics to cater to the various issues of castes results in widening the participatory base of the electoral democracy. Referring this to be the 'second democratic upsurge', Yadav (2000) believes that this makes electoral politics more sensitive to the issues of the socially marginalized, and hence, ensures their greater participation in the arena of democratic politics. In his opinion this is happening in Indian electoral politics since the 1990s. The involvement of a number of members of the Thakur family of the Matua sect in electoral politics of the state hence might be indicative of the,

'...significant rise in their sense of efficacy and their involvement in more active forms of political participation' (Yadav 1999, 2397). The entry of caste-related political dynamics in the discourses of electoral democracy in West Bengal, as was witnessed in the first decade of the present century, appeared to be a mark of the emergence of a new politics (Sinharay 2012). But, Guha (2019) tends to dismiss this claim on the ground that the apparent increase in the electoral participation of the Matuas has not resulted in the magnification of the domain of political participation of the SCs in general. Since the beginning of the new century, he argues, the proportion of SC MLAs to the total MLAs in the state has remained constantly low. The proportion remaining unchanged in spite of the continuing electoral success of the AITC and the concurrent debacle of the LF since 2011, also puts up factual challenge to the thesis that the loosening strength of the Left politics in West Bengal is associated with the growth of the political participation of the lower castes. Not only the Left parties, he contends, the other mainstream political parties are also not showing any serious effort to enhance the political participation of the lower castes by providing them the opportunity to contest from unreserved seats. So, the argument about the emerging new politics of caste in West Bengal, marked by the increasing representation of the lower castes in the domain of institutional politics, remains a contentious issue.

The increasing involvement of the Matuas of the Namasudra caste in electoral politics as is evident from the recent elections also cannot be generalized for all other lower castes. As their presence in districts other than Nadia and North 24 Parganas is considerably low, so they are not in a position to represent the other lower castes in electoral competition there. The differential in socio-economic status of the different Dalit communities is also a concern. While the literacy of some communities such as the Namasudras and Pods, as reflected in the Census of India 2011, is almost 80 per cent, the same figures for some other communities such as the Bagdi, Bauri and the Chamar stand at about 61 per cent, 51 per cent and 60 per cent respectively. There are differences in the degree of urban influences too. While almost 31 per cent of the Namasudras live in the urban areas the same for the Rajbanshis and Bagdis are as low as 12 per cent and 10 per cent respectively. The degrees of urbanity of other Dalit communities such as the Bauris, Pods and the Chamars are located in between these two extremes. There are occupational specificities as well. While the percentages of cultivators among the Rajbanshis and Namasudras are almost 23 per cent and 15 per cent respectively their proportion among the Bauris (about 3%) and Chamars (about 5%) are indeed very low. Quite expectedly the percentages of agricultural labourers among the Bauris (about 30%) and Chamars (about 32%) are significantly high. Such socio-economic status differentials among some of the major Dalit communities imply that there would be little commonalities of needs, aspirations and demands among them. To be specific, the Census 2011 figures indicate that there is, '...very little ground for the Bagdis or Bauris to make common cause with the Namasudras in the latter's particular demands regarding jobs, seats, education and relief and rehabilitation measures' (Samaddar 2013, 79).

The issue of the involvement of the lower castes in electoral politics thus could be viewed from the standpoint of collective bargaining by the respective caste groups with the state. Here it is to be kept in mind that only two numerically dominant Dalit communities, namely the Namasudras and the Rajbanshis are engaged in this effort at collective bargaining. For the Namasudras, being largely a migrant community in West Bengal, the issues related to citizenship status and refugee rehabilitation are their major concerns. Perhaps, this explains their increasing involvement in electoral politics since 2003, the year when the then NDA-led central government amended the Citizenship Act. In their struggle to repeal this Act the Namasudras later got the ready support of the Muslims in West Bengal since the issue of illegal immigration also affected the latter.

Particularly, the Muslims were and are still concerned with the attitude of the BJP to designate the Muslim immigrants as 'infiltrators' while considering the Hindu migrants to be 'refugees'. But since the 2003 amendment treated all the post-1971 migrants to be illegal, these two groups strategically came closer. The subsequent publication of a report of the Government of India in 2006 (popularly known as the Sachar Committee Report), which pointed out the 'development deficit' suffered by the Muslims in West Bengal, annoyed them further

(Government of India 2006). In a similar fashion to the Matuas the Muslims as a result were also getting alienated from the LF. This had been evident in the 2009 Lok Sabha Election, when a fairly large section of the Muslim population in West Bengal withdrew its support from the LF (Chatterjee and Basu 2014). Moreover, the proposed land acquisition for the chemical hub in Nandigram and for some other projects in South 24 Parganas district, where Muslims are present in significant numbers, created an apprehension among them that for these projects, lands of the Muslims would be acquired more. In the Assembly Election of 2011, the Matuas and the Muslims significantly voted against the LF to bring the AITC into the state power of West Bengal. Figure 4.2 about the Muslim vote share of the AITC and the LF from 2009–2016 depicts this.

The Muslims with 27.01 per cent of the total population of West Bengal (West Bengal Religion Census 2011) engaged themselves in effective bargaining with the AITC. Assuming the office of the chief minister of West Bengal in 2011, Mamata Banerjee announced a monthly stipend for the Muslim clerics in the state only to be struck down later by the Calcutta High Court. There had been some more proposals: to build a hospital for the Muslims, separate engineering examinations for the minorities and earmarking of fund to maintain mosques and so on. (Majumdar 2014). All these resulted in the AITC's gain of 20.7 per cent more Muslim votes in the 2014 Lok Sabha

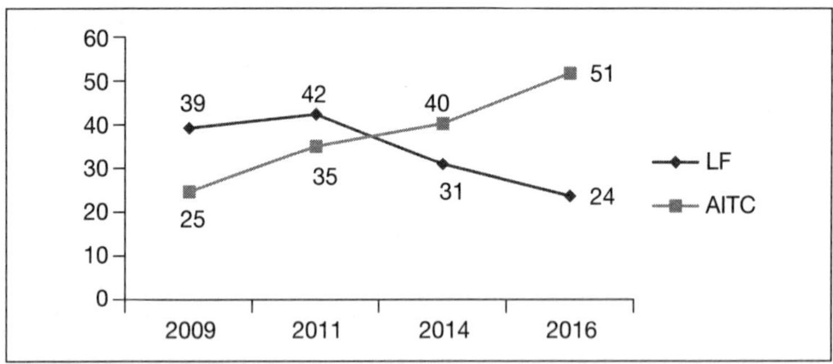

Figure 4.2 *Comparative Vote Shares of the AITC and the LF among Muslims (2009–2016)*

Source: CSDS Data Unit, NES 2009 and 2014; West Bengal Assembly Election Study 2011 and 2016.

Election compared to that of the 2009 (Chatterjee and Basu 2017). The bonhomie of the Muslims with the AITC continued after 2014 as well. In the Assembly Election of 2016 the AITC secured 51 per cent of the Muslim votes which reached almost 70 per cent in the 2019 Lok Sabha Election, as pointed out by the West Bengal Assembly Election Study 2016 and NES 2019 respectively. The bargaining of the Muslims with the AITC had been so prominent that almost 60 per cent of the sampled electorates in the 2016 West Bengal Assembly Election Study, agreed with the statement that Mamata Banerjee's government gives undue favour to the Muslims.

Although both the Matuas and the Muslims had been negotiating with the AITC government since 2011, but the trajectories of this for the two groups differed. This particularly concerned with the nature of politicization of the respective groups. Unlike the Muslims, who largely behaved like a pressure group to extract developmental benefits from the AITC in exchange of their electoral support to it, the Matuas, especially the members of the Thakur family of Thakurnagar became insiders of either the AITC or the BJP by joining these and competing elections on behalf of them. In the absence of a consolidated Dalit identity, for the reasons discussed earlier, this might appear to be a satisfaction of the aspirations of political mobility of the Matuas, more specifically, the members of the Thakur family. Thus, it would bear the risk of creating a situation marked by multi-level alienation. First, the Thakur family could be alienated from the rest of the Matuas. Second, the Matua as a sect could be alienated from the rest of the Namasudras. On an even higher level, this could alienate the Namasudras as a whole to the other constituents of the SCs. Moreover, given the Bhadralok domination of the mainstream political parties in West Bengal, which is evident in the social composition of the AITC also, it would bear the risk of the appropriation of the Dalit interest by the Bhadraloks. A hint of this could be traced from the opinion of Manjul Krishna Thakur, the Sahasanghadhipati of the Matua Mahasangha and a minister in the AITC government. During an interview with Prasanka Sinharay on 13 November 2012 he remarked on the dalit refugee issue, 'There is no problem on the issue these days. Earlier there were arrests and all, which has now been absolutely stopped. We cannot change the law; it's a central government issue. As of now there is no problem' (Sinharay 2013, 6). Strikingly, the Sahasanghadhipati of the Mahasangha could not find any problem with the refugee issue at a time when the primary demand of the Mahasangha was to repeal the Citizenship (Amendment) Act, 2003. Perhaps, his AITC identity was pressing enough, which led him to ignore the cause of the Dalit identity rooted in the grave concern of the future of the refugees. It was indeed very difficult even for a representative of the Dalit community itself to articulate the cause of her/his caste identity, transgressing the normative and cultural limits of the overwhelmingly caste-neutral institutional political sphere of West Bengal.

The ineffectiveness of caste as an instrument of electoral mobilization in West Bengal was also apparent in the decision of Abdur Rezzak Mollah to abandon the Social Justice Forum formed in 2014 by his initiative. The forum was supposed to contest the forthcoming Assembly Election in 2016 with the ultimate purpose of forming a government with a Dalit as its chief minister and a Muslim as the deputy. A veteran minister of land and land reform in the last LF government in West Bengal and subsequently expelled from the CPI (M) for anti-party activities, Mollah was experienced enough to perceive the caste-and religion-neutral political polarization existing at the ground level. Possibly, on the basis of this perception he decided to join the AITC and contested the Assembly Election of 2016 on behalf of it. In a similar manner to the politically inexperienced Matua leader, a politically matured Muslim leader also had to surrender to the caste-and community-independent political ethos of West Bengal.

This was also proved by Manjul Krishna's statement, 'We cannot change the law' as mentioned above. Here the 'we' certainly was not the Matuas or the Namasudras, the community to which he belongs. This 'we' rather was the collectivity composed of the Bhadraloks in the institutional political domain of the government represented by the AITC, who out of their unconditional faith in the modernist notion of federal democracy viewed the 'law' enacted by the central government as something beyond the capacity of the state government to intervene. Such an emphasis on the legality and constitutionality, the hallmark of elite politics (Guha 1988), by a member of the subaltern category could be a classic example of the engulfment of the autonomous political space of the subalterns by the elite political norms and discourses.

The elite appropriation of the subaltern political space was also evident from the division in the Thakur family along political lines emerging out of the resignation of Manjul Krishna Thakur from AITC and his joining hands with the BJP, with his son Subrata Thakur on the eve of the by-election to the Bongaon parliamentary constituency in early 2015. Boro Ma, Mrs Binapani Devi, the Matua matriarch, publicly blessed her daughter-in-law Mamatabala Thakur, and subsequently Mamatabala won the by-election defeating Subrata. The attempt to bargain with the institutional political parties by becoming part of these, has ultimately resulted in such an enthrallment of the elite political aspirations into the imagination of the subaltern that has ultimately weakened the hold of the tradition on subaltern political culture. This was clear from the loosening of the traditional control of Binapani Devi over the Matuas in general, since she was not in a position to influence or direct their overall electoral preference. This had its impact felt with the defeat of the AITC in the three assembly constituencies of Ranaghat (northwest), Ranaghat (south) of Nadia district and Bagda of North 24 Parganas in the 2016 Assembly Election where the Namasudras are present in large numbers. Their disenchantment with the AITC continued to increase since then. In the Lok Sabha Election of 2019 the BJP registered a huge gain of almost 48 per cent of the Namasudra votes while the AITC lost about 8 per cent of its support among the same community, as reports the NES 2019 data.

However, the National Register of Citizens (NRC) operation in Assam where four million people could not find their names in the register of Indian citizens, among which a large number are claimed to be the Namasudras, provided fertile condition for the unity of the divided Namasudras again. In West Bengal, the Namasudras largely under the Matua Mahasangha immediately took the streets to protest against this move of the BJP government in Assam. Mamata Banerjee was also quick enough to rip the potential benefits emerging out of this on the eve of the Parliamentary Election 2019. To garner the support of the Matuas, she visited Thakurnagar in November 2018 to attend the birth centenary celebrations of Binapani Devi. She conferred Bengal's highest civilian award the 'Banga Bibhushan', to her and declared a university to be set up after the name of Harichand Thakur. In early November, she also declared formation of two development boards for the Matuas and the Namasudras.

From the participation of the Matuas in institutional politics, it cannot possibly be taken as an indication of the increasing importance of the Dalits in Bengal politics. This is due to some factors particularly related to the caste. First, their numerical presence is prominent only in two districts, namely North 24 Parganas and Nadia of West Bengal. In these two districts also they are a decisive factor only in two parliamentary constituencies as far as electoral competition is concerned. Beyond these two districts their presence in the other districts of West Bengal is indeed very scanty. Not only the Namasudras, the presence of other SC communities such as the Bagdi and Bauri is also quite skewed in the different districts of West Bengal. Second, unlike the demands of the Dalits elsewhere in India, to the Matuas the issue of Indian citizenship is more pertinent. The identity of lower caste crossed by the identity of 'refugee' adds further complication to the process of identity construction of the Matuas. The legal issue pertaining to citizenship is a restricting condition to the Matuas, since no political party under the constitutional framework of India can provide electoral assurance to this effect. Third, there have been considerable socio-economic differentials among the various SC communities in West Bengal. In such a situation it is difficult, if not impossible, for any community to forge unity with others on certain common causes. Finally, the caste-neutral nature of popular discourse of West Bengal also restricts to some extent the articulation of caste-based issues in the domain of formal politics. In West Bengal, it is indeed difficult for any political party to count on its caste-based support. Conversely, the electorates also do not view electoral contests through the lens of caste. Starting with the local to the national level, caste perhaps has rarely been an electoral issue in West Bengal. Hence, the issues pertaining to the possible dalitization of Bengal politics, as traced by Sinharay (2012) or emergence of a new politics of identity contingent upon the decline of Left politics (Bhattacharyya 2011) appear to be contentious. Given the upper caste hegemony in West Bengal, it might be too early to say that the recent mobilizations of the Namasudras will pose a significant challenge to it (Samaddar 2013). This position also enjoys factual support of the relevant NES and West Bengal assembly election data of the CSDS since 2011, which have failed to trace any definite polarization of political parties emerging along caste lines.

SECTION II: ASSERTIONS OF REGIONAL IDENTITIES

Kamtapur Agitation

The negotiation of the Rajbanshis, the largest Dalit community in West Bengal, with the political parties active in the democratic political space has chalked out a completely different path. Having 17.71 per cent of the total SC population of the state, according to the Census of India 2011, the presence of the Rajbanshis is more pronounced in the north Bengal districts of Cooch Behar, Jalpaiguri, Uttar Dinajpur and Dakshin Dinajpur. In all these districts the Rajbanshis compose more than 50 per cent of the total SC population, while the highest being about 75 per cent in Cooch Behar (Census of India 2011b).

While the basic demands of the Namasudras veer around the issues of migration, refugee settlement and rehabilitation, and citizenship status, the Rajbanshis of North Bengal have raised the demands of regional autonomy in the shape of a separate Kamtapur, sometimes also called Uttarkhand within the Indian Union. The proposed state comprises the plains of Darjeeling, Jalpaiguri and a part of Cooch Behar district of north Bengal. They are demanding the separate state to safeguard their identity and to protect their distinct cultural heritage and language. Through a separate state of their own they aspire to take active part in the economic and political decision-making process affecting their community lives.

The Rajbanshis are primarily a cultivating community of north Bengal. They are also known as 'Deshi' or 'Bahey'. There has been enough confusion about the history of these people. The Cooch Behar state was generally recognized to be the place of origin of the tribe, who were indiscriminately designated to be the Koch, Rajbansi and Pali (Hunter 1974). Sanyal (1965, 10) notes that they, 'belong to the great Bodo family that entered India in the 10th century BC, from the east and settled on the banks of the Brahmaputra and gradually spread over Assam and the whole of North and East Bengal.' Another account considers the Kochs to be Hinduized or semi-Hinduized Bodos who abandoning their original Tibeto-Burman speech have adopted the northern dialect of Bengali (Chatterjee 1951). Risley (1892, xvii) observes, '...the great majority of the Kochh inhabitants of Rungpore now invariably describe themselves as Rajbanshis or Bhanga Kshatriya...'. Hence, it appears that the same group of people is termed interchangeably as Koch or Rajbansi. Hunter (1974), however, finds out a socio-economic distinction between the two. In Jalpaiguri and Cooch Behar, the name Rajbansi, literally meaning 'royal race', 'is adopted primarily by the cultivators and other respectable men', while that of Koch 'being restricted to labourers and specifically to the palanquin bearers' (pp. 347–348). Thus, it is a matter of pride for them to be called as Rajbanshis and to uphold this they invoke the status of Kshatriya although, 'there is no historical foundation for the claim of the Rajbanshis to be provincial variety of the Kshatriyas...' (Risley 1892, 491). The transformation of Koch into Rajbansi, by which they are known today in Jalpaiguri and Cooch Behar is a story of the transformation of a tribe into a caste or more generally 'Hinduisation of the Indo-Mongoloid of North Eastern India' (Chatterjee 1951, 120). Historically, the Rajbanshis identify themselves with the Cooch Behar state which continued its existence since 15th century to mid-20th century, when the last king Jagaddipendra Narayan Bhup Bahadur, agreed to make Cooch Behar a part of the Dominion of India in 1949. Since the kings and the subjects were all from the same race, so the Rajbanshis consider Cooch Behar to be the state of their own king. Their claim of Kshatriya status might be an offshoot of such a racial affinity with the members of the royal family of Cooch Behar.

To understand the recent movement of regional autonomy based on the Rajbansi identity, perhaps it is instructive to go back to the assertion of the Kshatriya identity of the Rajbanshis in the late 19th and early 20th century. With the unfolding of British rule, a middle class among the Rajbanshis were growing up. Interestingly, this middle class had a leaning towards Bengali culture and language. With further expansion of colonial rule, certain newer possibilities opened up such as job opportunities in the tea industry, in government service, in education and others consequent upon the expansion of the market due to the commercialization of agriculture. A sizeable portion of these opportunities were being monopolized by the immigrant upper caste Hindus from outside the region, primarily, the Bengalis. Not only monopolizing the economic opportunities, the upper castes used to look down upon the Rajbanshis as well, which irked the sentiments of the emerging Rajbansi middle class considerably (Karlsson 2000). 'The educated middle class among the Rajbanshis' argues Ray (2002, 119) 'attempted to unite and harness all classes of the community for the realization of its own aims.' With the beginning of Census operation in 1891, the Kshatriyaization movement started under the leadership of Haramohan Roy Khazanchi, a landlord of Rangpur district (presently in Bangladesh), later it passed on to the lawyer Panchanan Barma in 1901. Under Barma's leadership the reform movement to attain the Kshatriya identity got tremendous fillip. Observance of ritual impurity following a death in family for 12 days instead of the customary 30 days, assuming of more Kshatriya like surnames such as 'Singha', 'Barman' and 'Roy' along with different combinations such as 'Singha Roy', 'Roy Barman' replacing the vaishnavite surnames like Das. Wearing of sacred thread and many other ritualistic reform strategies were adopted to assert and prove their Kshatriya identity to the colonizers, especially the census operators. Literate sections of the community became busy in reinventing the history of the caste to prove that the Rajbansis are different from the Kochs. Myths in support of their Kshatriya status was also constructed referring to their Kshatriya ancestors who had to flee to this part in North Bengal to save them from the wrath of Parasurama.

The movement of the Rajbanshis at present although rooted in this history of identity assertion got a new political dimension in the wake of Indian Independence, when the princely state of Cooch Behar joined the Indian Union in 1949 and its subsequent status of becoming a district of West Bengal in 1950. The reduction of the ancient

Koch kingdom to a district was not acceptable to certain sections of the Rajbanshis.. In 1950 itself the Hit Sadhini Sabha was formed to demand statehood status of Cooch Behar under the Indian Union (Goswami 2014). The joining of Indian Union and turning out to be a district under West Bengal also resulted into larger influx of outsiders, the Marwaris and mostly Hindu Bengalis, into Cooch Behar. Moreover, due to partition of India, Rajbansi refugees from East Pakistan also entered the region in greater numbers. This resulted in an alteration of the economic and cultural mosaic of Jalpaiguri and Cooch Behar. The outsiders being economically and technologically superior to the Rajbanshis gradually extended their grip over the predominantly agrarian economy of North Bengal. The land reform policies, the enactment of the Estate Acquisition Act of 1953 and its more forceful implementation by the LF government in West Bengal since 1977, dealt further blow to the landowners among the Rajbanshis. It helped the outsiders in either receiving land patta or getting registered as sharecroppers. Gradually in Jalpaiguri the number of landholders increased among the Marwaris and the upper caste Bengali middle class people while their number among the Rajbanshis continued to decline. Since the Marwaris or the Bengali *babus* or the Bhadraloks (Xaxa 1980) were far detached from agriculture so their control over land brought in significant changes in agriculture as well as culture of the region. The entire gamut of the economy, politics and culture gradually came to be dominated by the outsider new settlers: the Bhatias as designated by the Rajbanshis. 'The indigenous people (Deshi) raised the question of the right of "son of the soil". They publicly express their hatred against the new settlers (Bhatia)', argues Adhikary (2010–2011: 1235).

Thus, the entire Rajbansi movement should be viewed as the effort of the indigenous Rajbanshis of North Bengal known as *Deshi* to safeguard their economic interest and cultural distinctiveness from the onslaught of the outsider non-Rajbanshis, known to be the *Bhatia*. After the Hit Sadhini Sabha, a number of organizations political as well as cultural have raised the same issue. Among them the prominent ones are the Uttar Khanda Dal (UKD) formed in 1969 and Uttarbanga Tapasili Jati o Adivasi Sangathan (UTJAS) formed in 1979. These along with many other small-scale organizations such as Kamtapur Gana Parishad (KGP) like the Asom Gana Parishad (AGP), All Kamtapur Students' Union like the All Assam Students' Union (AASU) and All Bodo Students' Union (ABSU) in Assam culminated in the creation of the Kamtapur People's Party (KPP), a civil society organization, and Kamtapur Liberation Organization (KLO), a militant organization, in the 1990s. In 1998 the Greater Cooch Behar People's Association (GCPA) was formed. In 2006 Atul Roy, the leader of the KPP, broke away from the party and formed the Kamtapur Progressive Party. Some of these organizations, particularly the GCPA raised legal questions regarding the merger of Cooch Behar state with West Bengal. By and large all these organizations demanded the formation of a separate Kamtapur state for the Rajbanshis in the Indian Union and inclusion of Kamtapuri language of the Rajbanshis in the Eighth Schedule of the Indian Constitution.

The emergence of so many organizations and fractions within a relatively short span of time might be a proof of the weakness of the Rajbansi movement. The cause of such weakness can be attributed to the complexities involved in the process of identity construction of the Rajbanshis. The complexity primarily was on account of the multi-layered dimensions of their identity. The history of the people since the colonial period had revealed their effort to negotiate with their multiple identities as Koch, Rajbansi and Kshatriya. There have been differences among the Rajbanshis themselves regarding the Kamtapuri language too. The Rajbansi intelligentsia tend to deny that it is an original language as claimed by the protagonist of the statehood demand (Bagchi 2014). The former considers it to be a dialect of standard Bengali. The Rajbansis not being a homogeneous category, their attitude and relationship to the Bengalis and Bengali culture also varied. In fact, it sometimes hindered the development of the ethnic identity of the Rajbanshis since their internal divisions often prevented the definite identification of the 'ethnic other'. Moreover, being a socio-economically backward community, the process of identity construction of the Rajbanshis had become ambivalent as it continuously oscillated between the two poles of ethnicity and class. While in reality the Rajbansi social, economic and cultural life always experienced the threat of cultural marginalization crossed by economic exploitation, this complex interaction, however was unable to inform the more abstract process of identity construction of the people.

In the 2001 Assembly Election the KPP joined the AITC-led Bangla Bachao Front, which failed to win a single seat in the districts of Jalpaiguri and Cooch Behar. The LF, considering the identity assertion of the Rajbanshis as a conspiracy of the 'National and International reactionary, communal and imperialist forces' (Dakua 2007, 64) to malign the government, had a crackdown that crushed the KLO with the subsequent arrest of its prominent leaders. In 2012 under the AITC regime, the GCPA revived its demand expecting leverage out of their earlier association with the present Chief Minister Mamata Banerjee. Far from giving any serious heed to their statehood demand, she announced the formation of the Rajbansi Bhasa Academy, which would work for the development of the languages of the Rajbansis. The frustrated Rajbanshis in reaction voted for the BJP in the 2014 Lok Sabha Election (Datta 2018). The CSDS data show that in comparison to 2009 in the National Election of 2014 the Rajbansi vote share of the AITC also increased but certainly the rate of increase was more for the BJP. The following diagram (Figure 4.3) about the relative Rajbansi vote share of the AITC and the BJP in different elections in West Bengal from 2009–2016 reveals this.

Perhaps, this had prompted the AITC government to form the West Bengal Rajbanshi Development and Cultural Board on 7 June 2017 to promote the socio-economic and cultural development of the

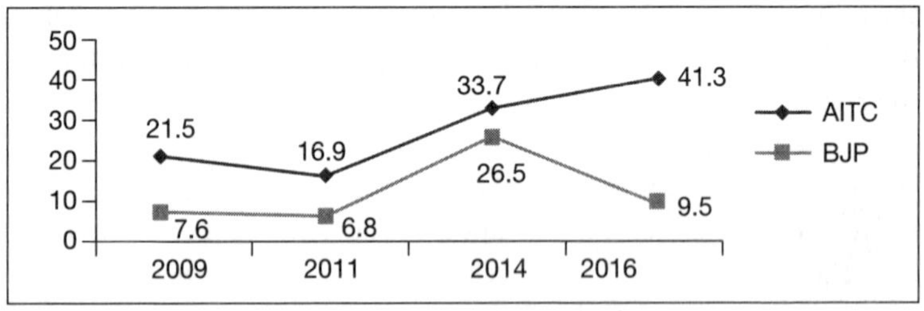

Figure 4.3 *Rajbansi Vote Share of AITC and BJP (2009–2016)*

Source: CSDS *Data Unit*, NES 2009 and 2014; West Bengal Assembly Election Study 2011 and 2016.

Rajbanshis. Later in February 2018, Mamata Banerjee came up with the assurance to recognize Kamtapuri as an official language. Critics along with the political adversaries of Mamata Banerjee believe that while these steps might benefit the AITC electorally, but certainly it would provide further impetus to the statehood demand not only of the Rajbanshis but in neighbouring regions also. That the formation of the development board for the Rajbanshis was not enough to secure their electoral support became evident from the results of the 2019 general election. The dissipation of the Rajbanshis from the AITC reached such a height that almost 75 per cent of the sampled Rajbansi electorate, as reports the NES 2019 data set, opted for the BJP against a dwindling 9 per cent for the AITC. The significant increase in the Rajbansi vote share of the BJP was also the chief architect of its victory in seven parliamentary seats out of eight in the North Bengal region.

Gorkhaland Agitation

Along with the Rajbanshis, during the same period the LF government had to negotiate with the movement of regional autonomy of the Gorkhas in the Darjeeling district as well. The district has three hill subdivisions, namely Darjeeling Sadar, Kurseong and Kalimpong, and a plains subdivision, namely Siliguri. In 1835 the king of Sikkim gifted the area except Kalimpong to the East India Company and Kalimpong was annexed from Bhutan in 1865. Since the mid-19 century, Darjeeling started to accrue significant revenue to the colonizers from tea, coffee and cinchona plantation. As all these plantations in the hilly terrain required hard work, the British encouraged the influx of the Nepalese to settle in the hills who were known for their ability to carry on sustained work.

The Gorkha community is composed of this Indian Nepali-speaking population. The Gorkhaland movement, as it is known today, finds its root in the historical aspiration of the Gorkhas in Darjeeling for self-rule. The Bengali middle class, emerging as a direct offshoot of British economic and educational policies, extended their control over the Gorkhas in the hills of Darjeeling since the middle of the 19th century. To safeguard the social, economic, cultural and political lives of the

Gorkhas against the subjugating attitude of the dominant Bengalis, the Hill Men's Association comprising the Nepali, Bhutia and Lepcha communities first gave the call of a separate administrative unit in Darjeeling including the Duars portion in Jalpaiguri on geographical and ethnic lines in 1907. The Association also submitted a petition in this effect to the Simon Commission in 1929. It again demanded the separation of Darjeeling from Bengal when the Government of India Act, 1935 was passed. Meanwhile, language issue came to reinforce the cause of Gorkha ethnicity. The Nepali language used in Darjeeling had its own distinctiveness. Known as Gorkhali or Gorkha Bhasa, it emerged out of the amalgamation of several dialects of the different castes and tribes among the Nepalis such as the Sherpa, Limbu and Rai. Gorkhali was emerging out of the necessity of social intercourse among the Nepali people working in the tea gardens and marketplaces (Ghosh 2009). In this sense it assumed the status of lingua franca of the Darjeeling hills. Even the non-Nepali communities of the hills such as the Lepcha and Bhutia adopted it. The consolidation of Gorkhali as a link language received further momentum with the formation of the Nepali Sahitya Sammelan in 1924 'which became the forum of the emergent Gorkha intelligentsia' (ibid., 11).

The emerging Gorkha intelligentsia, comprising the newly developing Gorkha middle class came to form the All India Gorkha League in 1943. On the eve of Indian Independence the League raised the regional autonomy demand of Darjeeling. The credit of the League lay in the fact that its consideration of the Gorkha nationality extended beyond the limits of Darjeeling, to appeal to the Gorkhas residing in Meghalaya, Assam, Uttar Pradesh and so on. The demand of autonomy was also supported by the CPI (Datta 1991). On 31 July 1950 the Treaty of Peace and Friendship was signed between the Governments of India and Nepal, known to be the Indo-Nepal Treaty of 1950, which started to complicate the situation. The Article 7 of the treaty maintains, 'The Governments of India and Nepal agree to grant, on reciprocal basis, to the nationals of one country in the territories of the other the same privileges in the matter of residence...' (Government of India 1950). Clearly this had erased the distinctions between the Indian born and Nepal born Nepali speakers. On the basis of the treaty, the Indian-born Nepalese could also be treated as foreigners like the Nepal born ones. The anxiety of the Gorkhas was increasing since the treaty paved the way for their eviction from India. Even the ex-Prime Minister Mr Morarji Deasi considered Nepali to be a foreign language (Ghosh 2009). Moreover, the influx of Bengali refugees in the Terai and Duars region of Darjeeling and Jalpaiguri district respectively from erstwhile East Pakistan due to Indian Partition reduced the predominance of the Gorkhas here. By increasing the population pressure on land many times this has resisted not only agricultural growth, but also tea industry received a serious jolt. The salt was added to the injury when Nepali-speaking migrants were evicted in large numbers from Assam and Meghalaya in the early 1980s. Possibly, the historically developing Gorkha identity along with the dubious status of their citizenship right in India were the fundamental reasons for the demand of a separate Gorkhaland state raised by Subhash Ghising-led Gorkha National Liberation Front (GNLF) in 1986. Apart from demanding a separate Gorkhaland state to be carved out from West Bengal, there had also been demands for granting the constitutional citizenship rights to the Gorkhas, inclusion of the language of the Gorkhas in the Eighth Schedule of the Indian Constitution and abrogation of Article 7 of the Indo-Nepal Treaty. The demands clearly revealed the nationality aspirations of the Gorkhas based on the emerging notion of the Gorkha ethnic identity pitted against the cultural and economic dominance of the Bengalis.

The GNLF adopted several strategies such as bandh, asking people of the hills not to pay taxes and refund the bank and cooperative loans, non-cooperation with the state government since to the GNLF it was primarily meant for the Bengalis. It also gave a call to social boycotting of the people who were opposed to the movement (Datta 1991). The LF government and its Chief Minister Jyoti Basu, like the Rajbansi movement, here also found the 'foreign hand' and outsiders' interest to create law and order crisis in the LF ruled state (Karlsson 2000). Failing to see the dynamic interface of economic discrimination and the threat of cultural marginalization behind such an ethnic upsurge of the Gorkha sub-nationality, the LF government wanted to suppress the movement through the sheer application of force. Consequently, there had been enough bloodshed, loss of lives and property in the hills during 1986 to 1988. Finally, in July 1988, on the request of the then Prime Minister Rajiv Gandhi, Ghising agreed to have an autonomous hill council comprising of the hill subdivisions and some areas of the Terai region, dropping the demand for a separate Gorkhaland state. Since its inception, the Darjeeling Gorkha Hill Council (DGHC) had been facing the problems of inadequate transfer of funds from the state government coupled with other structural impediments. There had also been charges of nepotism and corruption on the functioning of the Council. Ghising as the chairman of the DGHC also did not show any positive mood to work for the satisfaction of the unfulfilled cultural aspiration of the Gorkhas either.

That the DGHC was not a solution to the cultural aspiration of self-rule of the Gorkhas was gradually being felt by the common Gorkhas. Realizing the growing discontent among the people, Ghising in 2000 demanded the inclusion of the DGHC in the Sixth Schedule of the Constitution by recognizing Darjeeling as a tribal region. But perhaps being part of the institutional power structure in the form of the DGHC and getting used to its benefits, however limited, Ghising and the GNLF were not in a position to launch a people's movement strong enough to attain the goal of self-determination of the Gorkhas. The grievances persisted at the level of the Gorkha society were evident when a breakaway fraction of the GNLF formed a separate organization called Gorkha Janmukti Morcha (GJMM) under the leadership of Bimal Gurung, once a close associate of Subhash Ghising, to revamp the movement for a separate Gorkhaland state in 2007.

In a similar vein to the GNLF, the GJMM also in its statehood movement took the recourses to bandhs, asking people to pay no state government taxes, non-payment of electricity and telephone bills and so on. As the CPI (M) during the period was facing severe opposition in the plains emerging out of the Singur, Nandigram and related issues, so it was rather easy for the GJMM to consolidate the anti-CPI (M) sentiment in the hills. The degree of politicization of ethnicity, which was rather low in the DGHC era of the last two decades, became highly enlarged to characterize the CPI (M) as a party of the Bengalis.

Gorkha ethnicity under the GJMM in this manner was not only pitted against its declared 'other': the Bengali identity, but also the CPI (M). At a time, when throughout Bengal the discontent against the CPI (M) was simmering, such an amalgamation of Gorkha ethnicity with the dominant political mood allowed the GJMM some extra space to mobilize the people politically. It had its reflection in the ensuing Lok Sabha Election in 2009, where the CPI (M) in Darjeeling had to withstand a loss of almost 8 per cent votes compared to what it could secure in 2004, as reveals the data of the Election Commission of India. Jaswant Singh of the BJP, through the support of the upbeat GJMM, won the Darjeeling Lok Sabha constituency by securing 51.5 per cent of the votes. In the 2011 Assembly Election, in its first electoral contest the GJMM won all the three seats in the hills, namely Darjeeling, Kalimpong and Kurseong by securing 79.79 per cent of the votes. In contrast, the GNLF, the torchbearer of the Gorkhaland movement, contesting its first Assembly Election in 1996 could only secure 53.38 per cent of the votes in the same three seats, as reports the Election Commission of India. These are evidences of the level of ethnic polarization which came to characterize the political mosaic of the hill society in West Bengal at the end of the first decade of the new century.

Just after assuming state power in West Bengal in 2011, the AITC-led government of West Bengal engaged itself in a tripartite agreement with the GJMM and the Central Government to form the Gorkhaland Territorial Administration (GTA), yet another semi-autonomous council in July 2011. The GTA under the command of Bimal Gurung was to replace the earlier DGHC led by Subhash Ghising and was expected to bring peace and development initiatives in the hill areas of Darjeeling. To consider the GJMM's demand to include the Gorkha predominant areas of Terai and Duars region in the GTA a high power committee was formed. Apparently, the GTA was more autonomous than the DGHC, since it had command over more departments and greater number of elected members than the latter. It was perhaps also the first time in the history of the struggle of the Gorkha sub-nationality, that the state came to recognize 'Gorkhaland' as the nomenclature of the GTA suggests. While signing the DGHC accord the GNLF had agreed to drop the Gorkhaland demand, the GJMM agreed to form the GTA while not dropping the statehood demand.

That the GTA was a temporary arrangement came to the fore gradually. This was evident through various strategies adopted by the mainstream politics to appropriate the emerging voice of Gorkha unity developed through the historical process of ethnic identity formation of the various hill communities. Attempt towards this was evident in the projects to grant ST status, Gorkha certificate to various hill communities and formation of development councils for them. Allegations have been there that the process of granting ST status and Gorkha certificates instead of doing justice to the cause of Gorkha ethnicity is driven primarily to satisfy the political aspiration of the mainstream. The reservation benefits in the form of according ST status or issuing Gorkha certificates, allegedly, have been granted to some selected communities skipping others. Seen from the distinct angle of the unity of various communities under the Gorkha identity, this is perhaps a design to bring in crack therein. The same is true for the development councils formed at the initiatives of the state government under the AITC. By forming development councils for various hill communities it is perhaps trying to undermine the very basis of the historically evolved Gorkha identity. This is evident from the letter dated 17 June 2015, written by K. B. Yogi, President, Gorkha Yogi Kalyan Sangh to Chief Minister Mamata Banerjee on the issue of the constitution of the Sherpa Development Board by the Government of West Bengal. In the letter, as reproduced by Dewan (2016), Yogi accuses Mamata Banerjee for her selective and discriminatory action to help a few section of the hill communities who are already well-off socially, educationally and politically compared to some other sections of neglected, marginalized and deprived communities such as Thami, Bhujel, Mangar and Yogi. To Yogi, it was the execution of her hidden agenda to create internal rift within the Gorkha/Nepali community (ibid.). Yogi/Jogi is quite a backward community in Darjeeling hills and Duars region of West Bengal. Their total population in West Bengal is less than 2000. K. B. Yogi in another letter to Mamata Banerjee written on 19 September 2013 (ibid.) claims that it is the most backward among the Nepalese community in West Bengal.

By the end of 2017, the Mamata Banerjee government has formed 15 development councils for specific hill communities (Chowdhury 2019). While development of the communities is the stated goal but apprehensions are there regarding the divisive impact these councils might have on the ethnic unity of the Gorkhas, which historically has been forged through cultural, particularly, linguistic amalgamation of the different communities. However, for the AITC it would have very clear political dividends. First, the engulfment of the divisions among the communities might lower the tone of the Gorkhaland agitation. Second, these might also marginalize the BJP in the hills, which through the support of the GJMM, has won the Darjeeling parliamentary constituency in the last two elections. Here it should be noted that the development councils are kept under the control of the Tribal Development and Backward Classes Welfare Departments of Government of West Bengal not the GTA (ibid.). Through these councils, therefore, the AITC might expect to enhance its support base among the different hill communities by depleting the influence of the BJP. A hint of this can be found in the result of the Assembly Election of 2016, where the AITC secured almost 31 per cent of the votes polled in the two constituencies it contested in the hills, namely Darjeeling and Kurseong. Harka Bahadur Chhetri, the ex-GJMM leader and sitting MLA from Kalimpong, contesting as an AITC supported independent candidate, secured almost 41 per cent votes, as reports the data of the Election Commission of India. Finally, the development councils could split the GJMM also. This, in fact had happened. In June 2017, the state government proposed to introduce Bengali as a second language in schools of West Bengal. The GJMM perceiving it to be an assault to the linguistic identity of the Gorkhas, called an indefinite strike for the statehood demand. During the 104-days long bandh, factionalism within the GJMM became apparent as one faction of the GJMM led by Binay Tamang declared to call off the strike to facilitate talks with the state government, which was opposed by Roshan Giri, the general secretary of the GJMM. Binay Tamang later became the caretaker chief of the GTA. In March 2018, the Tamang faction decided to pull out of the NDA on account of the perceived failure of the BJP to give proper attention to the demand of Gorkhaland statehood. Tamang joined the public meeting of the anti-BJP parties called by Mamata Banerjee in Kolkata on 19 January 2019 and even participated in the dharna of Mamata Banerjee against the centre's alleged misuse of the CBI in February 2019.

The Gorkhalamd movement, as it stands now, is in a situation of flux. The divided GJMM appears to be too feeble organizationally to invigorate the movement for a separate Gorkhaland state. Among the mainstream political parties, the ruling AITC so far has been successful in making considerable inroads into the support base of the ethnic parties in the hills, most importantly the GJMM, through the formation of the development councils and thereby inflicting cracks in its organization. The dominant faction of the GJMM, now at the helm of the affairs of the GTA, perhaps for its political survival, has been toeing the line of the ruling AITC, which had made its anti-Gorkhaland stance amply clear through its actions. The present situation can be a mark of the appropriation of the ethnic parties by the mainstream political parties, the AITC in this case. Conversely, it might also be a temporary strategic retreat of the GJMM. Whatever be the case, how far the fundamental issue of satisfaction of the aspiration of Gorkha self-rule can be attained through such political manoeuvring remains the question. It would perhaps be a mistake to conceive the issue of ethnic identity of the Gorkhas as chiefly political.

This is also evident from the survey data of the West Bengal Assembly Election Study 2016. During the course of the study almost 63 per cent of the sampled electorates have agreed that Mamata Banerjee's government has mishandled the Gorkhaland issue. Seen from the vantage point of electoral politics, nobody possibly can deny that Mamata Banerjee's steps had been instrumental in extending AITC's support base to the hills. But that does not imply that the issue of unfulfilled cultural aspirations of the Gorkhas has been resolved. People's overall disapproval, as reveals the survey data, might be a pointer to the fact that the Gorkhaland issue should not be or cannot be tackled politically alone; it has rather a sharp cultural edge. The Gorkha identity is a result of the historical extension of the colonial and postcolonial economic relations in the hill areas of West Bengal. The Gorkhas were subjugated by the colonizers and their Bengali middle class associates, not only politically but also economically and culturally. In response, the Gorkha identity also emerged with the necessary cultural overtone to combat the cultural dominance of the non-Gorkhas. So far the state response to the cause of Gorkha ethnicity has missed this important point of cultural aspiration of the Gorkha community. Not only the Gorkhas, the state response to the identity assertion of the Rajbanshis and the Dalits, as have been discussed earlier, and to that of the adivasis of Lalgarh, as will be discussed now, has remained devoid of such cultural sensitivity.

Lalgarh Movement

Lalgarh is a village in Binpur–I community development (CD) block under the newly formed Jhargram district of West Bengal. During the movement of 2008 it was however a part of the Paschim Medinipur district. It is the headquarters of Binpur–I CD block, which has a ST population of 28.15 per cent and 25.02 per cent SC population (Census of India 2011a). Having its epicentre at Lalgarh the movement spread in almost 10 blocks of Paschim Medinipur district and in a number of adjacent blocks of the districts of Bankura and Purulia in West Bengal. Popularly this region is known to be the *Junglemahals* because of its large forest tract. Geographically the region is part of the Chotanagpur plateau region. Culturally the people of the region, mostly adivasis, feel racial, linguistic and emotional proximity with the adivasis of Chotanagpur. Politically, they inhabit the southwestern part of West Bengal, having the state boundary with Jharkhand in the west and northwest.

The series of events giving birth to the protest movement launched primarily by the adivasis in Lalgarh first received wider attention of the general public with the landmine explosion allegedly targeting the convoy of West Bengal Chief Minister Mr Buddhadeb Bhattacharya and the then union Steel and Mines minister Mr Ram Vilas Paswan, when they were returning from the inauguration of the Jindal Steel Works Special Economic Zone (SEZ) in Salboni of Paschim Medinipur district on 2 November 2008. Almost 5000 acres of land, including forest land, were acquired for the project (Ray 2008). Threatened to be alienated from the land and forest, the vital sources of their livelihood, the adivasis in and around the area were discontented. Since 2005 this area of Paschim Medinipur district along with the adjacent regions in Purulia and Bankura district of West Bengal had been in news for the political activities of the Communist Party of India (Maoist). The activists of this Maoist organization were supposedly behind the explosion.

It has been a common practice of the police, as alleged, to harass and arrest adivasis whenever there is a Maoist attack in the area. This time the target was no other than the chief minister and the police forces increased their repressive actions many times by indiscriminately harassing and arresting the adivasis belonging to almost 35 villages surrounding Lalgarh. They did not spare the teenagers and women also. One adivasi woman lost her eyes while another suffered multiple fractures as she was kicked on her chest. Allegation had been there that the police did not even spare a pregnant woman. Police brutality of such an extent crossed every limit of tolerance of the adivasis. The Bharat Jakat Majhi Madwa Juan Gaonta, the supreme social organization of the Santhals, assumed the leadership of the movement. The spontaneity of the movement rose to such a height that Nityananda Hembram, the 'Disham Majhi', the traditional chief of the organization, had to confess that the movement was not under the control of the organization; on the contrary, the organization was being controlled by the movement (Ray 2008). Apart from Bharat Jakat Majhi Madwa, several other smaller adivasi outfits joined the movement and argued in favour of armed resistance to uphold the cause of their existence. In the next few days the movement spilled over like wildfire into the entire Junglemahal area covering the adivasi-predominant ten blocks of Paschim Medinipur district and the neighbouring Bankura and Purulia districts.

Concerned with the rapid spread of the movement moving beyond their control, Bharat Jakat Majhi Madwa decided to confine the movement within the limits of Lalgarh only on the condition that the government agrees to stop the continuing police repression and accedes to their other demands. But the adivasis of Junglemahals were in no mood to put any limit to their ever-expanding agitation. Hence, the smaller adivasi organizations such as Jumit Gaonta and Kudmi Chatra Sangram Committee active at the forefront of the movement came together on 14 November to form the Pulishi Santrash Birodhi Janaganer Committee (People's Committee Against Police Atrocities [PCAPA]) to guide the movement (*Telegraph* 2008). The leadership of the movement in this fashion passed away from the traditional elderly adivasis to a firebrand group of young people.

The PCAPA was essentially a democratic organization of the oppressed people (Bora and Das 2009; Shell 2009). In every village under its operation a 10-member village committee comprising five men and five women was set up. Centrally there was a coordination committee composed of two members (one man and one woman) from each of these village committees. Any decision or plan of action taken or adopted by the PCAPA, thus, fully reflected the approval of the villagers at the grass-roots level.

PCAPA put forward a 13-point charter of demands, the pivotal among them being, the Superintendent of Police (SP) must come to Lalgarh and hold his ears publicly and apologise for victimizing and arbitrarily arresting innocent common people. The other guilty police officers have to rub their noses from all the way to Dalilpur chawk to Chhotopeliya village.[2] PCAPA also demanded that police camps must not be setup in schools, panchayat offices or hospitals. All the existing camps in such premises will have to be removed. Later some other demands were also added to these, the most important among these being the protection of adivasis' traditional right over water, forest and land (*jal*, *jangal* and *jamin*) of their region. They opposed the capitalist pattern of development through industrialization resulting in dispossession, displacement and marginalization of the adivasis. Instead, they put forward the thesis of pro-poor development strategy reflected through opening up of schools, health centres, provision of drinking water and so on.

To satisfy their aspiration for dignity and pro-poor development initiatives, the movement of the adivasi people continued for weeks. The flare of its spontaneity touched the adivasi pockets of very far-off

[2] For details about the demands visit: http://sanhati.com/wp-content/uploads/2008/11/lalgarh1830.jpg (accessed on 4 December 2009).

places such as Kharagpur, Keshiary and Debra, and in some places of the districts of Birbhum, Bardhaman and North 24 Parganas.

Gaining assurances from the administration about acceding to most of their demands in a meeting held between the representatives of the administration and PCAPA, the 32-day long blockade programme was lifted. Government released the arrested persons against whom no charges were framed, declared compensations for the persons injured in police action and subsequently removed police camps from schools.

In the meantime, organizations such as Ganapratirodh Committee and Adivasi-Anadivasi Aikya Committee were floated allegedly by the ruling CPI (M) and some other political organizations, notably Jharkhand Mukti Morcha (JMM) to combat the Maoists. To curb the apprehended growing influence of the Maoists over the adivasis, the district administration also redeployed police force in Lalgarh. Perceiving it as a breach of promise, the PCAPA gave a call for social boycott of the police and the administration. Determined to finish off the growing influence of the banned CPI (Maoist), the Central Government and to some extent a hesitant state government of West Bengal sent joint forces composed of the central paramilitary forces and state police forces in the middle of June 2009 in Lalgarh and its adjacent areas. In spite of this, the Maoist continued their strategy of guerrilla warfare killing a number of persons mostly members of the ruling CPI (M). The presence of the joint force had brought life to a standstill in Lalgarh. The adivasi women who used to earn subsistence by collecting sal and kendu leaves from the forests were not daring to come out of their houses out of a perceived fear of harassment in the hands of the joint forces. Schools were closed and converted into the camps of the joint forces. With the closure of the schools mid-day meal was also unavailable. All these had compounded the problems of the extremely poor adivasis. In protest, the PCAPA had organized several dharnas, rallies and strikes with the demands of withdrawal of joint forces and commencement of much promised development works without delay.

Right from the beginning of the Lalgarh movement, Junglemahals witnessed two streams of protest movements. On the one hand the

Maoists, active in organizing the downtrodden adivasis in the region for quite some time, intensified their struggle against the state apparatus, the PCAPA on the other hand continued with their programme of non-violent non-cooperation to the police and district administration. Many a quarter, including the mainstream political parties of West Bengal, the intellectuals and last but not the least the media houses had been busy in finding out the 'link' between these two organizations and their respective agitation programmes. Such a conjectural understanding about the isomorphism of the two organizations, operating in the same area with almost identical rank and files, was natural since both these, although in different forms, were opposing the state machinery. But from what one should not lose sight at is the vast area which came under the movement of the PCAPA along with the degree of spontaneity at which the adivasis participated in it. The grassroots democratic and gender-neutral organizational policies adopted by the PCAPA, infused enough energy and vibrancy in the movement, lending it a distinct mass character. This was revealed by the participation of adivasi women in large numbers in the movement. The Maoists who had command over a limited area in the Junglemahals did not seem to have the organizational potentiality to lead a mass movement of such a great scale. It was true that with the distancing of the Bharat Jakat Majhi Madwa from the movement on the one hand and with the increasing level of police operation the scale of the movement started to shrink. Gradually it got confined in Lalgarh and a few villages surrounding it. Due to such a reducing operational space, it then seemed possible and also feasible for the Maoists to provide backup to the movement.

Not the adivasis of the Junglemahals alone, presently the adivasis in the entire central Indian plateau region, starting from Chhatisgarh, Jharkhand to Orissa have been on the path of revolt, however intermittently, against the state acting as a facilitator of the free market economy. These movements should be viewed as the collective protests of the most downtrodden against the ever increasing and sharpening exploitation of global capital operating under the neoliberal framework. The basic issue has been of course the question of survival which is turning out to be a difficult proposition to ensure due to the severe repression unleashed by the profit-hungry capitalist forces, national and multinational.

The economic deprivation of the adivasis has continued to be a fact since the British era. Even after independence, the scene has remained unchanged. In 2004 five adivasis died of hunger and malnutrition at Amlasol, a village under the Banshpahari Gram Panchayat of Binpur–II Block in Paschim Medinipur district of West Bengal. This incident caught the attention of the government, and developmental measures began to be taken, which however, were not of much impact. The root of such discrimination is traced in economic inequality, primarily. The Amlasol incident, along with many other such incidences are the outcomes of the historical inequality in land relations, of which the adivasis perhaps are the worst victims. The adivasis of Chotanagpur, since the early days of colonial annexation, have been subjected to quite crude exploitative land relations in the forms of landlordism, absentee landlordism and zamindari tenure system. Moreover, the development projects such as irrigation, mining and setting up of industries also displace the adivasis in large numbers. They are mostly landless labourers, not land owners. So, it seems that deprivation is integrally linked with the existence and identity of the adivasi. Quite evidently, being an adivasi refers to two simultaneous form of discrimination: economic exploitation by the upper classes and cultural humiliation and oppression by the mainstream population. Such merger of economic and socio-cultural inequality was enough to generate a feeling of relative deprivation among the adivasis which might have led them to revolt against the discriminatory institutions. The adivasi movement at Lalgarh was also no exception. But the idiosyncratic feature of the movement perhaps lay in its ethnic identity assertion, an identity which is developed through their historical experience of exploitation and oppression continuing for centuries. The manner in which the adivasis attempted to have political solutions to the problems of their cultural marginalization merits attention here.

In ethnic movement, or nativistic movement to use Ralph Linton's (1943) words, there has always been a conscious effort to revive or perpetuate selected aspects of the culture of the ethnic groups mobilized. This found some relevance in the context of the mobilization of the adivasis of Junglemahals too. The movement of the adivasis here has originated and developed along the ordinates of adivasi cultural pattern. During the course of the movement there had been sincere invocation to adivasi tradition and cultural practices.

First, the movement's attachment to adivasi cultural tradition could be revealed by the enthusiastic participation of the women in large numbers. The tradition of adivasis movements in Chotanagpur region since the late 18th century bears testimony to this. Second, the movement originating in the small village of Lalgarh took no time to spread across a huge area covering a number of neighbouring districts. This was also in tune with the prototype of adivasi movements, which rather than the medium of formal organization, relies more on spoken utterances, coupled with a little bit of writing, and other aural and visual means such as community gathering with traditional dresses, musical instruments, weapons, sounds of the drums and horns to transmit the rebel spirit (Guha 1999). Third, the adivasis' attachment to their tradition is revealed in their call of 'Sarjam Gira' implying bitter struggle against the government. A similar call in this effect was given during the Santhal Insurrection of 1855 against the colonial authority, as well.

Fourth, the Lalgarh movement stands as yet another instance of adivasis' traditional hatred towards the police as a wing of the 'modern' state to maintain the law and order. Rather than law, maintenance of law and order was a function of the customary practices of the adivasi societies, marked by the overwhelming participation of the communities (Chatterjee 2002). The British rule for the first time replaced such customs with law. The adivasi uprisings against the colonizers, besides the economic issues, hence should also be considered as a clash between two worldviews, namely the 'modern' and the 'traditional'. The hatred shown by the adivasis of Lalgarh towards the police during the entire course of the movement might have its anchor in this historical duality. Along with social boycott of the police, the nature of the punishments to the guilty police personnel demanded by the adivasis of Lalgarh, was the proof of the hold of tradition upon the adivasis in contemporary time. Fifth, the adivasis at Lalgarh had demanded that Santhali should be the medium of instruction up to high school levels. They also had demanded further development of the 'Ol Chiki' script for the Santhali language. Needless to mention that these linguistic aspirations have always remained an archetypal cultural substance of ethnic identity assertion. Finally, the adivasis at Lalgarh had protested against the neoliberal model of development focused on large-scale industrialization. They had resented such *Ghorar Dimer Unnayan* or 'non-sensical/mare's-egg development' (Sarkar and Sarkar 2009, 13) which, to their view, would only alienate them from the *jal*, *jangal* and *jamin* (water, forest and land) of the region over which they believe to have customary rights. Besides causing further displacement, they also perceived it as an affront to their dignity or 'izzat' (Dasgupta 1985, 117).

These cultural issues were the stimulus for the movement. Undoubtedly, at the beginning, construction of ethnic identity or its protection had not been the main concern of the movement. The root cause of the movement presumably lay in the socio-economic deprivation faced by a large section of the poor adivasis of the Junglemahals. Quite interestingly, the adivasis submerged into extreme poverty, malnutrition and even starvation, went for political solution of their problems instead of the immediate economic ones. No serious economic demand, apart from compensation, was there in their charter of demands. Instead they demanded long denied dignity and prestige from the government which, as they perceived it, had only neglected and ignored them so far. In an ethnically-divided social structure this is the classic situation under which ethnic identity gets constructed or reconstructed to provide the necessary reinforcement for political mobilization. The movement of the adivasis at Lalgarh and other adjoining areas of the Junglemahals had exhibited such tendency, which was evident from the statement of Chhatradhar Mahato, the erstwhile (at present arrested) spokesperson of the PCAPA when he argued,

> We, the sons of the soil, want the right to the land, jungle and water of Jangalkhand. We want total autonomy because our people and land should be ruled by us.... We will soon set up a united ethnic platform to raise our demand for autonomy. (Cited in Mandal 2009)

Unfortunately, the CPI (M)-led LF government was not in a position to come up with a proper assessment of identity assertion of the adivasis of this region. It is always the case that in an underdeveloped economy the process of ethnic identity construction of the culturally-excluded people gets the necessary reinforcement from their economic or class-based exploitation. The growing middle class proclivity of the CPI (M) coupled with their recent rush to attract global capital made them insensitive, perhaps, to the issues of cultural marginalization, economic exploitation and the dynamic interface of these. The movements of the downtrodden people at present, everywhere, are getting informed by this complex combination of the questions of identity and class. The Lalgarh movement represents a delicate intertwining of ethnicity and class, which does not allow itself to be approached from the traditional binary of 'ethnicity' or 'class'. The CPI (M)'s perception of these movements as law and order problems created by the conspiracy of the anti-Left forces, national as well as international, which need to be crushed through administrative power of the state might be an offshoot of its failure to get into such complicated conflict at the core of the movement. Moreover, by attributing the root cause of the movement to the political aspiration of the opposition AITC, 'supported' by the Maoists, it neglected the autonomous agency of the subaltern, in this case the adivasis, in redrawing the exploitative and oppressive elite power structure.

It is true that the Lalgarh movement, like those of the Rajbanshis and Gorkhas, has failed to achieve the much cherished goals of self-rule of the adivasis, but, like the Singur and Nandigram agitations, it had a direct and one-to-one relation with the declining importance of parliamentary Left politics in West Bengal. The Central as well as the LF government's deployment of the joint forces to quell the voices of the adivasis had resulted in the gross violation of their human rights. The adivasis' obstinate resistance to the growing transgression of their right to dissent, and its violent suppression by the arrogant state government led by the CPI (M) created a legitimacy crisis of the government and the ruling party. This was evident from the support of the civil society composed of the intellectuals, human rights activists and other organizations to the cause of the oppressed adivasis at Lalgarh. In a multi-party democracy, this would obviously create greater space of operation to the opposition parties. The AITC led by

Mamata Banerjee, much like the mobilizations in Singur, Nandigram, Cooch Behar and Darjeeling, actively stood by the protesters and tried to mobilize their support for the party. In fact, during her campaigning for the Lok Sabha Election of 2009 Mamata Banerjee shared the dais with Chhatradhar Mahato, the then convenor of the PCAPA and expressed her unequivocal support to his cause (Chattopadhyay 2011). She also protested against the deployment of the joint forces to combat the Maoists in Junglemahals in 2009 (*Indian Express* 2009b). From a rally in the Junglemahals in August 2010, she demanded the withdrawal of the joint forces (Chattopadhyay 2011). Together with Singur and Nandigram, the adivasis' agitation at Lalgarh gave more concrete shape to her call for *poriborton* (change). It is true that to the adivasi culture and tradition, the discourse of popularly-elected representative government appears opaque. But the Lalgarh movement stands as a classic example of the reinforcement which the mostly unorganized or less organized popular mobilizations of the so called 'pre-modern' adivasis can provide to electoral or largely speaking, democratic politics.

Whether the PCAPA at Lalgarh was a frontal organization of the Naxalite political outfit, the Communist Party of India (Maoist), is a debatable issue, but there is a possibility that the latter might have some influence on the former. This not only reveals the salience of extra-parliamentary Left activism in West Bengal, but, more importantly, it had been a proof of the tradition of overwhelming participation of the adivasis in Naxalite movements as well, which Duyker's (1987) painstaking analysis of the Naxalbari movement in West Bengal brings into the fore. Whether predominance of the ethnic issue of the adivasis over class consciousness in Naxalbari uprising of the late 1960s, as claimed by Duyker, can be equally found in the Maoist movement at Junglemahals at present remains a contentious issue, but questions can be raised about the level of class consciousness running through the Maoist politics. This was evident when the then Maoist leader Kishenji supported Mamata Banerjee's rally at Lalgarh on 9 August 2010 (NDTV 2010). He even wished to see Mamata Banerjee as the next chief minister of West Bengal (Biswas 2015). It is a wonder indeed that a prominent Maoist leader like Kishenji went on to misjudge a politician, busy in ascending to political power in a bourgeois democratic political framework. Perhaps faced with the difficult task of waging class war against the CPI (M)-led state government, he wanted to unite all the opposition forces, even the TMC. This was perhaps not a sign of matured class politics, an important hallmark of the praxis of revolutionary Marxism. The Maoists had to pay a heavy price for such misjudged preferences. Within months of Mamata Banerjee becoming the chief minister, Kishenji was killed in an encounter with the joint forces in November 2011. She also appeared to be ambivalent about keeping her pre-electoral assurance of releasing the political prisoners (Chattopadhyay 2011). The joint forces are yet to be withdrawn, although prior to 2011, while in opposition, Ms Banerjee had consistently demanded that. Chhatradhar Mahato and some of his associates are still behind the bars charged under the Unlawful Activities Prevention Act (UAPA) and sentenced to life imprisonment in 2015.

From the foregoing discussion the significant influence of identity assertion on electoral politics is apparent. It is true that communities assert their identities when autonomy, the basic condition of their existence, faces the threat of extinction. But question may be there regarding the political autonomy of the processes set into motion by the communities to maintain and protect their autonomy. In spite of all the claims of the NSM theorists about the autonomous or non-institutional political orientation of the identity-related issues, it is also a fact that direct political initiatives often become instrumental in achieving the appeals to identity (Touraine 1988). In a multi-party political framework this assumes immense significance since the politics of identity can hardly aspire to be insulated from the influence of the political competition operating at the level of society. Conversely, the democratic political parties busy in the electoral arena also cannot ignore the cause of identities for their perceived electoral implications. The mobilizations of the Rajbanshis Gorkhas and the adivasis of Lalgarh in West Bengal can be of immense analytical potential to unveil the intricacies involved in the relationships between identity assertions of communities and the emerging contours of party competition.

The three movements discussed in this section more or less represent the prototype of ethnic movements. The issues of homeland, common language, shared history and so on—the hallmarks of classical ethnic movements were present in these movements—as well. Along with the cultural dimensions, these movements should also be viewed as the outbursts of the economically marginalized segment of the population, since in all these movements the poor and the underprivileged people participated in significant numbers. The CPI (M) ruled government of West Bengal, for the avowed cultural overtone of the movements, initially showed considerable indifference towards these. Not the CPI (M) alone, liberal democrats elsewhere also tend to ignore the ethnic movements as they expect the so called primordial ties binding the ethnic groups together to wither away under the sway of modern democracy. Quite striking was the failure on part of the CPI (M) to locate the interlocking of cultural oppression and economic exploitation as represented by the movements. Its inability to locate the class potential of the movements led it to judge the movements as nothing more than mere law and order issues. Consequently, without any effort to arrive at any political solution to the people's aspiration of self-rule via autonomy, it attempted to forcibly suppress the movements. Such faulty approach of the CPI (M), far from bringing down the scale of the movements, only helped in their expansion and augmentation. The Kamtapur, Gorkhaland and Lalgarh agitations during the first decade of the present century had exhibited this. The CPI (M) had to pay a heavy price for its misunderstanding the movements and the resultant arrogance. Mamata Banerjee, who had openly revealed her sympathy towards the cause of these people's movements, ultimately captured the state power in 2011.

The defeat of the CPI (M) and the ascendance of the AITC to the state power of West Bengal in 2011 might be considered as an example of the manner in which identity politics can determine the course of electoral trend in any democracy. But, concern is there about the extent the AITC can maintain its earlier sympathetic stance towards the identity assertions of these ethnic groups at present. Operating under the same liberal democratic set-up, how far it can do justice to the aspiration of self-rule of the marginalized communities, perhaps is the moot question. So far the trend is not encouraging. Mamata Banerjee at present is not only appearing to be busy in disconnecting her earlier ties with the movements and its leaders, but also attempting to inflict cracks among the historically developed inter-ethnic solidarity of the communities. Given the increasing weaknesses of the CPI (M) and the INC, this perhaps paves the way for the rise of the BJP as a viable contender of the AITC in the arena of party competition. How far the BJP can utilize the opportunity thrown up by such identity assertions, will certainly determine the course of West Bengal politics in the days to come.

Poriborton

West Bengal since 2009

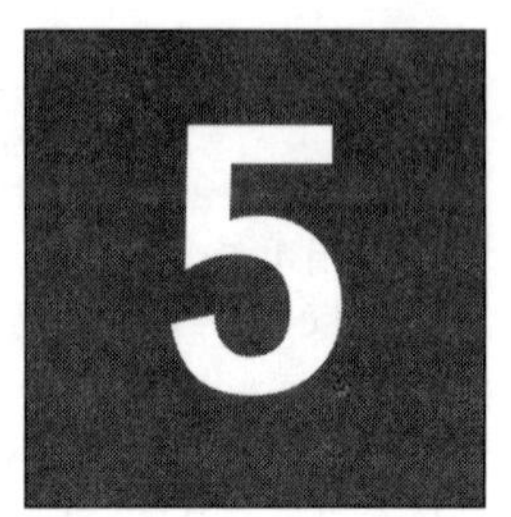

The 15th Parliamentary (Lok Sabha) Election 2009 had been a watershed in the course of democratic politics in West Bengal. This election for the first time in the history of the uninterrupted rule of the LF since 1977 had put up a stiff challenge to its political supremacy. The alliance of the AITC and the INC by securing 44.67 per cent (more than 1% what the LF had secured) of the votes and winning 25 out of a total of 42 parliamentary seats had dealt almost a mortal blow to the political hegemony of the LF (see Table 5.1).

In the 2011 Assembly Election, the LF was voted out of power to give the opposition alliance spearheaded by the AITC the first chance, since 1977, to form a non-Left government in West Bengal. In the next two elections, namely the Lok Sabha Election of 2014 and the Assembly Election of 2016, the AITC continued to increase its vote

Table 5.1 *Party Vote Share by Election (2009–2016)*

	Elections			
Parties	*2009 Lok Sabha Election*	*2011 Assembly Election*	*2014 Lok Sabha Election*	*2016 Assembly Election*
Left	43.3	41.1	29.5	26.4
AITC	31.2	38.9	39.3	44.7
BJP	6.2	4.1	16.8	10.2
INC	13.5	9.1	9.6	12.1

Source: Election Commission of India.

Note: All figures are in per cent.

share, while the Left maintained its declining trend. The BJP so far had a mixed fortune here. During the 2014 Lok Sabha Election it registered a spectacular increase in its vote share. Although many political researchers trace this to be the rise of the BJP in West Bengal politics, but the decline in its vote share in the 2016 Assembly Election casts doubt to this. Keeping aside the debate, what one cannot, possibly deny is that the BJP certainly has put its footprint in West Bengal politics. This is clear from the increase in its vote share in the 2016 Assembly Election in contrast to the 2011. The exemplary continuance of the LF rule since 1977 and the eventual turnaround in the electoral fortune of the LF in 2011 certainly have its antecedents in the policy framework under which the LF government has been operating from time to time.

Needless to mention, the ideology of any political organization in control of a state gets reflected in its policies. The fruit or desired effect of any policy is a function of its social test, that is, how far or in what manner the people at large are influenced by it. Through this line of causality one can trace the link between policies adopted by the state and the evolving nature of party competition at the social level. The policy discourse located at the state level, aimed at fulfilling the socio-economic and political aspirations of the stakeholders, has a direct bearing in the nature and dynamics of party competition characterizing the socio-political space. Here attention needs to be paid to the policies adopted by the LF government in West Bengal since 2006 to ascertain the change brought in by these in the nature of party competition leading to its debacle in 2011. A similar attempt is also called for to examine the policies adopted by the incumbent AITC government at present to get hold of its possible imprint on it. Such an exercise gains more importance because after wresting the state power from the LF in 2011 the initial euphoria, perhaps was enough for the AITC to win the Parliamentary Election of 2014 without a very critical consideration of its schemes and policies by the electorates. The policies and schemes of the AITC government were put to some test in the Assembly Election of 2016, while the detailed scrutiny of these are awaited.

POLICIES OF THE LF GOVERNMENT: IMPLICATION FOR PARTY COMPETITION

Development of agriculture through institutional reform had always been a policy thrust of the CPI (M)-led LF since its ascendance to state power of West Bengal in 1977. The resultant increase in productivity, as has been discussed earlier in Chapter 1, led to considerable decline in the extent of rural poverty during the 1980s. The improvement in some of the important economic indices had serious implication for the overall development of social lives of the people. Although in the long run the land reform initiative could not be transformed into agrarian reforms, still the LF government's effort to alter the property relations in the rural area, with all its limitations, are considered to be creditworthy by the people of West Bengal and beyond. This was evident from the data of West Bengal Assembly Election Study 2011, where the electorates of West Bengal have attributed the reason of LF's such a long stint of power to this, as can be revealed from Table 5.2.

It is observed from Table 5.2 that about 81 per cent of the sampled electorates, covered under the study, are of the opinion that the successive LF governments in West Bengal have been successful in improving agricultural production. The same data source also reflects that almost half of the electorates give the credit to the continued LF regime for effective land distribution (data with the authors). Such a favourable rating of the electorates about the LF is important since people are rating a government's policies which is at the reign of power

Table 5.2 *Whether the Left Front Government has Failed or Succeeded in Agricultural Production*

Opinion	Frequency	Per cent
Fully succeeded	1,381	30.54
Somewhat succeeded	2,276	50.33
Somewhat failed	566	12.52
Fully failed	298	6.6
Total	4522	100.0

Source: CSDS Data Unit, West Bengal Assembly Election Study, 2011.

Note: Adjusted for the 'Don't Know' category.

for almost the last three and half decades, a period long enough to generate anti-incumbency of the highest order. It is also significant since this has been the opinion of the people about a government's performance in the agricultural sector which of late has been criticized to be anti-agricultural by the opposition parties' contingent upon its industrialization rush at Singur, Nandigram and elsewhere in the state. Significantly, such a favourable opinion about the agrarian policy of the CPI (M) was expressed by the electorates during the 2011 Assembly Election, which the party was going to lose eventually. Hence, it is amply clear that the LF's agricultural policy has contributed positively in developing a 'permanent incumbency' (Bhattacharyya 2004), which has been instrumental in making the party competition favourable to it by pushing the opposition to the margins of West Bengal polity. The same electorate however had come up with a reverse opinion about the LF government's performance in attracting investments for industrial development of the state, as depicts Table 5.3.

When asked to express their opinion about the performance of the LF government in attracting investments, almost 62 per cent of the sampled electorates indicated towards its failure in this regard, which was essential to improve the industrial condition of the state. The opinion of the people does not seem to be too ungrounded, since during the long 34-years rule only two large-scale industries, namely Haldia Petrochemicals and Bakreshwar Thermal Power Plant could be set up in West Bengal by the LF government.

Table 5.3 *Whether the Left Front Government has Failed or Succeeded in Attracting Investments*

Opinion	Frequency	Per cent
Fully succeeded	321	10.89
Somewhat succeeded	802	27.2
Somewhat failed	746	25.3
Fully failed	1,080	36.62
Total	2,949	100.0

Source: CSDS Data Unit, West Bengal Assembly Election Study, 2011.

Note: Adjusted for the 'Don't Know' category.

For the poor industrial development of the state, the CPI (M) however blames the unfavourable attitude of the successive Congress ruled central governments. It particularly holds responsible the central government's denial of public-sector investments and licenses for setting up private industries (CPI [M] 2007) in West Bengal. It also refers to the freight equalization policy for coal and iron ore which also robbed West Bengal of its mineral advantages. Later, being a Marxist party its traditional opposition to the free market economy also proved to be a significant impediment in attracting private investments for industrial development. The attitude of the people towards such an ineffective industrial outlook of the LF government of West Bengal did have its imprint on various elections where the growing unpopularity of the CPI (M) in the urban areas was increasingly becoming evident.

The LF's policy anchored in agriculture continued to give it political dividend both in the Lok Sabha Election of 2004 and Assembly Election of 2006, which it had won quite convincingly. But the gradual erosion of its constituencies among the urbanites and industrial sector was increasingly becoming the points of concern. Convincingly winning the 2006 Assembly Election, the LF finally decided it time to address these. This was more so because on account of dwindling agricultural output and industrial stagnation, the West Bengal economy as a whole was approaching a point of staggering halt. Ultimately, succumbing to the increasing pressure of the neoliberal economic arrangement, the Buddhadeb Bhattacharya-led LF government in West Bengal began to shift its traditional focus on agriculture and opted for massive industrialization under the aegis of private capital, which obviously necessitates huge amount of land to be acquired among other things. The government's attempt to acquire land for industries brought the people, mostly of the rural areas, to the path of mass resistance at Singur, Nandigram, Lalgarh, Bhangar and some other places, which has already been discussed in the last two chapters. The course of events that followed exhibited an amazing show of a communist party, deviated from its ideological standpoint of spearheading social movements of the exploited and oppressed segments of the population, actively became engaged in suppressing those, even with the application of force by a combination of the state machinery and, allegedly, cadre power. It hardly requires mention that such a policy of hasty industrialization under the aegis of multinational capital led the people of West Bengal in the Assembly Election of 2011 to come up with a mandate of change by electing the AITC to rule the state, deserting the CPI (M)-led LF coalition. The desperate attempt of the CPI (M), along with its partners in the LF, to get accommodated in the global capitalist economic order, moving just in the opposite direction to their avowed ideology, possibly blurred their differences with other democratic political parties. This has been evident from the dramatic shifting loyalty of the electorate of West Bengal from the LF to the AITC since 2009. Moreover, in selecting the sites for the industries and chalking up the land acquisition process, the ruling communist coalition accorded more priority and even justified the profit motives of the capitalists by sacrificing the interests of the affected or displaced persons. For this, the CPI (M) increasingly came to be labelled as 'anti-poor', which Table 5.4, developed out of the CSDS conducted West Bengal Assembly Election Study 2011 data, describes quite succinctly.

To explore this, the sampled respondents were asked to rate the success or failure of the LF government in defending the dignity of the poor. It can be seen from Table 5.4 that to a majority of them (55%) the government has failed to protect the dignity of poor. This is interesting indeed because the opinion was expressed towards a

Table 5.4 *Whether the Left Front Government has Failed or Succeeded on Dignity for Poor*

Opinion	*Frequency*	*Per cent*
Fully succeeded	704	16.2
Somewhat succeeded	1,252	28.8
Somewhat failed	1,063	24.45
Fully failed	1,328	30.55
Total	4,347	100.0

Source: CSDS Data Unit, West Bengal Assembly Election Study, 2011.

Note: Adjusted for the 'Don't Know' category.

government which is known largely for its pro-poor policy priorities. The crisis of legitimacy which the LF government had to suffer since 2009, is also apparent here. The resultant feeling of anti-incumbency to the LF government altered the whole gamut of party competition in West Bengal subsequently. The anti-Left alliance, led by Mamata Banerjee, achieved considerable electoral success in the 2009 Lok Sabha Election and ultimately wrested the state power from the LF in the Assembly Election of 2011.

That the policies adopted by any political party or coalition running the government have serious implications for the party competition existing at the micro level of the society can be gauged by the motivation of the electorates in settling their electoral preferences. This was revealed from the explanation of the LF leaders, where they had identified two reasons for their poor show in the 15th Lok Sabha Election of 2009. First, they talked about the overall wave in favour of the INC-led United Progressive Alliance (UPA) in that election, which might have influenced the electorates of West Bengal too. Second was the successful consolidation of anti-Left votes by the INC–AITC alliance (Chatterjee and Basu 2014). Although the LF leaders were right in picking up the opposition alliance as the potential reason of their decline, but their first contention seemed to lack factual support. This is due to the fact that a majority of the sampled electorate during the course of the survey under NES 2009 reported to consider the performance of the state government, more than the central government, in determining their electoral preferences (ibid.). This assumes significance, as under the democratic federal framework the policies of the state government have more visibility than those of the central government. The electoral choices of the people at the local level possibly are shaped more by the trends operative under the overall political and policy climate of the state.

The AITC government ascending to state power in West Bengal took some positive initiatives to improve the conditions of public infrastructure in the state. Against the deteriorating condition of the roads and electricity in West Bengal during the dying phase of the LF rule, such initiatives of the newly-elected AITC government helped it a lot to consolidate its electoral position. Table 5.5 presents a snapshot

Table 5.5 *Electorates' Assessment of the Work Done by the Mamata Banerjee Government in the State in the Last Five Years*

Public Infrastructure	*Improved*	*Remained Same*	*Deteriorated*
Condition of road	58.9	28.6	8.8
Supply of electricity	63	27.9	4.7
Supply of drinking water	46.2	34.6	14.4
Quality of education in government schools	35.1	35.1	16.9
Medical facilities in government hospital	35.5	36.4	14
Law and order situation	24.5	34	23.2
Public bus/public transportation services	30.3	41.6	11.5

Source: CSDS Data Unit, West Bengal Assembly Election Study 2016.

Note: All figures are in per cent.

of the electorates' assessment of the AITC government's initiatives in this direction, during the course of the 2016 Assembly Election Study.

From Table 5.5 it can be observed that the AITC government had been successful in improving the conditions of roads, electricity and supply of drinking water. The respondents were sceptical to some extent about its performance in imparting quality education in government schools and providing medical facilities in government hospitals. The opinion of the respondents about medical facilities in government hospitals is striking since the Mamata Banerjee government had taken some measures to improve it. Mention can be made here about the fair price medicine shops and fair price diagnostic centres opened up by the AITC government, adopting the PPP model in the government hospitals with the intention to assist the poor patients. The West Bengal Assembly Election Study 2016 data set, however, finds out that only about 23 and 11 per cent of the respondents had been benefitted from the fair price medicine shops and fair price diagnostic centres respectively. From such figures the failure of the AITC government's intervention in the health sector is apparent. The score card of the AITC government as far as maintaining the law and order situation and improving public transportation services, as reveals Table 5.5, is also not encouraging since a majority of the respondents had failed to trace any significant change in this direction.

In addition to these initiatives, the incumbent AITC government of West Bengal has been making concerted effort to consolidate its constituency among the different cross-sections of the West Bengal electorates. Among these, three sections, namely, the rural, the women and the Muslims deserve special attention here. These three sections have remained the chief architects of the electoral success of the AITC since the Lok Sabha Election of 2009. A brief analysis of the policies and welfare schemes undertaken by the AITC government in West Bengal to cater the aspirations of these sections is pertinent here to understand the relation between these programmes and the nature of party competition. This is important even more to understand the sociological antecedents of particular electoral outcomes.

As reveals the Lokniti CSDS Assembly Election Studies data set, the AITC in alliance with the INC secured 44 per cent of the rural votes in the 2009 Lok Sabha Election. In the Assembly Election of 2011 maintaining the same alliance it increased the share of its rural votes by 4 per cent to reach 48 per cent. Contesting the 2014 Lok Sabha Election alone, it has secured 41 per cent of the rural votes. From the figures it is apparent that the AITC has been developing a strong support base among the rural areas of West Bengal since 2009. If the anti-land acquisition movement led by Mamata Banerjee at Singur, Nandigram paved the way for penetration of the AITC among the rural populace, especially the farmers till 2011, then the adoption of certain new schemes and effective implementation of the existing ones after assuming the state power in 2011, have been instrumental in consolidating it. Among some others, the key to it might lie in the implementation of the Mahatma Gandhi National Rural Employment Guarantee Act (MGNREGA) by the AITC government. The NES 2014 data reveal that compared to schemes such as Indira/Rajiv Awas Yojana, free medical facilities (National Rural Health Mission) and Pension (Old Age/Widow/Disability etc.), the number of beneficiaries under MGNREGA stands much higher in West Bengal (almost 27%). In the Assembly Election of 2016, about 31 per cent of those who have heard about the policy, reported to have benefitted out of it. Interestingly, among the beneficiaries, almost 60 per cent, as reveals the NES 2014 data set, give the credit for it to the local politicians. The influence of policies and welfare schemes on the nature of party competition at the grass-roots level possibly finds its concrete expression here. It might well be the case that a large section of the beneficiaries do not properly know whether MGNREGA is a policy of the central or the state government. To them the local politicians who are implementing it matter most. While determining the electoral choices, naturally, the political affiliation of these local politicians comes to exercise greater influence on the electorates.

The AITC government of West Bengal has introduced a large number of schemes to improve the socio-economic conditions of the people. With an aim to extend its support base primarily to the rural areas, a good number of such schemes are meant for the rural population. As reflected by the West Bengal Assembly Election Study 2016 data set, the most successful one among these schemes is the Khadya Sathi Scheme since almost 70 per cent of the sampled electorates have reported to have benefitted out of this. Khadya Sathi is one of the flagship programmes of the West Bengal government, implemented by the Food and Supplies Department. It appears to be a combined scheme of NFSA (National Food Security Act) of the Central Government and the RKSY (Rajya Khadya Suraksha Yojana) designed by the state government of West Bengal. The main purpose of this project is to ensure food and nutrition by supply of food in an affordable subsidized price. Popularly, the programme is well known as Rice at ₹2 per kg.

There are about 8.87 crore beneficiaries of the scheme at present in West Bengal. Among these the NFSA beneficiaries are 6.01 crores as mentions the Department of Food and Supplies, Government of West Bengal (2019), RKSY programme has two components RKSY–I and RKSY–II (Department of Food and Supplies, Government of West Bengal 2017). Under RKSY–I, the beneficiaries get rice and wheat at ₹2 per kg and there are about 1.5 crore beneficiaries of this scheme. About 1.4 crore beneficiaries, under the RKSY–II, get rice and wheat at ₹13 per kg and ₹9 per kg respectively as reports the Department of Food and Supplies, Government of West Bengal (2019). Thus, almost

7.47 crore beneficiaries get rice and wheat at ₹2 per kg. The prices of rice and wheat under NFSA stand at ₹3 and ₹2 per kg, respectively. The state government, hence, provides subsidy of ₹1 to rice and sells it at ₹2 per kg. The NFSA adopted by the UPA–II government at the Centre on 10 September 2013, although is not typically designed for the rural people, but a considerable emphasis on the rural area is there since it purports to cover 75 per cent of the rural population in contrast to 50 per cent of the urban population of the country, as the gazette notification of the Government of India (2013) stipulates. The identification of the beneficiaries under the NFSA is left to the states. The government of West Bengal, has selected people of the Junglemahals, hills, Aila-affected areas, farmers of Singur, tea garden workers and the members of the extremely backward Toto tribe of North Bengal to be covered under the scheme as declared by West Bengal Chief Minister Mamata Banerjee on 27 January 2016 (*Financial Express* 2019). The selection of the beneficiaries is suggestive, since the socio-economically backward rural people of the Junglemahals, the hills of Darjeeling and the farmers of Singur had been the chief architects of Mamata Banerjee's electoral success of 2011.

In the year 2015 the AITC government has introduced the Sabooj Sathi scheme which aims to distribute bicycles to the students of class IX to XII in all government run/government aided/government sponsored schools to encourage students in higher education and to reduce drop outs.[1] The government has a target to distribute 40 lakh bicycles under the scope of the scheme. The students of the rural area are expected to benefit more out of this where the scope of public transport system is rather less developed or a majority of whom cannot afford the price of it. Although not at the scale of Khadya Sathi, Sabooj Sathi scheme is also attaining success as almost 28 per cent of the sampled electorate (CSDS 2016 West Bengal Assembly Election Study) or any of their family members had received bicycles from the scheme. Such a scheme can be considered as an attempt of the AITC to bring the party competition in the rural areas of West Bengal more to its favour.

[1] Source: https://wb.gov.in/portal/web/guest/sabooj-sathi (accessed on 25 February 2019).

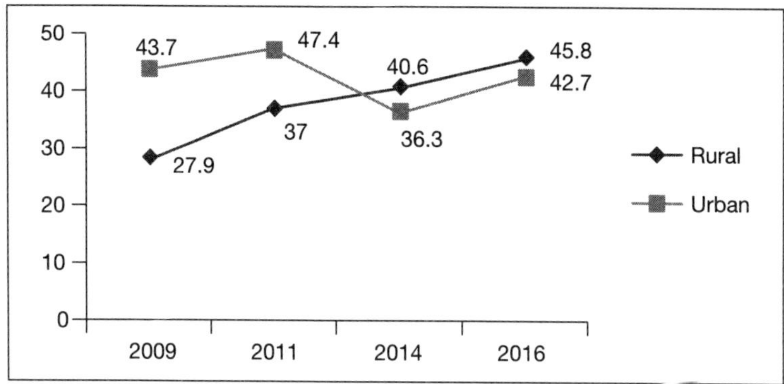

Figure 5.1 *Rural and Urban Vote Share of AITC in West Bengal (2009–2016)*

Source: CSDS Data Unit, NES 2009 and 2014; West Bengal Assembly Election Study 2011 and 2016.

Along with Khadya Sathi and Sabooj Sathi, there are some other schemes of the AITC government which lay considerable emphasis on the rural, primarily, the agricultural population.[2] Figure 5.1 clearly reveals the electoral dividend which these rural centric schemes have paid to the AITC in different elections in the state since 2009.

Since 2009 the AITC has been successfully increasing its popularity among women. This is evident from the 12 per cent increase in its women vote share in the Lok Sabha Election of 2014 compared to that of 2009. In 2016 Assembly Election by registering 47.1 per cent of the women's votes it improved its tally among the women electorates by almost 5 per cent compared to that of the 2014 Lok Sabha Election.[3] Considered in the background of the neglect of women's issues by successive LF governments (Chatterjee and Basu 2009, 2017; Ray 1998), the pro-women schemes adopted by the AITC government at present, may be a positive factor for it. The most important scheme in this direction is the Kanyashree Prakalpa. Launched in 2013 this scheme aims to reduce child marriages and school dropout rate among

[2] Details of the schemes are available at: https://sarkariyojana.com/west-bengal/ (accessed on 26 February 2019).

[3] Source: NES 2014 and West Bengal Assembly Election Study 2016.

girls from poor families by incentivizing them with scholarships. This is a conditional cash transfer scheme designed by the Department of Women Development and Social Welfare, Government of West Bengal. Recently, the amount of annual scholarship under this scheme has been increased, and most importantly, the conditionality pertaining to family income has also been withdrawn to bring all the girls studying in government schools or government aided schools under the scheme's coverage (Banerjee 2018). Presently, there are 17,402 registered institutions, more than 1.52 crore enrolled applicants, about 1.49 crore sanctioned applications with more than 56 lakh unique beneficiaries under the scheme.[4] As a mark of recognition, the government of West Bengal received the highest prize, 'United Nations Public Service Award' for the Kanyashree Prakalpa on 23 June 2017 (*Outlook* 2017). In spite of all these, this scheme of the government of West Bengal is yet to achieve the success which other of its programme Khadya Sathi has achieved. Among the sampled electorates of the West Bengal Assembly Election Study 2016, 23.52 per cent have reported to get benefit out of the Kanyashree scheme as against almost 70 per cent of the Khadya Sathi scheme.

The AITC government in West Bengal has also launched a scheme for distributing bicycles to Adivasi girl students from 'Left Wing Extremism affected' blocks of the Junglemahal region (Chatterjee and Basu 2017). There is yet another women-focused scheme named Rupashree. Under this scheme all girls whose family income from all the sources does not exceed ₹1.5 lakh annually, will get a one-time financial assistance of ₹25,000 at the time of their marriage.[5] The AITC apparently has earned considerable political mileage through such schemes aimed at improving the status of women, especially those of the poor families belonging to the backward regions. This has enabled it to overcome several allegations raised by the opposition parties about the deteriorating women's safety conditions in West Bengal. Despite the fact that West Bengal ranked second in 2016,

[4] Source: https://www.wbkanyashree.gov.in/kp_4.0/index.php (accessed on 25 February 2019).

[5] Source: https://sarkariyojana.com/west-bengal/ (accessed on 29 July 2019).

only behind Uttar Pradesh, as far as the rate and incidences of crime against women is concerned (NCRB 2016), still it was not a major issue here in the 2016 Assembly Election. Along with the NCRB data, the NES 2014 data also noted that a majority, about 46 per cent, of the respondents believed that women's safety had deteriorated during the last five years in West Bengal. The same data also pointed out that about 68 per cent of them believed that Mamata Banerjee had failed in ensuring safety of women in the state. Interestingly, the West Bengal Assembly Election Study 2016 data, like the NES 2014 data, show that issues related to women's safety such as discrimination against women, poor treatment of women and sexual harassment of women were major issues for a negligible portion of the voters. This is a classic example of the effect of welfare schemes on conditioning the trend of party competition. In spite of all their concerns about the deteriorating safety conditions of the women under the AITC rule, they came to regard Mamata Banerjee as the most efficient leader to address the issue of women's empowerment. Perhaps, the everyday experience of gender discrimination reinforced by poverty make the poor dependent upon the welfare schemes through which they can gain some material benefits. The party or the coalition which ensures these turns out to be their natural electoral choice. The overall conditions of deteriorating safety conditions for women, possibly, become secondary to them in such a deplorable condition of social living. This can be clearly seen from the steady growth of popularity of the AITC and the decline of the Left among the women in the various elections they contested in the state since 2009 (Figure 5.2).

Besides the women, the AITC government has also undertaken a number of schemes for the socio-economic upliftment of the Muslims, such as the monthly stipend for the Clerics, building up hospitals for them and some other which have already been mentioned in Chapter 4. Considered against the socio-economic and cultural backwardness of the Muslim population in West Bengal during the LF rule, as mentions the Sachar Committee Report (Government of India 2006), these have so far paid rich electoral dividend to the AITC. To understand the consolidation of Muslim votes by the AITC, Table 5.6 which depicts the voting pattern of the Muslims since the Assembly Election of 2006 is necessary.

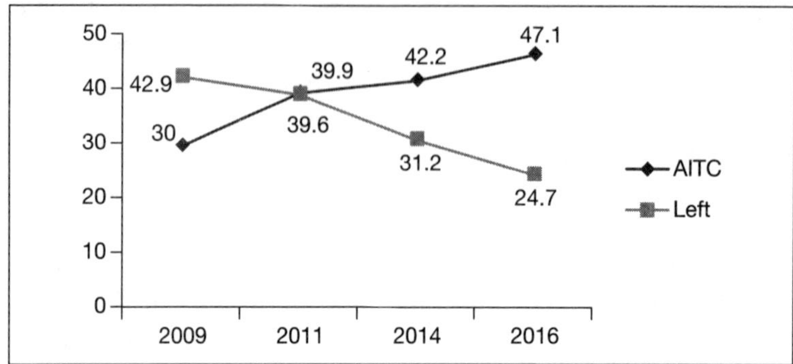

Figure 5.2 *Women Vote Share of the AITC and the Left (2009–2016)*

Source: CSDS *Data Unit*, NES 2009, 2014 and West Bengal Assembly Election Study 2011, 2016.

Table 5.6 *Muslim Vote Share of Different Political Parties in the Assembly Election since 2006*

	Assembly Elections		
Parties/Coalitions	*2006*	*2011*	*2016*
Left	46	42	24
AITC	20	35	51
BJP	0	2	6
INC	26	15	14

Source: CSDS Data Unit, West Bengal Assembly Election Studies 2006, 2011 and 2016.
Note: All figures are in per cent.

Table 5.6 reveals that during the three successive assembly elections since 2006, the AITC has managed to enhance its share of Muslim votes more than the other contesting parties. It has not only secured the majority of Muslim votes, but also increased its tally by almost 31 per cent in the Assembly Election of 2016, compared to that of the Assembly Election of 2006. That the AITC has gained considerable advantage in the party competition out of its support base among the Muslims, can be revealed by the fact of almost 22 per cent decline in the LF's share of Muslim votes during the same period. AITC's increasing popularity among the Muslims viewed against the declining electoral popularity of both the Left and the INC among them might be indicative of the emerging nature of political dynamics in West Bengal within the minority.

Such a gain in the Muslim votes of the AITC however appears to have a direct relation with the welfare programmes/schemes taken up by the AITC government for their socio-economic upliftment. What is important here is to discuss the influence of these strategies on politics in general, which in turn shapes the electoral preferences of the Muslims. Critics along with other political parties opposing the AITC readily term these as move by the AITC to attract the Muslim electorates. Not only them, a sizeable section of the sampled respondents (about 40%) of the West Bengal Assembly Election Study 2016, had also expressed the similar opinion. Even before, Narendra Modi during one of his electoral campaign for the Lok Sabha Election 2014, in West Bengal alleged Mamata Banerjee and the state government under her command for extending undue privileges to the Muslims. Modi's charges against Ms Banerjee should be judged in the context of post-Partition West Bengal, where a good number of Muslims had migrated and still are migrating from erstwhile East Pakistan and present day Bangladesh. Terming these Muslim immigrants as illegal infiltrators, Modi and the BJP wants them to be deported to Bangladesh. The BJP comes down heavily on Mamata Banerjee for 'spreading a red carpet' (Ghosh 2014) for them. From the point of view of secularism, what is of critical importance here is the distinction made by the BJP between Hindu and Muslim migrants from Bangladesh while the former would be accommodated and the latter deported (NDTV 2014). Obviously, this stand of the BJP appeared to be a threat to the Muslim population of Bengal in general and to those among them who have migrated from Bangladesh, in particular. This provided an opportunity for the AITC to cover some extra miles in the field of inter-party competition of Indian democracy. Mamata Banerjee severely criticized Modi for dividing the electorates along religious lines to rip electoral benefits. As a direct offshoot of this she could get hold of the Muslim sentiments of West Bengal and, as the NES 2014 data set reflects, even topped the list among all the prominent leaders of different political parties, contesting the 2014 election, as the one best suited for the betterment of Muslims in the country. This proves the influence of welfare schemes or programmes in creating an almost polarized party competition situation in West Bengal with the BJP expected to be backed by the Hindus while the Muslims rallying behind Mamata Banerjee-led AITC. Such polarization of the electorates along religious lines, in spite of their relative cost benefit outcome for the competing parties, is indeed a concern for secular democracy, a dominant aspiration of the Indian nation state. The weak presence of the Left parties, with their ideological stress to transcend this divide, might have some implication for the crystallization of such divisions.

The schemes, in spite of their effectiveness to the AITC in building up its electoral constituencies, run the risk of becoming discriminatory. It is not only due to the alleged politically selective implementation of the schemes. Fundamentally, any scheme or programme, however impartially it is implemented, for its in-build criteria of selection of beneficiaries might create a feeling of deprivation among the excluded people. They may question the validity of the criteria for inclusion and exclusion laid down in the scheme. Moreover, the schemes are developed in tune with the existing social cleavages. As these cleavages are indeed innumerable in number, so it is perhaps impossible for any government to include all these under the coverage of its welfare schemes. Such a feeling of relative deprivation, as mentioned in the previous chapter, was expressed by K. B. Yogi, president, Gorkha Yogi Kalyan Sangh to accuse the AITC government for not granting a development council for the 'backward' Yogi community, while the same for some other relatively 'advanced' communities was formed. The feeling of relative deprivation among salaried persons in West Bengal emerging out of the lesser rate of Dearness Allowance (DA), which they are getting compared to the central and state government employees in some other states, is a pointer to this. Different organizations of the state government employees have been fighting a legal battle for quite some time to resolve the issue. Moreover, the reluctance of Mamata Banerjee to implement the benefits of the Seventh Pay Commission in West Bengal, as note Chatterjee and Basu (2017), has also been augmenting such feeling of relative deprivation. Hence, feeling of deprivation becomes an unavoidable consequence of such an approach of welfare, which might have its influence on the existing as well as evolving pattern of party competition. This is evident from

Table 5.7 *Party Preference of the Beneficiaries and Non-beneficiaries of Different Schemes of AITC Government in West Bengal*

Schemes	Benefitted or Not	Voted AITC	Voted LF
Kanyashree	Benefitted	53.8	18.9
	Not benefitted	41.7	29.3
Yubashree	Benefitted	69.6	10
	Not benefitted	43.1	27.2
Shikshasree	Benefitted	61.1	9.2
	Not benefitted	42.2	29.5
Sabooj Sathi	Benefitted	56.4	18.5
	Not benefitted	41.4	28.2
Khadya Sathi	Benefitted	50	24.3
	Not benefitted	38	28

Source: CSDS Data Unit, West Bengal Assembly Election Study 2016.

Table 5.7, constructed out of the CSDS West Bengal Assembly Election Study 2016 data set. It depicts the political preferences of the beneficiaries vis-à-vis the non-beneficiaries of various schemes adopted by the Mamata Banerjee-led AITC government in West Bengal.

As in the election of 2016 the LF was the chief competitor of the AITC, so the table restricts the pattern of electoral preferences between these two parties or coalition only. Here it can be observed that the majority of the beneficiaries of the various schemes opted for the AITC while voting. This is quite expected, but surprisingly, a relatively good portion of them also voted for the opposition particularly, the LF. This was evident in the three important programmes, that is, Kanyashree, Sabooj Sathi and Khadya Sathi, where the LF secured more than 18 per cent of the votes of the beneficiaries of the programmes. Among the non-beneficiaries, the support for the AITC experienced an almost steep decline marked by a noteworthy rise in the support for the Left parties. It is interesting to note that among the beneficiaries almost 55 per cent reported to receive the help of local party leaders in getting the benefits while about 28 per cent were helped by the sarpanch or the pancahayat pradhans.[6] Taken together, more than 80 per cent of the beneficiaries, as the data suggests, were assisted by the politically influential persons of the local level in receiving the benefits of the schemes. To some analysts this situation closely resembles clientelist politics where 'parties and their local agents link access to government services and benefits from government welfare schemes' (Schneider 2014, para 1) to ascertain the electoral choices of the people. It is quite natural for the non-beneficiaries to vote against the AITC but it should be more concerned with that segment of the beneficiaries who had voted for the Left parties. Perhaps, the AITC needs to be more vigilant to monitor the defectors among the beneficiaries, other than the traditional supporters, who have opted for the LF. But that requires a well-knit organization with a meaningful presence in the daily lives of the people, what compared to the BJP and which the CPI (M) once had, the AITC does not seem to have as of now. On the contrary, news of in-fighting, factionalism and corruption of the party workers are regularly coming up. Mamata Banerjee, in her several public meetings had warned the party workers to stay away from these. Her apprehension about the corrupt practices of the party workers was not ungrounded, since almost 53 per cent of the sampled respondents of the West Bengal Assembly Election Study 2016 considered the AITC government to be corrupt. To counter the charges of corruption put up by the opposition on her party leaders on account of their alleged involvement in the Saradha scam and Narada sting operation, during the run up to the 2016 Assembly Election she appealed, 'I am the candidate in all 294 seats, cast vote for me' (Ghosh 2016). This was indeed a desperate attempt on her part to keep herself ahead of the party, the image of which might has been blotted by the corrupt practices and in-fighting of the workers. That this has been blotting the image of Mamata Banerjee was clear from the decline in her popularity. This could be revealed from the trend of her declining choice as the most preferred chief minister of West Bengal from 44.3 per cent in 2011 Assembly Election to 38 per cent in 2016.[7]

[6] Source: Compiled from West Bengal Assembly Election Study 2016.

[7] Source: West Bengal Assembly Election Study 2011 and 2016.

The extent of the feeling of deprivation, implicit in these politics, can be gauged from the fact that among the non-receivers of the benefits of all the schemes mentioned above, the support of the AITC not only shrunk but it also went below 44.91 per cent, which the party could secure in the 2016 Assembly Election in West Bengal as a whole. Conversely, the support of the Left parties among them registered almost an equal increase to take it above 26.4 per cent, its overall vote share in the 2016 election (source: the Election Commission of India). In the case of the Khadya Sathi scheme, the LF's vote share crossed its all West Bengal count but the rise was not that steep compared to other schemes. If this trend continues, then further swelling in the support base of the LF among the non-beneficiaries may pose challenge to the electoral supremacy of the AITC. This, however, is an overall concern in the macrosociology of power as argues Lehman (1969), '...if the power-wielder's opponents "call" his threats or promises somewhat regularly, he may have to spend more and more units of resources for each new validation of his credibility' (p. 458). For any populist welfare regime, as in the case of the AITC at present in West Bengal, the need of such continual enhancement of inducement is felt even more. This calls for an escalation of the range and scope of the benefits offered to the electorates by the incumbent AITC government to reduce the scale of the feeling of deprivation. Given the financial constraints under which the state governments have to operate within the Indian Union, this might often be problematic. In the 2019 general election this has been felt particularly in the Junglemahal region. Despite all the effort of Mamata Banerjee since the *poriborton* in 2011 to nurture this region, in the 2019 general election AITC's vote share here has registered a decline of almost 5 per cent compared to that of 2014, as reflects the statistics of the Election Commission of India. Negating Mamata Banerjee's claim of Junglemahal's development represented through her rhetoric *Junglemahal Haschhe* (Junglemahal is laughing), the BJP in the 2019 election not only has secured 48 per cent of votes, but won all the five seats of this region, namely Purulia, Jhargram (ST), Bankura, Medinipur, Bishnupur (SC) as well.

The effort of the AITC to build up its own constituency, notwithstanding, some critiques consider the pro-poor thrust of these schemes to be the proof of the ubiquity and indispensability of Left politics in general. In fact, some of them are of the opinion that it is indeed very difficult for any political party or coalition to denounce the substance of Left politics in West Bengal since it possesses a historically-developed distinct Leftist political culture (Kumar and Guha 2014). Even Mamata Banerjee, during the campaigning for the 2011 Assembly Election, remarked that except some, not all communists were bad (Biswas 2011). She even claims to be the Left (Samaddar 2018). This was possibly due to her much-projected simple lifestyle which had remained an authentic representation of the common people, mostly the poor folk. Banerjee (2010, 21) argues, 'She projects herself as the girl next door, wrapped in a crumpled sari, ready to help her neighbours, and visiting every corner of West Bengal to improve the lot of the poor!' Traces of Left political orientation could also be found in her political approach and rhetoric. Through her opposition to FDI in retail, issues of pension funds, protecting the state's right in the Lokpal Bill and some other typical agenda of the Left, she could get hold of the sentiments of that segment of the Left supporters who gradually were becoming disillusioned with the compromising outlook of the CPI (M) and other Left parties (EPW 2012).

However, to trace the imprint of this political gesture of Mamata Banerjee on the transformation and evolution of party competition in post-LF West Bengal, one needs to consider the role of values and interests, the two chief coordinates of political competition in democratic polity. Tavits and Letki (2013, 247) consider interest-based competition to represent the 'classic economic Left-Right dimension of social protectionism versus market liberalism', while value-oriented competition accords priority to the issues of culture, identity, populism and other related non-economic factors. Since the policies, schemes or programmes of any party reflect the existing social cleavages: divisions or the different strata of the social stratification, so party competition as shaped and expressed through the welfare schemes are the direct manifestations of the social fault lines represented by the cleavages. Party competition in Indian democracy represents both the interest and the value dimensions since the nearly two centuries of colonial rule created some deep-rooted socio-economic as well as cultural cleavages into the structure of Indian society. The policies adopted by the successive governments in the post-Independence India have so far failed to bridge these inequalities, while the adoption of the neoliberal economic framework in the early 1990s might have helped in their augmentation. The Left parties, especially in West Bengal, particularly for the Left political heritage existing here, act more on the interest-based competition to cater to the aspirations of the economically deprived populace. The ideological deviation of the Left, as has been manifested in its growing insensitivity to the marginalized people, has taken away from it the important resource to engage in the contemporary arena of party competition. The reorienting and reorganizing bid of the Left parties, particularly its dominant partner the CPI (M), in West Bengal today must receive the necessary ideological reinforcement to reappear as an important participant in the arena of the political competition.

The AITC since 2011, keeping the LF behind, has engaged itself as a dominant partner in the domain of party competition. Through the schemes, discussed above, it tries to cater to the interests of the underprivileged, poor and backward sections of the population. So far these have successfully contributed in the expansion of the AITC's support base. But rooms of apprehensions are indeed there, since without the backing of a sound pro-poor ideological standpoint these schemes might turn out to be unorganized largesse. In that case, these very schemes might become antithetical to the goal of development through self-reliance. The lack of ideology of the AITC towards this direction has been reported by many scholars and critiques (Banerjee 2010; Datta-Ray 2016; De 2017). The apparent replacement of ideology with opportunism and convenience has its consequence in vitiating the interest-based party competition. With the entry of the BJP with its value-based agenda, focused on the identity of Hindutva, the two dimensions of party competition are actually competing to gain the much desired support of the electorates of Bengal. Besides catering to the economic interest of the marginalized people through the schemes, Mamata Banerjee is also seen to be busy in snatching away the substance of BJP's value-based agenda. For this she is making every attempt to prove herself a devoted Hindu. To showcase the 'pure'

Hindu identity of Bengali Hindus she comments, 'We worship Durga, BJP sells Ram' (*Times of India* 2018). The same attempt was evident in AITC's decision to observe Ram Navami in 2018. Similarly, her appeals to Matua and Namasudra identity, Rajbansi identity, identities of different hill communities in Darjeeling and so on might serve the proof of this.

This oscillation of the AITC between the anchors of interest and value-based party competition has rendered enough volatility in the domain of party competition in West Bengal. Such fluctuation between the two almost opposed genres of party competition perhaps is a reflection of the week ideological orientation of the AITC. While the CPI (M) lost much of its political relevance due to its detachment from the Left ideological discourse, its ardent opponent, the AITC is approaching the difficult terrain of party competition devoid of any definite ideology to support its stand. This is a possible source through which opportunism may creep in the politics of AITC. The signs are already there. Mamata Banerjee has been attempting to cover this up through her charisma. Putting oneself over and above the party to run a one-person show in the political dynamics of a multi-party democracy raises pertinent questions about its sustainability. With passage of time her charisma getting routinized, this might give birth to authoritarianism. Allegation in this direction has already been there. Mahasweta Devi, famous novelist, the Magsaysay and Padma Vibhushan awardee, and one of the prominent supporters of Mamata Banerjee's call for *poriborton*, criticized the AITC government as 'fascist' for not granting permission to the APDR (Association for the Protection of Democratic Rights), a democratic rights organization to hold a rally in Kolkata in November 2011 (*Hindustan Times* 2011). Ms Banerjee, with utmost decency in showing respect to the novelist's age, refused to accept her criticism. Some other similar types of allegation have also been there. People of West Bengal, had been witness to these sorts of authoritarian behaviour from the CPI (M) leaders during the fag end of their 34-years long rule. Ideological dilution of the party resulting in the disintegration of the party-society had been responsible for this.

At present these issues are not bothering the AITC since it is riding on a massive popular support. The recently held panchayat election in

West Bengal in 2018 has also more or less confirmed it. In this election, marred by considerable violence and allegations of malpractices raised by the opposition parties, the AITC won almost 96 per cent, 87 per cent and 78 per cent of the seats in the zila parishad, panchayat samiti and the gram panchayats respectively as reports the West Bengal State Election Commission (Source: http://www.wbsec.org/PublicPages/Home.aspx). The various welfare schemes, as discussed earlier, have been instrumental for this. In the context of democratic politics of West Bengal today, the opposition parties primarily the CPI (M) and the INC, already enfeebled by the populist measures of the AITC, are finding it increasingly difficult to articulate their voices as opposition. This is perhaps paving the way for the entry of the BJP in West Bengal politics. Enjoying the advantage of being in power at the Centre since 2014, it is making concerted effort to occupy the opposition political space in West Bengal by capitalizing on the weaknesses of the CPI (M) and the INC. So far the BJP's record is mixed one. In 2014 Lok Sabha Election it won two seats securing 16.8 per cent of the votes, which went down to 10.2 per cent in the Assembly Election of 2016 (source: Election Commission of India). In this election it could win only three assembly seats. But in the by-elections held since 2016 it has been improving its position by making its claim to be the main opposition party in West Bengal stronger. In the recently held Panchayat Election of 2018, although far behind the AITC, it remained ahead of the LF and the INC to finish as the runner-up.

In contrast to the rural areas, the BJP is appearing to be a major threat to the ruling AITC in the urban areas. In the 2014 Lok Sabha Elections it secured almost 25 per cent of the urban votes which was 19 per cent more than what it secured in 2009 Lok Sabha Elections (NES 2009 and 2014). The same data source indicates that although the AITC secured 36 per cent of the urban votes in 2014, but the concern perhaps was the 8 per cent decline of its urban vote share compared to the 2009. The BJP's rising curve got somehow thwarted in the Municipal Elections of 2015 and the 2016 Assembly Election. But again it seemed to regain the momentum to some extent as was evident from the results of the Panchayat Election in 2018 and the by-elections since 2016. In the Lok Sabha Election of 2019 the momentum gained enough strength since in this election the BJP, beside securing 40.2 per cent of votes (a gain of almost 23% from 2014), also managed to win 18 parliamentary seats (a gain of 16 seats compared to 2014). Keeping into consideration the continuing declining tone of the LF and the INC and the simultaneous gain of the BJP, it would not be too farfetched to expect it to appear as an important participant in the domain of party competition in West Bengal in the days to come.

CONCLUSION

The politics of West Bengal since the 1990s stands as a classic instance of the unfolding of democratic politics in the new global order. This was the period when the collapse of communism in Soviet Russia, bringing an end to the cold war, left the developing countries in Asia, Africa and Latin America with very little option but to accept the Washington Consensus as the most preferred path of their development. Designed by the IMF, the World Bank and the United States Department of the Treasury, this Consensus during the 1980s recommended free market operation and reduction in state involvement, the principal doctrines of neoliberal globalization as the panacea for the problem of economic backwardness of the developing countries. India, accepting the Consensus agreed to undertake the SAP and adopted its new economic policy in 1991 accordingly. The LF spearheaded by the CPI (M) had to face a steep challenge on account of such a change in the macroeconomic policy of the national government. Although neoliberalism talks about greater economic freedom, but it is a political project as well since it advocates limited role of the state as a necessary condition to maintain and uphold the free market spirit. Communists throughout the globe for greater emphasis on centralized state and wider scope of the public sector found themselves at odds with the tenets of neoliberal reform and began to negotiate, adjust, compromise and/or counter its prescriptions. The LF government in West Bengal was also no exception to this trend. The redefinition of the activities of the state, restricting its scope, presented a great political obstacle to the CPI (M) to carry forward its much professed state-guided reform of the economic and political structure of West Bengal. The ensuing dialogue of the CPI (M) with the political economy of neoliberalism and its influence on policies of the state opened up some new concerns and challenges, having far-reaching implication for the future course of democratic politics in the new world order.

But the process of the institutional reform by the CPI (M) soon had to face severe obstruction emanating from its endogenous dynamics. There were some important dimensions of it. First, after a decade of implementation of the land reform programme, specifically during the late 1980s and early 1990s, it got exhausted. It was not that the land redistribution programme covered all the landless people or the recorded tenants were conferred with ownership rights of their land under tenancy. There was also no concerted attempt at cooperativization either. To achieve these, a greater level of revolutionary commitment was required from the CPI (M), which perhaps due to its growing acclimatization with the structure of parliamentary democracy, the CPI (M) could not exhibit. In such a situation the process of political reform lost its economic imperative. Second, the ideological emphasis of the CPI (M) on all-peasant unity brought the middle and relatively rich peasant within the fold of the party along with the poor peasants and the landless labourers. This section of the middle peasantry along with their rich brethren was fundamentally antithetical to the interest and goal of the land reform.

For this ideological metamorphosis, the CPI (M) could not organize any viable opposition to neoliberal economic restructuring. Moreover, the middle class within the organization, expecting greater economic opportunity associated with market reform, also prevented the CPI (M) from voicing opposition against it. As it happened in other states, in West Bengal also the adoption of new economic policy by the central government in the 1990s resulted in the declining income from agriculture. The situation became more vulnerable since the condition of industrial development in the state was also in a deplorable condition. There was little effort on the part of the CPI (M)-led LF government to utilize the agricultural surplus gained in the 1980s for industrial development. To break the jinx, after a bit of initial hesitation, the CPI (M), during the mid-1990s recognized the importance of private capital investment for industrial development. The process which began during the end of the chief ministerial tenure of Jyoti Basu acquired greater momentum under that of Buddhadeb Bhattacharya. Under Bhattacharya, the CPI (M) became an apologist of global capital. A communist party with its supposed ideological anchor in the conflict between labour and capital was now transformed to seek compromise between the two.

Judging from the standpoint of a communist party committed to the cause of people's democratic revolution, the recent position of the CPI (M), quite obviously was a deviation. People were getting disappointed with the CPI (M) for many reasons. Most important among these being economic stagnation of the state, the sense of invincibility growing out of long stint at power, arrogance of the party workers in dealing with the people at large, conflating the civic space of the government by the party and encroachment of the party into the autonomous territory of the civil society and so on. Although, the CPI (M) advocated for decentralization, participatory governance, democratization and so on, but in reality all these remained only as rhetoric. Practically, too much party control robbed of the independent agencies of the civil society, community and the locality. Subverting the cause of grassroots democracy, the encroachment of the informal social space of the locality by the party created a condition of colonization of locality.

That the resultant dissatisfaction of the masses over the CPI (M) was increasing could be gauged from the continuously increasing electoral support for the opposition AITC since its inception in 1998. But that was perhaps not enough to dislodge the LF government. It continued to rule the state primarily on the basis of its rural support base developed out of its earlier effort at reforming the economic and political structure of the rural societies. The rural electorates, being apprehensive about the AITC for its landlord connection (Lofgen 2016), went on to support the LF. Convincingly winning the 2006 West Bengal Assembly Election, the LF government seriously undertook the industrialization drive. Considering its victory in the assembly election as people's mandate for industrialization they invited Tata Motors at Singur to set up their small car industry there and the Indonesia-based Salim Group to develop a chemical hub at Nandigram. In the subsequent years there was considerable resistance of the people to protest against the acquisition of land for these industries followed by the counter resistance by the state. The LF government in its rush to go for large-scale industrialization under private capital experienced significant decline in its legitimacy, while the AITC, under the firebrand leadership of Mamata Banerjee, led the anti-land acquisition struggles from the front and enhanced its acceptability to the overall people of West Bengal. The declining legitimacy of the LF and the simultaneous increase in the popularity of the AITC ultimately resulted in the wresting of state power by the latter from the former in the Assembly Election of 2011.

The incidences of Singur, Nandigram and Lalgarh raise serious concerns regarding democracy and sustenance of democratic institutions in the new global order. As an ideology, neoliberal globalization, as experience shows, is of full potential to increase economic inequality and socio-cultural vulnerability. Development under neoliberalism is exclusively aimed at earning profit for the industrial and business corporations from capital-intensive industrialization projects. Reduction in state involvement, as the proponents of the Washington Consensus prescribe, thus boils down to the protection of the interest of the corporations. Economic liberalization in this perspective implies allowing the corporations to gradually appropriate the public assets such as land, minerals and water. While limited state involvement creates favourable conditions for unrestricted capital accumulation, the ideology of free market marked by unfettered competition is put forward to provide justification for this. Ultimately it results in farther impoverishment for the already poverty-ridden mass of the developing third world. This top-down and technocratic development approach, as argues Escobar (1995), is fundamentally exclusionary in nature, since it excludes, '…what development was supposed to be all about: people' (p. 44). This makes the current development regime undemocratic. The replacement of the value of liberal democracy by liberal marketocracy (rule of the market) poses fundamental question for the sustenance of democratic institutions such as the state and the political parties. The philosophy of free market becomes incompatible with the ethos of democracy since the former increases inequality, reduces the scope of social justice, which the latter promises to reduce or eliminate. The end of history as declares Fukuyama (1989) might be a signal of the beginning of another history where the struggle would be to liberate liberalism from the aggression of neoliberalism.

The concept of democracy, thus, occupies a highly-contested space in the entire discourse of neoliberalism. Such fundamental contradiction by vitiating the democratic substance of popularly-elected governments creates an overall environment of democratic and/or trust deficit. The decline of LF rule in West Bengal, besides having its idiosyncrasies as reflected in its detachment from the people at large, from the social movements at the grassroots and excessive party control of the state administration has also largely been due to this. Such a trust deficit was felt in the case of Singur. In a representative democracy it is quite natural for the people to expect protection from the government in matters affecting their lives and livelihood. But in the land acquisition drive at Singur, the LF government failed to meet this expectation of the displaced people.

The feeling of trust deficit reached its peak in Singur on 2 December 2006 when under the patrolling of 6,000 policemen, combat force and rapid action force the acquired land was fenced off. There was a huge protest by the villagers. The police lathi charged the protesting villagers. The police action resulted in severely injuring about 100 villagers including women. This was one of the classic examples of application of brutal force in the implementation of 'development'. But the paradox was that it was done under the aegis of the representative government, elected by the same people whom now it violently coerced. Although for the architects of neoliberal development it was 'lesser' involvement of the state, but for the affected people it was nothing short of a highly proactive state duty bound to uphold the cause of 'development', which to them was basically harmful for their livelihood. The physical fencing off of the land for the industry perhaps stood as a symbol of fencing off development from the people. As the state acted as a facilitator in the whole process of excluding the people from 'development', so the question about its legitimacy would naturally arise. By forcing the people to sacrifice their land for the profit of the multinational capital, the state also under neoliberalism, appeared to be undemocratic. In Singur the primary allegation was about the action of the state in forcibly acquiring the land of the peasants, the only means of their subsistence. Herein lies the fundamental contradiction between neoliberalism and its professed policy of democratization via participation. The basic question thus, is it at all possible for a democratic government to sustain under neoliberalism or to put it more directly, is democracy compatible with the ideology of development under neoliberalism?

As the direct offshoot of people's disapproval of the manner in which the LF government was approaching the issue of land acquisition, the AITC and INC alliance came to power in West Bengal by winning 226 out of 294 seats in the Assembly Election of 2011. The AITC alone won 184 seats. The ascendance of the AITC to the power of West Bengal marks the change in the dominant party system represented by the CPI (M) for a relatively longer period. Although the events at Singur and Nandigram might have some facilitating influence on this, but the process actually began during the early part of the present century. The AITC with its rigid anti-CPI (M) stand had been instrumental in breaking the dominance of the CPI (M), as the results of different elections in the state since 2001 reveal. The importance of the events at Singur and Nandigram perhaps lay in its inflicting crack in the social base of the CPI (M), primarily in the rural area. The agricultural population, so far the largest constituency of the CPI (M), got ruptured. The AITC, leading the movements from the front, earned huge support of the agricultural labourers and the farmers: the traditional support base of the Left parties. This was revealed in the 2009 Lok Sabha Election itself, where the LF lost considerable support of these two agricultural categories (Chatterjee and Basu 2014). The Left also lost almost 16 per cent of its votes among the skilled and semi-skilled workers in the rural area in this election compared to the 2004 Lok Sabha Election (ibid.).

Along with the rural area the loss of legitimacy of the LF was also revealed in the urban areas, as well. The economic stagnation of the state had a negative impact on the business sector in the urban areas. The loss of LF's vote share among this segment of the urbanites was quite prominent in the 2009 Lok Sabha Election. This trend not only continued but enhanced further in the 2011 Assembly Election in West Bengal. Seen from the overall angle of class, it is indeed striking to note that in the 2011 Assembly Election, the INC and AITC alliance secured more votes of the poor than the Left. Compared to 2006 the AITC alliance gained 11 per cent more votes of the poor at the cost of a similar loss of the LF among them (source: West Bengal Assembly Election Study 2006 and 2011). Not only the poor, the LF also suffered significantly among the SCs and STs as well, while the popularity of the AITC increased notably among these categories (source: West Bengal Assembly Election Study 2006 and 2011). Taking all these into account it can be asserted that post Singur, Nandigram and Lalgarh there had been a lateral shift in the support base of the Left towards the AITC.

This shift undoubtedly was due to the ideological deviation of the CPI (M). With the encroachment of the middle class in significant numbers into the party, its ideological orientation towards the workers and the peasantry got diverted. The ideological deviation also resulted in the CPI (M)'s changing outlook to democratic institutions as well. The violent suppression of the mass movements by employing state forces, deserting the path of dialogue, was proof of this. This also resulted in its shrinking support base among different cross-sections of the West Bengal electorates as witnessed in the elections of 2009 and 2011. Quite prominent was the case of the young voters (aged between 18–25 years). That they had lost all interest in Left politics of the CPI (M) was evident from their withdrawal of support from the LF, which went down to 37 per cent in 2011 from 56 per cent in 2006 (West Bengal Assembly Election Study 2006 and 2011). During the same period the AITC alliance gained almost 21 per cent more young votes. The comparative performance of the LF and the AITC in the different elections since 2006 to 2011 and thereafter, signalled a drastic shift in the connotation of Left politics altogether. Replacing the Left-oriented CPI (M), the non-Left AITC took up the mantle of furthering the cause of the politics of the marginalized and the underprivileged. The significant increase in the support base of the AITC at the cost of LF, as the facts above indicate, might be an indication of the emergence of yet another dominant party system in West Bengal under the leadership of the AITC. But the question regarding the realization of this expectation remains. Although the continuous decline of the CPI (M) and the INC might be an indication of the emergence of the AITC-dominated party system but the quick inroad which the BJP is making into the mosaic of party competition in West Bengal since 2014, has been raising doubts about it.

The verdict of the 2019 Lok Sabha Election has, however, cleared the doubt by bringing in the BJP at the political mainstay of West Bengal. From the challenge thrown up by the BJP to the AITC in this election, it is apparent that far from being an AITC-dominated party system; West Bengal is heading towards a bi-polar party competition. The emerging bi-polarity is confirmed by the manner in which a significant chunk of the traditional Left and the INC voters have opted for the BJP, and, although in a relatively lower extent, for the AITC (Chatterjee and Basu 2019). As a result, both the AITC and the BJP have registered increase in their respective vote shares, while, the balance being tilted largely towards the BJP. This pro-BJP mood of the electorates can be explained from several angles. First, the Saradha and Narada scam and the alleged involvement of a number of frontline AITC leaders in these might have pulled down the image of the government before the electorates. Not the AITC bigshots alone, charges of corruption have allegedly been there against a number of local level leaders of the party, as well. Second, since its ascendance to state power in 2011, the AITC had relied upon populist measures to win over the electorates rather than undertaking serious measures to improve the conditions of agriculture and industry. Lack of determined vision towards sustainable economic development might have lowered the trust of the people over the government. Third, the excessive urge to remain in power in such a situation infused the culture of authoritarianism among the leaders and the rank and file of the AITC. Their alleged arrogant behaviour might have annoyed the people at large. Finally, the authoritarian outlook of the AITC led it to transgress the basic norms of democracy as was revealed in the Panchayat Election of 2018, where about a record 34 per cent of the seats were won by the AITC without a contest (*New Indian Express* 2018). There have been allegations against the AITC for not allowing the opposition forces to submit the nominations. Even the Supreme Court of India apprehended about the malfunctioning of democracy at the grassroots levels in West Bengal (ibid.). From the consolidation of the opposition votes in the BJP camp, it is evident that the electorates in general have picked it up as a potent means to redress their feeling of grievances and frustrations over the incumbent AITC government.

To understand the political antecedents of the emerging polarization of the electorates between the BJP and the AITC in West Bengal one need to look at the political processes operative here since the *poriborton* in 2011.

Forming the government, the first action of the Mamata Banerjee-led AITC–INC coalition government was to pass the Singur Land Rehabilitation and Development Act, 2011 only to be declared unconstitutional by the Calcutta High Court in June 2012. Afterwards, the Supreme Court on 31 August 2016 quashed the land acquisition at Singur for the Tata Motors Ltd. by the earlier LF government. The agitations at Singur, Nandigram and some other places in India propelled the UPA–II government to enact the Right to Fair Compensation and Transparency in Land Acquisition and Resettlement Act, in 2013 replacing the Land Acquisition Act of 1894. The new Act made it compulsory for the agencies, public as well as private, to obtain prior consent from the landholder before actually acquiring the land. Undoubtedly, Singur agitation left a permanent mark in the history of peasants struggle against land acquisition drive for industrialization under the aegis of capital, private as well as public. It seems to be a paradox as the state functioning under the overall model of neoliberal development has come up with such an Act, which will make the process of land acquisition for industries and other enterprises difficult. Effort to resolve the paradox is also at the corner. This is evident from the Narendra Modi-led NDA government, which since its ascendance to power at the national level in 2014, has been attempting to amend the Act to dilute the rights of the farmers and landholders over their land. Due to the opposition from other parties it is yet to achieve the targeted amendment so far. But, how long the opposing parties can withstand the pressure of the forces of the current development regime remains a crucial question.

By November 2016, Mamata Banerjee's government obeying the Supreme Court directive quite enthusiastically returned the 1,000 acre acquired land to almost 13,000 farmers of Singur. Since, returning the land of the 'unwilling' farmers had been her main demand during the agitation, which also happened to be her primary commitment during the subsequent elections, the Supreme Court's verdict added to her ongoing effort to build the electoral constituencies for the AITC. Since 2011 Mamata Banerjee was busy to develop and consolidate AITC's electoral support base. Apart from the schemes discussed earlier, the AITC government had spent ₹600 crore donations to neighbourhood clubs across Bengal, ever since it came to power in 2011 (*Hindustan Times* 2018). Doing this the government up to January 2018 had helped 15,000 clubs. Ms Banerjee's main argument for this was that besides the development of sports infrastructure, these neighbourhood clubs were engaged in different social work that help in generating a sense of mutual help among the members of the neighbourhood. Perhaps, on the basis of a similar understanding during the Durga Puja of 2018, the AITC government had spent ₹28 crore to assist 28,000 community Durga Pujas, each receiving ₹10,000. The opposition parties in their bitter criticism to this act of the government had questioned Ms Banerjee's invocation of the 'social work' done by the neighbourhood clubs. To them, it was a ploy to win their support in the election. Possibly, the members of the clubs were not only expected to vote for the AITC, but also to work for the party's interest in elections and to create a favourable attitude towards the party in the neighbourhood. Regarding the assistance to community Durga Pujas the opposition parties, particularly the CPI (M), criticized her to engage in 'competitive communalism' (Singh 2018, para 4). To them it was a bid on her part to attract the Hindu votes by balancing out her assistance to the Muslim imams and muazzins. That the assistance to the puja committees was meant to keep those under her command could be revealed from her statement, 'This is a small contribution from our side. But do keep this in mind that if someone tries to buy the puja committees with more money, do not surrender' (ibid., para 3). It seems that by this 'someone' she referred to the opposition parties, particularly, the BJP. The statement of Mamata Banerjee might be an indication of the increasing space which the BJP is attempting to acquire in the politics of contemporary West Bengal.

From the gesture of Mamata Banerjee to financially assist the neighbourhood clubs and community organizations aimed at, as the critiques argue, ripping electoral benefit out of this, question may emerge whether it was an attempt on her part to replace the party-society of the CPI (M). Although to answer this we have to wait for the future, but right now we can have some reflection on it from the party-society thesis of Bhattacharya (2009, 2016). First, the party-society, developed primarily by the CPI (M) in rural West Bengal, was a result of a very long drawn process where a section of school teachers, who were also members of the party, and some others, used to interact with the local people on a regular basis on a range of affairs affecting their public and private lives. It was not at all the case that just before or during election this would happen. They used to involve in collective bargaining with the state on behalf of the local people. Engaging them in the non-institutional microsetting of everyday politics, they could create a positive image of the party among the villagers. Second, the involvement of the school teachers in the everyday lives of the rural people was guided by a moral principle or ideology to work for the betterment of underprivileged people. Third, following the tenets of such ideology, the party-society attempted to achieve some kind of horizontal unity of the rural people mostly the peasantry. Although some members of the middle and rich peasantry might feature in it but certainly the large landholders were excluded. Finally, party-society's attempt was to achieve governmental benefits from the government but that was never in terms of financial assistance. It was primarily aimed at improving rural infrastructure related to betterment in the standards of education, health, social security, roads, electricity, drinking water, proper utilization of community resources like land, forest, water and so on.

Evidently, the effort of the AITC is different from these. The members of the party, rather than engaging them in everyday unstructured interaction with the villagers, appear to be more oriented to deliver the benefits of various schemes to the latter. Hence, it is a direct exchange relationship. Since, the exchange is not guided by any concrete pro-poor redistributive ideology, like that of the CPI (M) at its initial period of rule, so ultimately it reduces to a relationship between the powerful, by virtue of her/his membership to the ruling party, with the powerless. Since power, unchecked by moral and/or ideological constraint has a tendency to be corrupt, the charges of corruption have also been raised against the AITC leaders. Nath (2017) during the course of a group discussion in Bardhaman has come across people's opinion pointing towards this, 'CPM leaders were honest, they never demanded money for public services, but neither did they provide as many days of work or other benefits as swiftly as TMC does. TMC people ask for money, but in return the work is done' (p.23). By days of work the villagers referred to the number of days of work they could avail under the MGNREGA scheme and by TMC they referred to the AITC. Faction feuds among the AITC party members only help in augmenting the allegations of corruption against the party workers. Moreover, unlike the party-society of the CPI (M), the grassroots leaders of the AITC do not engage them in bargaining with the state for improvement of living conditions of the community. Although there have been development of roads, electricity and some other aspects of rural lives under the AITC regime, but still there are other dimensions which the local leaders or activists of the party could bring to the notice of the state through their efforts of collective bargaining on behalf of the people. Acting only as the facilitators for implementation of the schemes, they fail to reflect back the people's opinion about these to the higher level decision-makers. Finally, in the instance of the ruling CPI (M), the party-society, operating outside the institutional domain of formal politics, used to garner social support towards its institutional intervention. Hence, it had a distinct imprint in the attempted institutional reform of the rural Bengali society. But, as the AITC is yet to evolve any definite strategy towards reforming the institutional pattern, so financial assistance to the neighbourhood club may inspire them to perform better social work, as claims Ms Banerjee, but that in no way ensures their greater contribution in the task of social engineering to bring in a better society. Going by comparison, while during the first decade of LF rule in West Bengal the state exchequer recorded noteworthy growth, the same during the AITC's eight years of rule has resulted in incurring huge debt to maintain the economy. It is true that in 2011, the departing LF government left a debt burden of ₹1.93 lakh crore behind. But the AITC government is all set to double the figure by 2019 (Ghosal 2017). In fact, during 2019–2020 Bengal's public debt may rise to about ₹4.32 lakh crore (Ghosh 2019). So, the amount of loan, which the LF government took long 34 years to incur, the present AITC government has taken just eight years to double it up. How far the AITC government in West Bengal can sustain the ever-increasing demands of populist politics, in such a tight financial condition, is a serious matter of concern.

So far the welfare populism of AITC has been successful in garnering the electoral support of the majority of the electorates of West Bengal. This is reflected in the continuous increase of its vote share from 38.93 per cent in 2011 Assembly Election to 39.79 per cent in the Parliamentary Election of 2014, to reach 44.91 per cent in the Assembly Election of 2016, as reports the Election Commission of India. Along with the welfare schemes, the charisma of Mamata Banerjee is also instrumental for this. Particularly her 'lady next door' image and conduct has been leading the electorate to consider her as someone belonging to their immediate social lives. Although, some sections of the Bhadraloks might be critical about this, but her apparent 'simplicity' is enough to get hold of the imagination of the lower rung of the Bengali society. The AITC, quite obviously, appears to be very keen to maintain and further develop such an image of Mamata Banerjee. If one travels through the length and breadth of the state, she/he would come across numerous posters and hoardings of Mamata Banerjee with the captions such as *satotar pratik* (the symbol of honesty), *Mamata Banerjee r unnayan e samil hon* (participate in the development effort of Mamata Bannerjee) and so on. These give rise to a discourse, which shifts the focus of the people from the contemporary political trends to the figure of Mamata Banerjee as the epitome of honesty, fairness, transparency and such other values, irrespective of however corrupt, allegedly, her colleagues in the party might be. The portrayal of Mamata Banerjee as someone larger than her party, particularly the glorification of her personality traits to attract electorate may result in the detachment of the AITC from the domain of institutional politics. Liberal democracy in such a situation may encounter a serious challenge as politics increasingly becomes focused upon charismatic leadership at the cost of growing redundancy of the rational, formal and well-organized internal party structure. Not only in West Bengal, the same challenge is being witnessed in the national politics too, where there has been a conscious effort to project the image of Narendra Modi as an epitome of development. The slogans of *Abki Baar Modi Sarkar* (this time Modi government) raised by the BJP during the campaign for the 2014 Lok Sabha Election and *Phir Ekbar Modi Sarkar* (once again Modi government) being raised during the 2019 Lok Sabha Election are pointers to this. Since Narendra Modi, unlike Mamata Bannerjee, belongs to a well-knit political organization like the BJP, so the question arises to what extent the BJP can accommodate this or seen conversely, is the emphasis on Modi a sign of the diminishing significance of BJP as a democratic political party? In the midst of contestations about the distinctive role of charismatic leaders in bringing electoral success to the Right-wing populist parties compared to others, the question regarding the political trajectory of Mamata Banerjee-led AITC, hence, might become an interesting agenda for political analysis. We only have to wait for the future to gauge whether or not the populist welfare politics of Mamata Banerjee will take a Right-wing turn.

REFERENCES

Acharya, P. 1993. 'Panchayats and Left Politics in West Bengal'. *Economic and Political Weekly* 28 (22): 1080–1082.

———. 1994. 'Elusive New Horizons: Panchayats in West Bengal'. *Economic and Political Weekly* 29 (5): 231–234.

Adhikary, M. C. 2010–2011. 'Socio-Political Movement in Post Colonial North Bengal: A Case Study of the Rajbanshis'. *Proceedings of the Indian History Congress*, 71: 1233–1242.

Bagchi, A. K., and P. Das. 2005. 'Changing Pattern of Employment under Neo-liberal Reforms: A Comparative Study of West Bengal and Gujarat'. *Indian Journal of Labour Economics* 48 (4): 945–958.

Bagchi, R. 2014, 7 January. 'Gorkhaland & Kamtapur Movements'. *The Statesman.* Avaialble at: https://www.thestatesman.com/opinion/gorkhaland-amp-kamtapur-movements-33338.html (accessed on 16.11.2018)

Bandyopadhyay, D. 1997. 'Not a Gramscian Pantomime'. *Economic and Political Weekly* 32 (12): 581–584.

———. 2001. 'Tebhaga Movement in Bengal: A Retrospect'. *Economic and Political Weekly* 36 (41): 3901–3903, 3905–3907.

———. 2003. 'Land Reforms and Agriculture: The West Bengal Experience'. *Economic and Political Weekly* 38 (9): 879–884.

Bandyopadhyay, S. 1989. 'Social Protest or Politics of Backwardness? The Namasudra Movement in Bengal'. In *Dissent and Consensus: Protest in Pre-Industrial Societies (India, Burma and Russia)*, edited by B. Chattopadhyay, H. S. Basudevan and R. K. Ray, 170–232. Calcutta: K. P. Bagchi & Company.

———. 2004. *Caste, Culture and Hegemony: Social Dominance in Colonial Bengal.* New Delhi: SAGE Publications.

———. 2011. 'Who are the Matuas?' *Frontier* 43(37). Available at http://frontierweekly.com/archive/vol-number/vol/vol-43-2010-11/vol-43-37/matuas-43-37.pdf (accessed on 16 August 2018).

Bandyopadhyay, S., and A. Basu Ray Chaudhury. 2014. *In Search of Space: The Scheduled Caste Movement in West Bengal after Partition*. Kolkata: Mahanirban Calcutta Research Group.

Banerjee, A., P. J. Gertler, and M. Ghatak. 1998. 'Empowerment and Efficiency: The Economics of Agrarian Reform' (working paper No. 98-22, Department of Economics, Massachusetts Institute of Technology).

Banerjee, A.V., P. J. Gertler, and M. Ghatak 2002. 'Empowerment and Efficiency: Tenancy Reform in West Bengal'. *Journal of Political Economy* 110 (2): 239–280.

Banerjee, Abhijit, Ashok Sanjay Guha, Kaushik Basu, Maitreesh Ghatak, Mrinal Datta Chaudhuri, and Pranab Bardhan. 2002. 'Strategy for Economic Reform in West Bengal', *Economic and Political Weekly* 37 (41): 4203–4218.

Banerjee, P. 2006. 'Land Acquisition and Peasant Resistance at Singur'. *Economic and Political Weekly* 41 (46): 4718–4720.

Banerjee, P. S., and D. Roy. 2007. 'Behind the Present Peasant Unrest in West Bengal'. *Economic and Political Weekly* 42 (22): 2048–2050.

Banerjee, S. 2003. 'Bengali Left: From Pink to Saffron?' *Economic and Political Weekly* 38 (9): 864–865.

———. 2006. 'Elections, "Jatra" Style, in West Bengal'. *Economic and Political Weekly* 41 (10): 864–866.

———. 2008. 'A Political Cul-de-Sac: CPI(M)'s Tragic Denouement'. *Economic and Political Weekly* 43 (42): 12–15.

———. 2010. 'Washing Dirty Bengali Dhuti in Public'. *Economic and Political Weekly* 45 (3): 20–22.

Banerjee, T. 2018, 15 August. 'Family-income Cap Removed, Kanyashree Now for All Girls', *Times of India*. Available at https://timesofindia.indiatimes.com/city/kolkata/family-income-cap-removed-kanyashree-now-for-all-girls/articleshow/65408536.cms (accessed on 2 March 2019).

Bardhan, P. 2005. 'Nature of Opposition to Economic Reforms in India'. *Economic and Political Weekly* 40 (48): 4995–4998.

Bardhan, P., Michael Luca, Dilip Mookherjee, and Francisco Pino. 2014. 'Evolution of Land Distribution in West Bengal 1967–2004: Role of Land Reform and Demographic Changes'. *Journal of Development Economics* 110: 171–190.

Bardhan, P., Sandip Mitra, Dilip Mookherjee, and Abhirup Sarkar. 2009. 'Local Democracy and Clientelism: Implications for Political Stability in Rural West Bengal'. *Economic and Political Weekly* 44 (9): 46–58.

Bardhan, P., and D. Mookherjee. 2003. Political Economy of Land Reforms in West Bengal 1978–98 (working paper, Institute for Development, Boston University, Boston). Available at http://citeseerx.ist.psu.edu/viewdoc/download?doi=10.1.1.505.7117&rep=rep1&type=pdf (accessed on 25 November 2018).

———. 2010. 'Determinants of Redistributive Politics: An Empirical Analysis of Land Reforms in West Bengal, India'. *American Economic Review* 100 (4): 1572–1600.

Barua, K. 2010. 'Variation in Wage Earnings among Agricultural Labourers in Rural Bengal: A Fieldwork-Based Analysis'. *The Indian Journal of Labour Economics* 53 (4): 677–686.

Basu, J. 1977. Excerpts from the Message broadcast from the Calcutta Station of All India Radio on June 22, quoted from *Thirty Years Ago*. Available at: http://www.jyotibasu.net/?q=node/17 (accessed on 13. 04. 2017).

Basu, A. 1989. 'Democratic Centralism in the Home and the World: Bengali Women and the Communist Movement'. In *Promissory Notes: Women in the Transition to Socialism*, edited by S. Kruks, R. Rapp and M. B. Young, 215–232. New York, NY: Monthly Review Press.

Basu, D. 2001. 'Political Economy of "Middleness": Behind Violence in Rural West Bengal'. *Economic and Political Weekly* 36 (16): 1333–1335, 1337–1344.

Bengal Government. 1914. *Report of the Bengal District Administration Committee 1913–1914*. Calcutta: Bengal Secretariat Press.

Besley, T., and R. Burgess. 2000. 'Land Reform, Poverty Reduction, and Growth: Evidence from India'. *Quarterly Journal of Economics* 115 (2): 389–430.

Bhaduri, A. 2007. 'Development or Developmental Terrorism?' *Economic and Political Weekly* 42 (7): 552–553.

Bhattacharya, B. 2007, 25 February. 'Devil's Advocate' (interview). *ITV*. Available at: http://itv.in/index.php?option=com_video&view=detail&v_id=397&Itemid=8l (accessed on 27 January 2019).

Bhattacharyya, D. 1995. 'Agrarian Reforms and Politics of the Left in West Bengal'. *Proceedings of the Indian History Congress*, 56: 665–674.

———. 2004. 'West Bengal: Permanent Incumbency and Political Stability'. *Economic and Political Weekly* 39 (51): 5477–5483.

———. 2009. 'Of Control and Factions: The Changing "Party-Society" in Rural West Bengal'. *Economic and Political Weekly* 44 (9): 59–69.

———. 2010. 'Left in the Lurch: The Demise of the World's Longest Elected Regime?' *Economic and Political Weekly* 45 (3): 51–59.

———. 2011. 'Party Society, Its Consolidation and Crisis: Understanding Political Change in Rural West Bengal'. In *Theorising the Present: Essays for Partha Chatterjee*, edited by Anjan Ghosh, Tapati Guha-Thakurta, and Janaki Nair, 226–250. New Delhi: Oxford University Press.

———. 2016. *Government as Practice: Democratic Left in a Transforming India*. Delhi: Cambridge University Press.

Bhattacharya, M., and S. Bhattacharya. 2007. 'Agrarian Impasse in West Bengal in the Liberalisation Era'. *Economic and Political Weekly* 42 (52): 65–71.

Biswas, D. K. 1964. *Jaatibhed: Sri Sivnath Sastri*. Edited by D. K. Biswas. Kolkata: Sadharan Brahmo Samaj (In Bengali, 1370, *Bangabdo*, 2nd Edition).

Biswas, N. 2015, 20 July. 'Who Killed Kishenji?' *Sanhati*, Available at http://sanhati.com/articles/13994/ (accessed on 12 September 2017).

Biswas, S. 2011, 12 May. 'Who Says Communism is Dead in Bengal?' *BBC News*. Available at https://www.bbc.com/news/world-south-asia-13371621 (accessed on 15 June 2017).

Blumer, H. 1946. 'Collective Behavior'. In *New Outline of the Principles of Sociology*, edited by A. M. Lee, 167–222. New York, NY: Barnes & Noble.

Bora, M., and B. Das. 2009. 'The Movement in Lalgarh'. *Economic and Political Weekly* 44 (26–27): 15–17.

Bose, N. K. 1958. 'Some Aspects of Caste in Bengal'. *The Journal of American Folklore* 71 (281): 397–412.

Bose, R. 2011, 31 March. 'Why the Matuas Matter?' *The Hindu*. Available at https://www.thehindu.com/news/national/Why-the-Matuas-matter/article14967574.ece (accessed on 15 September 2018).

Bourdieu, P. 1977. *Outline of a Theory of Practice*. Cambridge: Cambridge University Press.

Boyce, K. J. 1987. *Agrarian Impasse in Bengal: Institutional Constraints to Technological Change*. Oxford: Oxford University Press.

Broomfield, J. H. 1968. *Elite Conflict in a Plural Society: Twentieth-Century Bengal*. Berkeley and Los Angeles: University of California Press.

Buhler, G., trans. 1886. *The Laws of Manu*. Oxford: Clarendon Press.

Burgmann, V. 2005. 'From Syndicalism to Seattle: Class and the Politics of Identity'. *International Labor and Working-Class History* 67: 1–21.

Cassandra. 1995. 'The Impending Crisis in Egypt'. *Middle East Journal* 49 (1): 9–27.

Census of India. 2011a. *C.D. Block Wise Primary Census Abstract Data (PCA)—West Bengal*. New Delhi: Office of the Registrar General & Census Commissioner, India. Available at http://censusindia.gov.in/pca/cdb_pca_census/Houselisting-housing-WB.html (accessed on 24 December 2018).

———. 2011b. *A-10 Individual Scheduled Caste Primary Census Abstract Data and its Appendix*. New Delhi: Office of the Registrar General & Census Commissioner, India. Available at http://www.censusindia.gov.in/2011census/PCA/SC.html (accessed on 15 February 2019).

Centeno, M. A., and J. N. Cohen. 2012. 'The Arc of Neoliberalism'. *Annual Reviews of Sociology* 38: 317–340.

Chakrabarty, B. 2014. *Communism in India: Events, Processes and Ideologies*. Oxford: Oxford University Press.

Chakrabarty, D. 2000. *Provincializing Europe: Postcolonial Thought and Historical Difference*. Princeton, NJ: Princeton University Press.

Chakraborti, A. K. 2003. *Beneficiaries of Land Reforms: The West Bengal Scenario*. Kolkata: State Institute of Panchayat and Rural Development (SIPRD).

Chakraborty, R. 1996. *Bange Baishnab Dharma* (in Bengali). Calcutta: Ananda Publishers.

Chambers, R. 1992. 'The Self Deceiving State'. *IDS Bulletin* 23 (4): 31–42. Available at https://opendocs.ids.ac.uk/opendocs/bitstream/handle/123456789/227/rc336.pdf;jsessionid=57DCE43C61D3C22ACB7B2953F080C7F5?sequence=2 (accessed on 16 November 2018).

Chandra, N. K. 2008. 'Tata Motors in Singur: A Step towards Industrialisation or Pauperisation?' *Economic and Political Weekly* 43 (50): 41–51.

Chatterjee, B. 1872. 'Bangadesher Krishak'. *Bangodarshan* 1(5): 307–314.

Chatterjee, J. 2002. 'The Historicity of the Jharkhand Movement: A Quest for Identity'. *Studies in Humanities and Social Sciences* IX (2): 113–132.

Chatterjee, J., and S. Basu. 2009. 'West Bengal: Mandate for Change'. *Economic and Political Weekly* 44 (39): 152–156.

———. 2014. 'Permanent Incumbency Shattered: Development Dilemma and Electoral Choice in West Bengal'. In *Party Competition in Indian States: Electoral Politics in Post-Congress Polity*, edited by S. Palshikar, K. C. Suri, and Y. Yadav, 284–308. New Delhi: Oxford University Press.

———. 2017. 'West Bengal Politics at the Crossroads'. In *Electoral Politics in India: Resurgence of the Bharatiya Janata Party*, edited by S. Palshikar, S. Kumar, and S. Lodha, 196–212. London: Routledge.

———. 2019, 28 May. 'Post-poll survey: When the Left Moved Right in West Bengal'. *The Hindu*. Available at https://www.thehindu.com/elections/lok-sabha-2019/when-the-left-moved-right/article27266690.ece (accessed on 9 June 2019).

Chatterjee, P. 1997. *The Present History of West Bengal: Essays in Political Criticism*. Delhi: Oxford University Press

———. 2004. *The Politics of the Governed: Reflections on Popular Politics in Most of the World.* New York, NY: Columbia University Press.

———. 2009. 'The Coming Crisis in West Bengal'. *Economic and Political Weekly* 44 (9): 42–45.

———. 2012. 'Historicising Caste in Bengal Politics'. *Economic and Political Weekly* 47 (50): 69–70.

———. 2016. 'Partition and the Mysterious Disappearance of Caste in Bengal.' In *The Politics of Caste in Bengal*, edited by U. Chandra, Geir Heierstad, and Kenneth Bo Nielsen, 83–102. New Delhi: Routledge.

Chatterjee, S. K. 1951. *Kirata-Jana-Krti: The Indo-Mongoloids: Their Contribution to the History and Culture of India*. Calcutta: The Asiatic Society.

Chattopadhyay, A. K. 2005–2006. 'Distributive Impact of Agricultural Growth in Rural West Bengal'. *Economic and Political Weekly* 40 (53): 5601–5610.

Chattopadhyay, S. S. 2006, 16–29 December. 'Land Reform Not an End in Itself. Interview with Nirupam Sen: West Bengal Industries Minister'. *Frontline* 23 (25) Available at: https://frontline.thehindu.com/static/html/fl2325/stories/20061229001903600.htm (accessed on 27.06.2018).

———. 2011, 22 October–4 November. 'Mamata vs. Maoists'. *Frontline* 28 (22). Available at: https://frontline.thehindu.com/static/html/fl2822/stories/20111104282203000.htm (accessed on 28.07.2018).

Chaudhury, B. B. 1979. 'The Transformation of Rural Protest in Eastern India 1757–1930'. *Proceedings of the Indian History Congress* 40: 503–541. Available at: http://www.jstor.org/stable/44141992 (accessed on 09 June 2018).

Chowdhury, B. 2019, 18 February. 'West Bengal: With 15 "development board", Funding, Mamata Banerjee Woos the Hills as BJP Slides'. *The Indian Express*. Available at https://indianexpress.com/elections/

with-15-development-boards-funding-mamata-banerjee-woos-the-hills-as-bjp-slides-5588498/ (accessed on 21 February 2019).

CMIE. 1993. *Performance of Agriculture in Major States, 1967–68 to 1991–92*. CMIE: Bombay.

Corbridge, S., Glyn Williams, Manoj Srivastava, and Rene Veron. 2005. *Seeing the State: Governance and Governmentality in India*. Cambridge: Cambridge University Press

CPI (M). 1964. 'Programme: Adopted at the Seventh Congress of the Communist Party of India at Calcutta, October 31 to November 7'. Available at https://s3.amazonaws.com/s3.documentcloud.org/documents/1305530/1964-programme-communist-party-of-india-marxist.pdf (accessed on 14 May 2018).

———. 2005. 'Political Resolution Adopted at the 18th Congress Communist Party of India (Marxist)'. Available at https://www.cpim.org/sites/default/files/documents/2005-18Cong-pol-res%20%281%29.pdf (accessed on 14 April 2019).

———. 2006. 'Singur: Myth and Reality'. *People's Democracy*, 30 (50).

———. 2007, 30 June. *Thirty Years of West Bengal Left Front Govt*. Available at https://www.cpim.org/content/thirty-years-west-bengal-left-front-govt (accessed on 12 August 2018).

———. 2015a. *Draft Review Report on the Political-Tactical Line* (*Adopted by Central Committee at its Meeting, January 19–21, 2015*, Hyderabad). New Delhi: CPI(M). Available at http://www.cpimodisha.org/sites/default/files/documents/Draf%20pol-tac-line-cc-adopted.pdf (accessed on 17 September 2018).

———. 2015b. *Draft Political Resolution for the 21st Congress* (*Adopted by the Central Committee at its January 19–21, 2015 Meeting, Hyderabad*). New Delhi: CPI(M). Available at https://cpim.org/sites/default/files/documents/20150204-draft-pol-resolution_0.pdf (accessed on 17 September 2018).

———. 2015c. *Report on Organization* (*Adopted by the Plenum on Organization Kolkata, December 27–31, 2015*). New Delhi: CPI(M). Available at https://cpim.org/sites/default/files/documents/2015-dec-plenum_report_organisation.pdf (accessed on 18 September 2018).

Dakua, D. C. 2007. 'A Journey from Hitasadhani to Greater Kuch Bihar'. In *Socio-political Movements in North Bengal (a Sub-Himalayan Tract)*, edited by S. Barma, 49–64. New Delhi: Global Vision Publishing House.

Das, R. 2016. 'The Politics of Land, Consent, and Negotiation: Revisiting the Development-Displacement Narratives from Singur in West Bengal'. *South Asia Multidisciplinary Academic Journal* 13: 1–17. Available at https://journals.openedition.org/samaj/4103 (accessed on 12 October 2018).

Dasgupta, A. 1982. 'The Fakir and Sannyasi Rebellion'. *Social Scientist* 10 (1): 44–55.

Dasgupta, B. 1972. 'The 1972 Election in West Bengal'. *Economic and Political Weekly* 7 (16): 804–808.

———. 1984. 'Sharecropping in West Bengal: From Independence to Operation Barga'. *Economic and Political Weekly* 19(26): A85–A96.

Dasgupta, S. 1985. 'Adivasi Politics in Midnapur c. 1760–1924'. In *Subaltern Studies IV*, edited by Ranajit Guha, 100–135. Delhi: Oxford University Press.

Datta, P. 1991. 'The Gorkhaland Agitation in West Bengal'. *The Indian Journal of Political Science* 52 (2): 225–241.

Datta, R. 2018, 8 March. 'West Bengal: Speaking their language'. *India Today*. Available at https://www.indiatoday.in/magazine/states/story/20180319-speaking-their-language-mamata-banerjee-ethnic-group-rajbongshi-1185638-2018-03-08 (accessed on 12 December 2018).

Datta-Ray, S. K. 2016, 25 March. 'Mamata Banerjee: I'm the Change'. *OPEN Magazine* Available at http://www.openthemagazine.com/article/india/mamata-banerjee-i-m-the-change (accessed on 02 March 2019).

De, A. 2017, 6 October. 'Sadly, Bengal is no state for dissent'. *Daily O*. Available at https://www.dailyo.in/politics/mamata-banerjee-dissent-bengal-bjp/story/1/19917.html (accessed on 02 March 2019).

Dewan, P. 2016. *Ethnicity and Politics of Identities: A Study on Gorkhaland Movement* (MPhil Dissertation Submitted to Sikkim University). Available at http://14.139.206.50:8080/jspui/bitstream/1/4580/1/Pratishtha%20Dewan.pdf (accessed on 10 January 2019).

Dimock, E. C., Jr. 1966. *The Place of the Hidden Moon: Erotic Mysticism in the Vaisnava Sahajiyā Cult of Bengal*. Chicago, IL: The University of Chicago Press.

Dirks, N. B. 1989. 'The Invention of Caste: Civil Society in Colonial India'. *Social Analysis: The International Journal of Social and Cultural Practice* (25): 42–52.

———. 2001. *Castes of Mind: Colonialism and the Making of Modern India*. Princeton, NJ: Princeton University Press.

Downs, A. 1957. 'An Economic Theory of Political Action in a Democracy'. *The Journal of Political Economy* 65 (2): 135–150.

Durkheim, E. 1982. *The Rules of Sociological Method*. Edited by Steven Lukes and translated by W. D. Halls. New York, NY: The Free Press.

Duyker, E. 1987. *Tribal Guerrillas: The Santals of West Bengal and the Naxalite Movement*, Delhi: Oxford University Press.

Echeverri-Gent, J. 1992. 'Public Participation and Poverty Alleviation: The Experience of Reform Communists in India's West Bengal', *World Development*, 20(10): 1401–1422.

EPW. 2012. 'The Tender Mercies of Mamata: Will the Trinamool Congress Manage to Pull off the High Stakes Game It Is Playing in West Bengal?' *Economic and Political Weekly* 47 (3): 7–8.

Escobar, A. 1995. *Encountering Development: The Making and Unmaking of the Third World*. Princeton, NJ: Princeton University Press.

Foucault, M. 1984. *The Foucault Reader*. Compiled and edited by Paul Rabinow. New York, NY: Pantheon Books.

Foucault, M. 1991. 'Governmentality'. In *The Foucault Effect: Studies in Governmentality: With Two Lectures by and an Interview with Michel Foucault*, edited by G. Burchell, C. Gordon, and P. Miller, 87–104. Chicago, IL: University of Chicago Press.

Franda, M. F. 1971. *Radical Politics in West Bengal.* Cambridge, MA: MIT Press.

Fukuyama, F. 1989. 'The End of History?' *The National Interest* 16: 3–18.

Gazdar, H., and S. Sengupta. 1997. 'Agrarian Politics and Rural Development in West Bengal'. In *Indian Development: Selected Regional Perspectives*, edited by J. Dreze and A. Sen, 129–204. New Delhi: Oxford University Press.

———. 1999. 'Agricultural Growth and Recent Trends in Well-being in Rural West Bengal'. In *Sonar Bangla? Agricultural Growth and Agrarian Change in West Bengal and Bangladesh*, edited by B. Rogaly, B. Harriss-White, and S. Bose, 60–91. New Delhi: SAGE Publications.

Ghatak, M., and M. Ghatak. 2002. 'Recent Reforms in the Panchayat System in West Bengal: Toward Greater Participatory Governance?' *Economic and Political Weekly* 37(1): 45–58.

Ghatak, M., Sandip Mitra, Dilip Mookherjee, and Anusha Nath. 2013. 'Land Acquisition and Compensation: What Really Happened in Singur?' *Economic and Political Weekly* 48 (21): 32–44.

Ghatak, M., and S. Roy. 2007. 'Land Reform and Agricultural Productivity in India: A Review of the Evidence'. *Oxford Review of Economic Policy* 23 (2): 251–269.

Ghosal, A. 2017, 10 February. 'By 2018–19 Trinamool government set to overtake debt raised by the Left'. *The Hindustan Times*. Available at https://www.hindustantimes.com/kolkata/by-2018-19-trinamool-government-set-to-overtake-debt-raised-by-the-left/story-Cp284HCJHl4Ycz6DwhrKjN.html (accessed on 02 March 2019).

Ghosh, A. 2001, December. 'Cast(e) out in West Bengal'. *Seminar*. Available at https://www.india-seminar.com/2001/508/508%20anjan%20ghosh.htm (accessed on 21 November 2016).

———. 2009. 'The Gorkhaland Redux'. *Economic and Political Weekly* 44 (23): 10–13.

Ghosh, D. 2014, 28 April. 'Come May 16, Bangladeshi Immigrants Must Pack Up: Narendra Modi'. *NDTV*. Available at http://www.ndtv.com/elections/article/election-2014/come-may-16-bangladeshi-immigrants-must-pack-up-narendra-modi-514883 (accessed on 15 December 2014).

Ghosh, P. 2019, 5 February. 'Bengal's Debt Pile Balloons'. *The Telegraph*. Available at https://www.telegraphindia.com/business/bengal-s-debt-pile-balloons/cid/1683764 (accessed on 08 March 2019).

Ghosh, S. 2016, 20 May. 'No, Not Ten, Mamata Had Only Two Factors Going for Her'. *The News Minute*. Available at https://www.thenewsminute.com/article/no-not-ten-mamata-had-only-two-factors-going-her-43547 (accessed on 02 March 2019).

Giddens, A. 2004. *The Third Way and its Critics.* Cambridge: Polity Press.

Goswami, U. 2014. *Conflict and Reconciliation: The Politics of Ethnicity in Assam.* New Delhi: Routledge.

Gough, K. 1974. 'Indian Peasant Uprisings'. *Economic and Political Weekly* 9 (32/34): 1391–1412.

Government of India. 1950. *Treaty of Peace and Friendship between the Government of India and the Government of Nepal.* Ministry of External Affairs. Available at https://mea.gov.in/bilateral-documents.htm?dtl/6295/Treaty+of+Peace+and+Friendship (accessed on 12 February 2019).

———. 1973. *Report of the Task Force on Agrarian Relations.* New Delhi: Planning Commission. Available at http://krishikosh.egranth.ac.in/handle/1/2041412 (accessed on 25 November 2018).

———. 2006. *Social, Economic and Educational Status of the Muslim Community of India: A Report.* New Delhi: Planning Commission. Available at https://sabrang.com/sachar/sacharreport.pdf (accessed on 15 October 2012).

———. 2010. *West Bengal Development Report.* New Delhi: Planning Commission.

———. 2013. *The National Food Security Act, 2013; No. 20 of 2013.* Ministry of Law and Justice. Available at http://www.egazette.nic.in/WriteReadData/2013/E_29_2013_429.pdf (accessed on 26 February 2019).

Government of West Bengal, 2004. *West Bengal Human Development Report 2004.* Development and Planning Department. Available at http://hdr.undp.org/en/content/west-bengal-human-development-report-2004 (accessed on 14 April 2018).

Govt. of West Bengal. 2004a. *Statistical Handbook, West Bengal,* Bureau of Applied Economics and Statistics. Kolkata: Government of West Bengal.

Govt. of West Bengal. 2004b. *District Statistical Handbook of Hooghly,* Bureau of Applied Economics and Statistics. Kolkata: Government of West Bengal

———. 2007. *Status Report on Singur.* Available at https://www.wb.gov.in/portal/documents/10180/0/Status+Report+on+Singur/25c3412f-997b-4fb7-8e52-a6faa5404647?version=1.0 (accessed on 18 January 2019).

———. 2017. *Khadya Sathi—Food Security Scheme for West Bengal.* Available at https://wbxpress.com/khadya-sathi-food-security-scheme/ (accessed on 12 March 2019).

———. 2019. *Ration Card Life Cycle Management.* Department of Food and Supplies, Government of West Bengal. Available at https://202.61.117.98/RCCount_District.aspx (accessed on 13 March 2019).

Guha, A. 2016. 'Why Caste Politics Failed in West Bengal?' *Frontier* 49 (2): 1–2. Available at http://www.frontierweekly.com/articles/vol-49/49-2/49-2-Why%20Caste%20Politics%20Failed%20in%20Bengal.html (accessed on 27 June 2017).

———. 2019. 'Is There A Second Wave of Dalit Upsurge in West Bengal?' *EPW Engage* 54 (2). Available at https://www.epw.in/engage/article/is-there-a-second-wave-of-dalit-upsurge-in-west-bengal (accessed on 12 February 2019).

Guha, R. 1988. 'On Some Aspects of the Historiography of Colonial India'. In *Selected Subaltern Studies* edited by R. Guha and G. C. Spivak, 37–45. Delhi: Oxford University Press.

———. 1999. *Elementary Aspects of Peasant Insurgency in Colonial India.* Durham and London: Duke University Press.

Gulati, A., and S. Bathla. 2001. 'Capital Formation in Indian Agriculture: Re-Visiting the Debate'. *Economic and Political Weekly* 36 (20): 1697–1708.

Guruswamy, M., Kamal Sharma, and Jeevan Prakash Mohanty. 2005. 'Economic Growth and Development in West Bengal: Reality versus Perception'. *Economic and Political Weekly* 40 (21): 2151–2157.

Habermas, J. 1981. 'New Social Movements'. *Telos* (49): 33–37.

Hanstad, T., and R. Nielsen. 2004. 'West Bengal's Bargadars and Landownership'. *Economic and Political Weekly* 39 (8): 853–855.

Harriss, J. 1992. 'Does the "Depressor" Still Work? Agrarian Structure and Development in India: A Review of Evidence and Argument'. *The Journal of Peasant Studies* 19 (2): 189–227.

———. 1993. 'What Is Happening in Rural West Bengal? Agrarian Reform, Growth and Distribution'. *Economic and Political Weekly* 28 (24): 1237–1247.

———. 2011. '"New Politics" and the Governmentality of the Post-liberalization State in India: An Ethnographic Perspective'. In *The State in India after Liberalization: Interdisciplinary Perspectives*, edited by A. Gupta and K. Sivaramakrishnan, 91–108. London: Routledge.

Harris-white, B. 2003. *India Working: Essays on Society and Economy*. Cambridge: Cambridge University Press.

Harvey, D. 2005. *A Brief History of Neoliberalism*. Oxford: Oxford University Press.

———. 2009. 'The "New" Imperialism: Accumulation by Dispossession'. *Socialist Register* 40 (40): 63–87.

———. 2018. 'Reading Marx's Capital Vol 1 – Class 13, Conclusion' (video). Available at: http://davidharvey.org/2008/09/capital-class-13/ (accessed on 24 January 2019).

Heller, P. 2001. 'Moving the State: The Politics of Democratic Decentralization in Kerala, South Africa, and Porto Alegre'. *Politics and Society* 29 (1): 131–163.

Hobsbawm, E. J. 1971. *Primitive Rebels.* Manchester: University of Manchester.

Hunter, W. W. 1868. *The Annals of Rural Bengal.* London: Smith, Elder and Co.

———. 1876. *The Indian Musalmans.* London. Trubner and Company.

———. 1974. *A Statistical Account of Bengal.* Delhi: D. K. Publishing House.

South Asia Citizens Web. 2007, January 29. *Interim Report of the Citizens' Committee on Singur and Nandigram.* South Asia Citizens Web. Available at http://www.sacw.net/Nation/Jan07reportSingur_Ngram.html (Accessed on 12 August 2014).

Karlsson, B. G. 2000. *Contested Belonging: An Indigenous People's Struggle for Forest and Identity in Sub-Himalayan Bengal.* New York, NY: Routledge.

Khasnabis, R. 1981. 'Operation Barga: Limits to Social Democratic Reformism'. *Economic and Political Weekly* 16 (25/26): A43–A45, A47–A48.

———. 1986. 'More on West Bengal Tenancy Reforms'. *Economic and Political Weekly* 21 (4): 178–180.

———. 1994. 'Tenurial Conditions in West Bengal: Continuity and Change'. *Economic and Political Weekly* 29 (53): A189–A199

———. 2008–2009. 'The Economy of West Bengal'. *Economic and Political Weekly* 43 (52): 103–115.

Kitschelt, H., and S. I. Wilkinson, 2007. 'Citizen–Politician Linkages: An introduction'. In *Patrons, Clients, and Policies: Patterns of Democratic Accountability and Political Competition*, edited by H. Kitschelt and S. I. Wilkinson, 1–49. Cambridge: Cambridge University Press.

Kohli, A. 1983. 'Parliamentary Communism and Agrarian Reform: The Evidence from India's Bengal'. *Asian Survey* 23 (7): 783–809.

———. 1987. *The State and Poverty in India: The Politics of Reform*. Cambridge: Cambridge University Press.

———. 1990. 'From Elite Activism to Democratic Consolidation: The Rise of Reform Communism in West Bengal'. In *Dominance and State Power in Modern India: Decline of a Social Order*, Vol. 2, edited by F. Frankel and M. S. A. Rao, 367–415. Delhi: Oxford University Press.

———. 1997. 'From Breakdown to Order: West Bengal'. In *State and Politics in India*, edited by Partha Chatterjee, 336–366. Delhi: Oxford University Press.

Krishnaji, N. 1979. 'Agrarian Relations and the Left Movement in Kerala: A Note on Recent Trends'. *Economic and Political Weekly* 14 (9): 515–521.

Kumar, A., and A. Guha. 2014. 'Political Future of Caste in West Bengal'. *Economic and Political Weekly* 49 (32): 73–74.

Lehman, E. W. 1969. 'Toward A Macrosociology of Power'. *American Sociological Review* 34 (4): 453–465.

Lenin, V. I. 1920. *Lenin Collected Works*. Vol. 31. Moscow: Progress Publishers.

Lieten, G. K. 1990. 'Depeasantisation Discontinued: Land Reforms in West Bengal'. *Economic and Political Weekly* 25 (40): 2265–2271.

———. 1992. *Continuity and Change in Rural West Bengal*. New Delhi: SAGE Publications.

Linton, R. 1943. 'Nativistic Movements'. *American Anthropologist* 45: 230–240.

Lofgen, H. 2016. 'The Communist Party of India (Marxist) and the Left Government in West Bengal, 1977–2011: Strains of Governance and Socialist Imagination'. *Studies in Indian Politics* 4 (1): 102–115.

Macaulay, T. B. 1919. 'Macaulay's Minute'. In *Selection from Educational Records Part I 1781–1839*, collected and compiled by H. Sharp, 107–17. Calcutta: Superintendent Government Printing.

Majumdar, A. 2014, 12 October. 'The Tiger that Mamata Banerjee is Riding'. *Hindustan Times*. Available at http://www.hindustantimes.com/comment/analysis/the-tiger-that-mamata-banerjee-is-riding/article1-1274603.aspx (accessed on 15 December 2014).

Majumdar, M. 2009. 'Democracy in Praxis: Two Non-Left Gram Panchayats in West Bengal'. *Economic and Political Weekly* 44 (9): 82–93.

Mandal, C. 2009, 31 August. 'We'll Fight for Jangalkhand Autonomy: Chhatradhar'. *Times of India*. Available at https://timesofindia.indiatimes.

com/city/kolkata/Well-fight-for-Jangalkhand-autonomy-Chhatradhar/articleshow/4952607.cms (accessed on 30 November 2009).

Manheim, K. 1979. *Ideology and Utopia: An Introduction to the Sociology of Knowledge*. London: Routledge & Kegan Paul.

Mani, L. 1987. 'Contentious Traditions: The Debate on Sati in Colonial India'. *Cultural Critique*, 7: 119–156.

———. 1998. *Contentious Traditions: The Debate on Sati in Colonial India*. Berkeley, CA: University of California Press.

Mathew, G. 2001. 'Panchayat Elections: Dismal Record'. *Economic and Political Weekly* 36 (3): 183–184.

Mishra, S. K. 2007. 'On Agrarian Transition in West Bengal'. *The Marxist* 33 (2): 1–22. Available at https://cpim.org/marxist/200702_marxist_s.misra-agri-wb.pdf (accessed on 07 December 2018).

Mohanty, M. 2007. 'Political Economy of Agrarian Transformation: Another View of Singur'. *Economic and Political Weekly* 42 (9): 737–741.

Mukarji, N., and D. Bandyopadhyay 1995. 'New Horizons for West Bengal's Panchayats: A Report for the Government of West Bengal'. *Indian Journal of Agricultural Economics* 50 (4): 688–698.

Mukherji, P. N. 2009. 'From Land Reforms to Economic Reforms: Dilemmas of Development in West Bengal'. *West Bengal Sociological Review* 2: 5–21.

Mukherji, P. N., and B. N. Ghosh. 2010. Democratic Centralism, Party Hegemony, and Decentralisation in West Bengal. *Sociological Bulletin* 59 (2): 199–215.

Nandy, A. 1975. 'Sati: A Nineteenth Century Tale of Women, Violence and Protest'. In *Rammohun Roy and the Process of Modernization in India*, edited by V. C. Joshi, 168–194. Delhi: Vikas Publishing House.

Natarajan, L. 1979. 'Indigo Cultivators' Strike–1860'. In *Peasant Struggles in India*, edited by A. R. Desai, 148–158. Delhi: Oxford University Press.

Nath, S. 2017. 'Everyday Politics and Corruption in West Bengal'. *Economic and Political Weekly* 52 (21): 22–25.

NCRB. 2016. *Crime in India 2016*. New Delhi: Ministry of Home Affairs, Government of India.

NDTV. 2010. 'Fully Support Mamata's Rally, says Maoist Leader Kishenji' (video). *NDTV*. Available at: https://www.ndtv.com/india-news/fully-support-mamatas-rally-says-maoist-leader-kishenji-426211 (accessed on 24 February 2019).

———. 2014, 9 May. 'After Calling Narendra Modi a "Donkey", Mamata Banerjee Now Calls Him "Danga Babu"'. *NDTV*. Available at http://www.ndtv.com/elections/article/election-2014/after-calling-narendra-modi-a-donkey-mamata-banerjee-now-calls-him-danga-babu-520703 (accessed on 15 December 2014).

Nielsen, K. B. 2010. 'Contesting India's Development? Industrialisation, Land Acquisition and Protest in West Bengal'. *Forum for Development Studies* 37 (2): 145–170.

———. 2018. *Land Dispossession and Everyday Politics in Rural Eastern India.* London: Anthem Press.

NCHRO. 2006, 5 December. 'Atrocities at Singur, West Bengal, India'. Available at https://www.nchro.org/index.php/2006/12/05/atrocities-at-singur-west-bengal-india/ (accessed on 26 September 2018).

Offe, C. 1985. 'New Social Movements: Challenging the Boundaries of Institutional Politics'. *Social Research* 52 (4): 817–868.

Outlook. 2017, 23 June. 'WB Govt. Honoured with UN Public Service Award for Kanyashree Prakalpa'. *Outlook*. Available at https://www.outlookindia.com/newsscroll/wb-govt-honoured-with-un-public-service-award-for-kanyashree-prakalpa/1083259 (accessed on 25 February 2019).

Patnaik, P. 2011. 'The Left in Decline'. *Economic and Political Weekly* 46 (29): 12–16.

Petras, J., and H. Veltmeyer. 2009. *Social Movements and State Power*. Kolkata: Update Publications.

Pillai, S. R. 2018. 'CPI (M) and the Agrarian Question'. *People's Democracy* XLII (49), Available at http://www.peoplesdemocracy.in/2014/1109_pd/cpim-and-agrarian-question (accessed on 13 June 2018).

Quinn, C. E., and A. C. Halfacre. 2014. 'Place Matters: An Investigation of Farmers' Attachment to Their Land'. *Human Ecology Review* 20 (2): 117–132.

Ramachandran, V. K. 2001. 'So why did the Left Front win?' *Frontline* 18 (11). Available at https://www.frontline.in/static/html/fl1811/18110220.htm (accessed on 01 November 2018).

Rawal, V., and M. Swaminathan. 1998. 'Changing Trajectories: Agricultural Growth in West Bengal, 1950 to 1996'. *Economic and Political Weekly* 33 (40): 2595–2602.

Ray, P. S. 2008. *Background of the Movement*. Available at http://sanhati.com/front-page/1083/#52 (accessed on 5 December 2009).

Ray, R. 1998. 'Women's Movement and Political Fields: A Comparison of Two Indian Cities', *Social Problems,* 45 (1): 21–36.

Ray, S. 2002. *Transformations on the Bengal Frontier: Jalpaiguri 1765–1948*. London: Routledge.

Raychaudhuri, A., and G. K. Basu. 2007. 'The Decline and Recent Resurgence of the Manufacturing Sector of West Bengal: Implications for Pro-Poor Growth from an Institutional Point of View'. Research Programme Consortium for Improving Institutions for Pro-Poor Growth, DFID, Discussion Paper Series, No. 10, 1–33. Available at http://www.ippg.org.uk/papers/dp10.pdf (accessed 10 July 2017).

Risley, H. H. 1892. *The Tribes and Castes of Bengal*. Vol. 1. Calcutta: Bengal Secretariat Press.

Rogaly, B. 1998. 'Containing Conflict and Reaping Votes: Management of Rural Labour Relations in West Bengal'. *Economic and Political Weekly* 33 (42/43): 2729–2739.

Roy Burman, B. K., Yogendra Singh, T. K. Oommen, P. C. Joshi, and S. C. Dube. 1974. 'Land Reforms in a Sociological Perspective'. *India International Centre Quarterly* 1(1): 51–68.

Roy, D. 2011. 'Caste and power: An Ethnography in West Bengal, India'. *Modern Asian Studies* 46 (4): 947–974.

———. 2014. *Rural Politics in India: Political Stratification and Governance in West Bengal*. Cambridge: Cambridge University Press.

Roy, N. 1952. *Bangaleer Itihas: Aadi Parba* (in Bengali). Kolkata: Dey's Publishing.

Roy, S. 1966. *Bharater Krishak Bidroha O Ganatantrik Sangram* (in Bengali). Kolkata: Radical Impression.

Rudra, A. 1981. 'One Step Forward, Two Steps Backward'. *Economic and Political Weekly* 16 (25/26): A61, A63, A65, A67, A68.

———. 1985. 'Agrarian Policies of Left Front Government in West Bengal'. *Economic and Political Weekly* 20 (23): 1015–1016.

Ruud, A. E. 1999. 'Embedded Bengal? The Case for Politics'. *Forum for Development Studies* 2: 235–259.

———. 2003. *Poetics of Village Politics: The Making of West Bengal's Rural Communism*. New Delhi: Oxford University Press.

Saha, A., and M. Swaminathan, 1994. 'Agricultural Growth in West Bengal in the 1980s: A Disaggregation by Districts and Crops'. *Economic and Political Weekly* 29 (13): A2–A11.

Salomon, C. 1991. 'The Cosmogonic Riddles of Lalan Fakir'. In *Gender, Genre, and Power in South Asian Expressive Traditions*, edited by A. Appadurai, F. J. Korom, and M. A. Mills, 267–304. Philadelphia, PA: University of Pennsylvania Press.

Samaddar, R. 2013. 'Whatever Has Happened to Caste in West Bengal?' *Economic and Political Weekly*. 48 (36): 77–79.

———. 2016, 19 May. 'Populist Governments with Strong Leaders Like Mamata Are Here to Stay'. *The Wire*. Available at https://thewire.in/politics/populist-govts-with-strong-leaders-like-mamata-are-here-to-stay-says-political-scientist-ranabir-samaddar (accessed on 12 January 2019).

———. 2018, 2 February. 'Interview: Mamata Banerjee is Reaping the Political Dividends of Her Populist Policies'. *The Wire*. Available at https://thewire.in/politics/interview-political-shifts-strategies-of-tmc-bjp-revealed-in-the-west-bengal-by-polls (accessed on 28 February 2019).

Sanyal, C. C. 1965. *The Rajbansis of North Bengal*. Kolkata: The Asiatic Society.

Sanyal, M. K., Pradip Kumar Biswas, and Samaresh Bardhan. 1998. 'Institutional Change and Output Growth in West Bengal Agriculture: End of Impasse'. *Economic and Political Weekly* 33 (47/48): 2979–2986.

Sarkar, A. 2006. 'Political Economy of West Bengal: A Puzzle and a Hypothesis'. *Economic and Political Weekly* 41(4): 341–348.

Sarkar, H. C., ed. 1914. *Life and Letters of Raja Rammohun Roy*. 2 ed. Calcutta: R. Cambray.

Sarkar, S. 2007, 9 January. 'A Question Marked In Red'. *Outlook*. Available at https://www.outlookindia.com/website/story/a-question-marked-in-red/233577 (accessed on 12 June 2017).

Sarkar, S., and T. Sarkar. 2009. 'Notes on a Dying People'. *Economic and Political Weekly* 44 (26–27): 10–14.

Schneider, M. 2014, 13 January. 'Can Benefits be Tied to the Vote?' *The Hindu Business Line*. Available at https://www.thehindubusinessline.com/opinion/can-benefits-be-tied-to-the-vote/article22995591.ece (accessed on 15 April 2019).

Scott, J. C. 1976. *The Moral Economy of the Peasant: Rebellion and Subsistence in Southeast Asia*. London: Yale University Press.

Sen Gupta, B. 1982, 31 December. 'CPI-M: Time to Take Stock'. *India Today*. Available at https://www.indiatoday.in/magazine/guest-column/story/19821231-promode-dasgupta-the-man-who-kept-the-left-front-government-strictly-under-control-772542-2013-07-25 (accessed on 26 July 2019).

Sen, A., and Sengupta R. 1995. 'The Recent Growth in Agricultural Output in Eastern India, with Special Reference to the Case of West Bengal'. Paper presented at the Workshop on Agricultural and Agrarian Structure in Contemporary West Bengal and Bangladesh, CSSSC, 9–12 January.

Sen, K. C. 1904. *Keshub Chunder Sen's Lectures in India*. London: Cassell and Company Limited.

Sengupta A., and Kundu, S. 2008. 'Factor Contribution and Productivity Growth in Underdeveloped Agriculture: A Study from Liberalised India'. *Indian Economic Review* 43 (2): 265–285.

Sengupta, S. 1981. 'West Bengal Land Reforms and the Agrarian Scene', *Economic and Political Weekly*, 16 (25–26): A69–A76

Shanin, T. 1966. 'The Peasantry as a Political Factor'. *Sociological Review* 14 (1): 1–5.

Sharma, A. 2008. 'Logics of Empowerment: Development, Gender, and Governance in Neoliberal India'. *Division II Faculty Publications* 43. Available at https://wesscholar.wesleyan.edu/div2facpubs/43 (accessed on 12 January 2019).

Sharp, H. 1920. *Selection from Educational Records Part I 1781–1839*. Calcutta: Superintendent Government Printing.

Shell, S. 2009. *Revolution in India: Lalgarh's Hopeful Spark*. Available at http://readingfromtheleft.com/PDF/Kasama/revolution_in_india_lalgarh.pdf (accessed on 26 July 2019).

Singh, S. S. 2018, 10 September. 'Mamata Banerjee's Sop for Durga Puja'. *The Hindu*. Available at https://www.thehindu.com/news/cities/kolkata/mamata-banerjees-sop-for-durga-puja/article24919062.ece (accessed on 06 March 2019).

Sinha, S. 2008. 'Singur Sowing Problems', *Mainstream,* XLVI (38). Available at: *https://www.mainstreamweekly.net/article919.html* (accessed on 16.09.2018).

Sinharay, P. 2012. 'A New Politics of Caste'. *Economic and Political Weekly* 47 (34): 26—27.

———. 2013. 'Caste, migration and identity'. *Seminar* 645 (May). Available at http://www.india-seminar.com/semsearch.htm (accessed on 23 November 2018).

———. 2014. 'West Bengal's Election Story: The Caste Question'. *Economic and Political Weekly* 49 (17): 10–12.

Slater, T. E. 1884. *Keshab Chandra Sen and the Brahma Samaj: Being a Brief Review of Indian Theism from 1830–1884.* Madras: Society for Promoting Christian Knowledge.

Smith, W. C. 1943. *Modern Islam in India: A Social Analysis*. Lahore: Minerva Book Shop.

Suryanarayana, P. S. 2005, 28 August. 'We Are Trying to Change the Mindset of Workers, says Buddhadeb Bhattacharjee'. *The Hindu*. Available at https://www.thehindu.com/2005/08/28/stories/2005082804290800.htm (accessed on 11 September 2018).

Tagore, D. 1876. 'Letter no. 84'. In *Maharshi Debendranather Patrabali* (in Bengali), edited by Priyanath Shastri, 115. Available at https://ia801605.us.archive.org/35/items/in.ernet.dli.2015.338171/2015.338171.Maharshi-Debendranather.pdf (accessed on 31 January 2018).

Tavits, M., and N. Letki 2013. 'From Values to Interests? The Evolution of Party Competition in New Democracies'. *The Journal of Politics* 76 (1): 246–258.

Tawa Lama-Rewal, S. 2009. 'The Resilient Bhadralok: A Profile of the West Bengal MLAs'. In *Rise of the Plebeians? The Changing Face of the Indian Legislative Assemblies*, edited by C. Jafferlot and S. Kumar, 361–392. New Delhi: Routledge.

The Financial Express. 2019, 27 January. '90 Per cent People in West Bengal Getting Rice at Rs 2 Per kg, says Mamata Banerjee'. *The Financial Express*. Available at https://www.financialexpress.com/india-news/90-per-cent-people-in-west-bengal-getting-rice-at-rs-2-per-kg-says-mamata-banerjee/1456494/ (accessed on 25 February 2019).

The Hindu. 2015, 27 June. 'Supporting Emergency Was a Mistake: CPI Leaders'. *The Hindu Available at: https://www.thehindu.com/news/national/supporting-emergency-was-a-mistake-cpi-leaders/article7359292.ece* (accessed on 14.02.2018).

The Hindustan Times. 2011, 22 November. 'Mahasweta Calls Mamata Government "Fascist"'. *The Hindustan Times*. Available at https://www.hindustantimes.com/kolkata/mahasweta-calls-mamata-government-fascist/story-qOsTwf1u-FLP59Iin42OT2O.html (accessed on 02 March 2019).

———. 2018, 24 January. 'Have Donated Rs 600 Crore to Neighbourhood Clubs Since 2011: Mamata Banerjee'. *The Hindustan Times*. Available at https://www.hindustantimes.com/kolkata/have-donated-rs-600-crore-to-neighbourhood-clubs-since-2011-mamata-banerjee/story-gFdo0KQp7aRu-ciAI8skt8L.html (accessed on 4 March 2019).

The Indian Express. 2009a, 6 December. 'Eye on Polls, Mamata Joins Matua Sect'. *The Indian Express*. Available at https://indianexpress.com/article/cities/kolkata/eye-on-polls-mamata-joins-matua-sect (accessed on 12 October 2018).

———. 2009b, October 14. 'Mamata demands withdrawal of joint forces from Lalgarh'. *The Indian Express*. Available at https://indianexpress.com/article/india/india-others/mamata-demands-withdrawal-of-joint-forces-from-lalgarh/ (accessed on 22 February 2019).

The New Indian Express. 2018, 3 July. '"Shocked" over huge number of uncontested seats in West Bengal panchayat polls: Supreme Court'. *The New Indian Express*. Available at http://www.newindianexpress.com/nation/2018/jul/03/shocked-over-huge-number-of-uncontested-seats-in-west-bengal-panchayat-polls-supreme-court-1837642.html accessed on 10.06.2019

The Telegraph. 2008, November 15. 'New voices in Lalgarh'. *The Telegraph*. Available at http://www.telegraphindia.com/1081115/jsp/bengal/story_10114172.jsp (accessed on 30 November 2009).

The Times of India. 2018, 27 November. 'We Worship Durga, BJP Sells Ram: West Bengal CM Mamata Banerjee'. *The Times of India*. Available at https://timesofindia.indiatimes.com/city/kolkata/we-worship-durga-bjp-sells-ram-mamata-banerjee/articleshow/66820022.cms (accessed on 02 March 2019).

Touraine, A. 1988. *Return of the Actor: Social Theory in Post-industrial Society*. Minneapolis, MN: University of Minnesota Press.

Turner, V. 1977. *The Ritual Process: Structure and Anti-structure*. New York, NY: Cornell University Press.

Varkey, O. 1979. 'The CPI-Congress Alliance in India'. *Asian Survey* 19 (9): 881–895.

Varshney, A. 1998. *Democracy, Development and the Countryside: Urban–Rural Struggles in India*. Cambridge: Cambridge University Press.

Warriner, D. 1969. *Land Reform in Principle and Practice*. Oxford: Clarendon Press.

Webber, J. R. 2015. 'Crisis and Class, Advance and Retreat: The Political Economy of the New Latin American Left'. In *Polarising Development: Alternatives to Neoliberalism and the Crisis*, edited by Lucia Pradella and Thomas Marois, 157–168. London: Pluto Press.

Webster, N. 1992a. *Panchayati Raj and the Decentralisation of Development Planning in West Bengal (A Case Study)*. Calcutta: K. P. Bagchi & Company.

———. 1992b. 'Panchayati Raj in West Bengal: Popular Participation for the People or the Party?' *Development and Change* 23 (4): 129–163.

———. 2009. 'School Provision, the Capacity to Aspire, and the State of Popular Representation in West Bengal'. In *Rethinking Popular Representation*, edited by Olle Törnquist, Neil Webster and Kristian Stokke, 79–98. New York, NY: Palgrave Macmillan.

West Bengal Religion Census, 2011. Available at: https://www.census2011.co.in/data/religion/state/19-west-bengal.html (accessed on 12.02.2019).

Williams, G. 2001. 'Understanding "Political Stability": Party Action and Political Discourse in West Bengal'. *Third World Quarterly* 22 (4): 603–622.

Williams, G., and S. Nandigama. 2018. 'Managing Political Space: Authority, Marginalised People's Agency and Governance in West Bengal'. *International Development Planning Review* 40 (1): 1–26.

World Bank. 2010. *The World Bank's Country Policy and Institutional Assessment: An IEG Evaluation.* Washington DC: The World Bank.

Wrenn, M. 2014. 'Identity, Identity Politics, and Neoliberalism'. *Panoeconomicus* 4: 503–515. Available at http://www.doiserbia.nb.rs/img/doi/1452-595X/2014/1452-595X1404503W.pdf (accessed on 12 March 2019).

Xaxa, V. 1980. 'Evolution of Agrarian Structure and Relations in Jalpaiguri District (West Bengal): A Case Study of Subsistence Setting'. *Sociological Bulletin* 29 (1): 63–85.

Yadav, Y. 1999. 'Electoral Politics in the Time of Change: India's Third Electoral System, 1989–99'. *Economic and Political Weekly* 34 (34/35): 2393–2399.

———. 2000. 'Understanding the Second Democratic Upsurge: Trends of Bahujan Participation in Electoral Politics in the 1990s'. In *Transforming India,* edited by Francine R. Frankel, Zoya Hasan, Rajeev Bhargava, and Balveer Arora, 120–145. New Delhi: Oxford University Press.

———. 2006, 16 May. 'The Opportunities and the Challenges'. *The Hindu* Available at: https://www.thehindu.com/todays-paper/tp-national/the-opportunities-and-the-challenges/article3133798.ece (accessed on 12.08.2010).

INDEX

ABOUT THE SERIES EDITORS AND AUTHORS

Suhas Palshikar taught politics at the Savitribai Phule Pune University, Pune, and has been associated with the Lokniti Programme for Comparative Democracy of the CSDS. He is also the Chief Editor of the journal *Studies in Indian Politics*. He has co-edited two volumes on electoral politics: *Party Competition in Indian States: Electoral Politics in Post-Congress Polity* (2014) and *Electoral Politics in India: Resurgence of Bharatiya Janata Party* (2017). His most recent publication is *Indian Democracy* (2017).

Rajeshwari Deshpande is a professor of politics at the Savitribai Phule Pune University, Pune. She is a member of the editorial managing team of the journal *Studies in Indian Politics* and coordinates a forum on teaching and learning political science in India in the journal. She has published over 20 research articles in journals and edited volumes in English as well as in Marathi. She has edited the book *Politics of Welfare: Comparisons across Indian States*, with Louise Tillin and K. K. Kailash (2015).

Jyotiprasad Chatterjee is presently Associate Professor in the Department of Sociology, Barrackpore Rastraguru Surendranath College, North 24 Parganas, West Bengal. His research interest includes social movements, sociology of ethnicity, the processes of ethnic identity construction and assertion, the dialectics of democracy and development. Under the scope of doctoral research, his endeavour has been to underscore the sociological dynamics of Jharkhand Movement in India. As a member of the Lokniti–CSDS network from West Bengal, he has been regularly taking part in different national-level scholarly debates and discussions regarding the evolving nature of political processes in India with particular reference to West Bengal. He has co-authored a book and has published a number of articles in scholarly journals, edited volumes and newspapers in the fields of social movements, social development, electoral behaviour, ethnic movements, sociology of gender, motherhood, etc. As a member of the team of Sociology of MHRD, Government of India project 'e-PG Pathshala', he has written two e-modules in the paper on social movements.

Suprio Basu is Assistant Course Director, Rural Awareness and Self Employment, Department of Sociology, University of Kalyani, West Bengal. He has been Lokniti–CSDS's coordinator of the state of West Bengal since 2006. His areas of specialization are rural sociology, women's empowerment, Self Help Group (SHG), study of democracy and decentralization. As a part of his interest in rural sociology and rural social transformation, he is actively involved with various governmental and non-governmental organizations working in the field. Beside co-authoring a book, he has also published several articles in prominent journals, edited volumes and newspapers.